Be prepared...
To learn...
To succeed...

MW01259990

Get **REA**dy. It all starts here. REA's preparation for the FCAT is **fully aligned** with the current Grade 10 Reading and Writing tests.

Free!
2 Practice Tests Online
www.rea.com/FCAT

Visit us online at ***www.rea.com***

Ready, Set, Go!®

FCAT 2.0

Grade 10 Reading & Writing Tests

3rd Edition

by John Allen

Research & Education Association

The benchmarks presented in this book were created and implemented by the Florida Department of Education (FLDOE). For further information, visit the FLDOE website at *http://fcat.fldoe.org.*

Research & Education Association
61 Ethel Road West
Piscataway, New Jersey 08854
E-mail: info@rea.com

Ready, Set, Go!
FCAT 2.0 Grade 10 Reading and Writing Tests
3rd Edition

Library of Congress Control Number 2011942944

ISBN-13: 978-0-7386-1021-4
ISBN-10: 0-7386-1021-6

Contents

Section 1: Reading Process

Section 2: Writing Process

Foreword

Education is no longer about teaching students what to think, it is about showing them *how* to think. Gone are the days of formal assessments that test only a student's ability to regurgitate information. The modern trend in education lies in the FCAT 2.0, an instrument that measures students' repertoire of analytical tools – not how much information they are capable of memorizing within a certain time frame.

As a tenth-grade English instructor, I know firsthand that the pressure to succeed on the FCAT is immense. It is the topic of our faculty meetings, it is the focus in our classrooms – it is the driving force of our instruction. Student performance is not only a direct reflection of an individual's ability – it is also an indication of teacher aptitude. Because of this, there has long been a desire for a resource that fits the needs of both student and teacher.

Working with this text will provide students with confidence and a sense of possibility, both of which are vital to doing well on an assessment of this magnitude. Once students find that the test is conquerable by way of practice, they gain tremendous confidence. Through the use of this guide, students are able to practice the skills they need for the FCAT 2.0; in fact, this is as close as they can get to the real thing.

Over the years, my sophomore students have struggled with FCAT guides because they seemed unapproachable and prosaic. They become plagued by boredom mere minutes into a lesson. Students need high interest; they need engaging material that they feel can help them grow. With the rich, relevant examples in this book that illustrate the benchmarks clearly and logically, students learn precisely what they are expected to know.

Through the use of REA's *FCAT 2.0 Grade 10 Reading and Writing Tests,* students are trained to know where to look and what to look for in a passage. As a result, they begin to understand the relationship between question and answer, which is quite a tricky feat. If there is doubt about how to approach a question, they are provided with useful tips that guide them through the thought process. Once their eyes are opened to the fact that the test is no longer something to fear, taking it becomes second nature.

Students need simplicity and clarity. They need to believe a task is doable or else it will not get done. They sometimes need to see a task modeled multiple times in order to do it themselves with certainty. Herein lies the beauty of this guide. A reading or writing element of the FCAT 2.0 is introduced, explained in language a student can comprehend, and modeled numerous times to ensure mastery. Students even get the opportunity to take it a step further with full-length practice exams; once they see it, review it, and absorb it, they will retain it.

Success is always about preparation. A runner cannot complete a marathon without training. A racecar driver would not get behind the wheel without first studying the track. An actor would not take the stage without rehearsing the play's lines. In the same way, a student is better prepared to face an assessment of this scale with the cognitive tools necessary to triumph.

> Meagan Stocks, B.S.
> 10th Grade English and Critical Thinking Teacher
> J.W. Mitchell High School
> New Port Richey, Florida
> *Former Member, FCAT Writing Test Development and Item Analysis Committee*

About Research & Education Association

Founded in 1959, Research & Education Association is dedicated to publishing the finest and most effective educational materials—including software, study guides, and test preps—for students in middle school, high school, college, graduate school, and beyond.

Today, REA's wide-ranging catalog is a leading resource for teachers, students, and professionals.

We invite you to visit us at *www.rea.com/FCAT* to find out how REA is making the world smarter.

Acknowledgments

We would like to thank REA's Larry B. Kling, Vice President, Editorial, for supervising development; Pam Weston, Publisher, for setting the quality standards for production integrity and managing the publication to completion; Alice Leonard, Senior Editor, for project management of new edition.

We also gratefully acknowledge the writers, educators, and editors of REA and BBE Associates, Ltd., for content development, and Matrix Publishing for page design.

Succeeding on the FCAT 2.0 Grade 10 Reading and Writing Tests

About This Book

This book, which includes access to free online practice, gives you everything you need to succeed on Florida's FCAT 2.0 Reading and FCAT Writing tests.

The total package includes:

- Focused subject review

- Strategies and tips just for the FCAT

- Six full-length practice tests (two online at www.rea.com/FCAT and two in the book split between Reading and Writing)

- Every test answer keyed to the corresponding Florida standard

About the Test

Who Takes the FCAT 2.0 and What Is It Used For?

The FCAT is given to public school students throughout Florida to measure achievement in the skills and competencies outlined in the Sunshine State Standards. The FCAT consists of four sections: Reading, Writing, Mathematics, and Science. FCAT Reading 2.0 is given to students in Grades 3 through 10 and is aligned with the Next Generation Sunshine State Standards. FCAT Writing is administered to students in Grades 4, 8, and 10 and is aligned with the Sunshine State Standards. Students must pass the reading portion of the tenth-grade FCAT 2.0 in order to receive a high school diploma.

When and Where Is the Test Given?

FCAT Reading 2.0 is administered to students in Florida public schools in April. Students who need to retake FCAT Reading 2.0 can do so in one of two sessions in October. FCAT Writing is administered to students at the end of February.

Is There a Registration Fee?

Because all Florida public high school students must take the FCAT 2.0 and pass the test in order to receive a high school diploma, no fee is required.

What Is the Format of FCAT Reading 2.0?

FCAT Reading 2.0 contains 70% informational text and 30% literary text. The passages are 300 to 1,500 words each, with the average being 1,000 words. The test consists of 50 to 56 multiple-choice questions. Students are given 140 minutes to complete the test.

Changes to FCAT Reading 2.0

FCAT Reading 2.0 features only multiple-choice items. It also has a more rigorous content than the previous test. Students will be asked more often to:

- Use reasonable prior knowledge, such as grade-appropriate vocabulary.

- Make reasonable inferences that are not explicitly text-based.

- Analyze information across a pair of texts, such as making comparisons of themes or main ideas.

What Is the Format of FCAT Writing?

FCAT Writing consists of one writing prompt, which is either expository or persuasive. Students will each receive a test booklet containing the prompt and a section for making notes. Students are given 45 minutes to plan, draft, and revise their essays based on the prompt.

Test Accommodations and Special Situations

Every effort is made to provide a level playing field for students with disabilities taking the FCAT 2.0 and seeking a standard high school diploma. Special accommodations are permitted for students who:

- have been assigned to a special program, according to State Board Rule 6A-6.0331, FAC, and

- have a current Individual Educational Plan (IEP).

Federal law requires the inclusion of exceptional education students in all regular assessment programs. The school, district, and state FCAT 2.0 score averages represent all students taking the test, including students with disabilities.

In addition, students with limited English proficiency (LEP) are expected to take the FCAT 2.0. LEP students may be exempt from participating in the statewide assessment program:

- if the student has been receiving services in an approved district LEP plan for one year or less, and

- if the student's LEP committee determines that the FCAT is not appropriate.

LEP students may take the FCAT using accommodations appropriate for the particular need of the student. It is the responsibility of local school educators to work with students and parents to identify the allowable testing accommodations.

Additional Information and Support

Additional resources to help you prepare to take the FCAT include:

- the official FCAT website at *http://fcat.fldoe.org*

- the Florida Department of Education website at *http://www.fldoe.org/*

How to Use This Book

What Do I Study First?

Read over the review sections and the suggestions for test-taking. Studying the review sections thoroughly will reinforce the basic skills you need to do well on the test. Be sure to take the practice tests in this book and online to become familiar with the format and procedures involved with taking the actual FCAT 2.0. Check your answers to see which skills you need to review.

Test-Taking Strategies

What to Do Before the Test

- Pay attention in class and do your homework. Beginning with the first assignment of the year, organize each school day so there is always time to study and keep up with homework. Knowing that you have completed all the activities in this book will give you extra confidence to do well on the test.

- Carefully work through the review sections of this book. Mark any topics that you find difficult so that you can focus on them while studying and get extra help if necessary.

- Take the practice tests and become familiar with the format of the FCAT 2.0. When you are practicing, simulate the conditions under which you will be taking the actual test. Stay calm and pace yourself. After simulating the test only a couple of times, you will feel more confident, and this will boost your chances of doing well.

- Students who have difficulty concentrating or taking tests in general may have severe test anxiety. Tell your parents, a teacher, a counselor, the school nurse, or a school psychologist well in advance of the test. They may be able to suggest some useful strategies to help you feel more relaxed so that you can do your best on the test.

- Get plenty of rest. Getting a good night's sleep the night before the test is essential to being sharp and focused.

What to Do During the Test

- Read all of the possible answers. Just because you think you have found the correct response, do not automatically assume that it is the best answer. Read through each answer choice to be sure that you are not making a mistake by jumping to conclusions.

- Use the process of elimination. Go through each answer to a question and eliminate as many of the answer choices as possible. By eliminating two answer choices, you will give yourself a far better chance of getting the item correct since there will only be two choices left to choose from.

- Work quickly and steadily and avoid focusing on any one question for too long. Taking the practice tests in this book and online will help you learn to budget your time on the actual test.

- Work on the easiest questions first. If you find yourself working too long on one question, make a mark next to it on your test booklet and continue. After you have answered all of the questions that you know, go back to the ones that you skipped.

- Be sure that the answer oval you are marking corresponds to the item number in the test booklet. Since the multiple-choice sections are graded by machine, marking just one wrong answer choice for a question can throw off your answer key and thus your score.

- Work from the answer choices. You can use a multiple-choice format to your advantage by working backwards from the answer choices to answer the question. You may be able to make an educated guess based on eliminating choices that you know do not fit the question.

FCAT 2.0 Benchmarks*

FCAT 2.0 Reading Benchmarks **Chapter 1**
LA.910.1.5.1 The student will adjust reading rate based on purpose, text difficulty, form, and style.
LA.910.1.6.1 The student will use new vocabulary that is introduced and taught directly.
LA.910.1.6.2 The student will listen to, read, and discuss familiar and conceptually challenging text.
LA.910.1.6.3 The student will use context clues to determine meanings of unfamiliar words.
LA.910.1.6.4 The student will categorize key vocabulary and identify salient features.
LA.910.1.6.5 The student will relate new vocabulary to familiar words.
LA.910.1.6.6 The student will distinguish denotative and connotative meanings of words.
LA.910.1.6.7 The student will identify and understand the meaning of conceptually advanced prefixes, suffixes, and root words.
LA.910.1.6.8 The student will identify advanced word/phrase relationships and their meanings.
LA.910.1.6.9 The student will determine the correct meaning of words with multiple meanings in context.
LA.910.1.6.10 The student will determine meanings of words, pronunciations, parts of speech, etymologies, and alternate word choices by using a dictionary, thesaurus, and digital tools.
LA.910.1.6.11 The student will identify the meaning of words and phrases from other languages commonly used by writers of English (e.g., *ad hoc, ex post facto, RSVP*).
LA.910.1.7.1 The student will use background knowledge of subject and related content areas, prereading strategies (e.g., previewing, discussing, generating questions), text features, and text structure to make and confirm complex predictions of content, purpose, and organization of a reading selection.
LA.910.1.7.2 The student will analyze the author's purpose and/or perspective in a variety of texts and understand how they affect meaning.

(continued)

* The benchmarks presented in this book were created and implemented by the Florida Department of Education (FLDOE). For further information, visit the FLDOE website at *http://fldoe.org/bii/curriculum/sss/*.

(continued)

FCAT 2.0 Reading Benchmarks
Chapter 2

LA.910.1.7.3 The student will determine the main idea or essential message in grade-level or higher texts through inferring, paraphrasing, summarizing, and identifying relevant details.

LA.910.1.7.4 The student will identify cause-and-effect relationships in text.

LA.910.1.7.5 The student will analyze a variety of text structures (e.g., comparison/contrast, cause/effect, chronological order, argument/support, lists) and text features (main headings with subheadings) and explain their impact on meaning in text.

LA.910.1.7.6 The student will analyze and evaluate similar themes or topics by different authors across a variety of fiction and nonfiction selections.

LA.910.1.7.7 The student will compare and contrast elements in multiple texts.

LA.910.1.7.8 The student will use strategies to repair comprehension of grade-appropriate text when self-monitoring indicates confusion, including but not limited to rereading, checking context clues, predicting, note-making, summarizing, using graphic and semantic organizers, questioning, and clarifying by checking other sources.

Chapter 3

LA.910.2.1.1 The student will analyze and compare historically and culturally significant works of literature, identifying the relationships among the major genres (e.g., poetry, fiction, nonfiction, short story, dramatic literature, essay) and the literary devices unique to each, and analyze how they support and enhance the theme and main ideas of the text.

LA.910.2.1.2 The student will analyze and compare a variety of traditional, classical, and contemporary literary works, and identify the literary elements of each (e.g., setting, plot, characterization, conflict).

LA.910.2.1.3 The student will explain how meaning is enhanced through various features of poetry, including sound (e.g., rhythm, repetition, alliteration, consonance, assonance), structure (e.g., meter, rhyme scheme), and graphic elements (e.g., line length, punctuation, word position).

LA.910.2.1.4 The student will identify and analyze universal themes and symbols across genres and historical periods, and explain their significance.

LA.910.2.1.5 The student will analyze and develop an interpretation of a literary work by describing an author's use of literary elements (e.g., theme, point of view, characterization, setting, plot), and explain and analyze different elements of figurative language (e.g., simile, metaphor, personification, hyperbole, symbolism, allusion, imagery).

(continued)

(continued)

FCAT 2.0 Reading Benchmarks
Chapter 3

LA.910.2.1.6 The student will create a complex, multi-genre response to the reading of two or more literary works, describing and analyzing an author's use of literary elements (e.g., theme, point of view, characterization, setting, plot), figurative language (e.g., simile, metaphor, personification, hyperbole, symbolism, allusion, imagery), and analyzing an author's development of time and sequence through the use of complex literary devices such as foreshadowing and flashback.

LA.910.2.1.7 The student will analyze, interpret, and evaluate an author's use of descriptive language (e.g., tone, irony, mood, imagery, pun, alliteration, onomatopoeia, allusion), figurative language (e.g., symbolism, metaphor, personification, hyperbole), common idioms, and mythological and literary allusions, and explain how they impact meaning in a variety of texts.

LA.910.2.1.8 The student will explain how ideas, values, and themes of a literary work often reflect the historical period in which it was written.

LA.910.2.1.9 The student will identify, analyze, and compare the differences in English language patterns and vocabulary choices of contemporary and historical texts.

LA.910.2.1.10 The student will select a variety of age- and ability-appropriate fiction materials to read based on knowledge of author's styles, themes, and genres to expand the core foundation of knowledge necessary to connect topics and function as a fully literate member of a shared culture.

Chapter 4

LA.910.2.2.1 The student will analyze and evaluate information from text features (e.g., transitional devices, table of contents, glossary, index, bold or italicized text, headings, charts and graphs, illustrations, subheadings).

LA.910.2.2.2 The student will use information from the text to answer questions or to state the main idea or provide relevant details.

LA.910.2.2.3 The student will organize information to show understanding of relationships among facts, ideas, and events (e.g., representing key points within text through charting, mapping, paraphrasing, summarizing, comparing, contrasting, or outlining).

LA.910.2.2.4 The student will identify and analyze the characteristics of a variety of types of text (e.g., references, reports, technical manuals, articles, editorials, primary source historical documents, periodicals, job-related materials, practical/functional text).

LA.910.2.2.5 The student will select a variety of age and ability appropriate nonfiction materials (e.g., biographies and topical areas, such as science, music, art, history, sports, current events) to expand the core knowledge necessary to connect topics and function as a fully literate member of a shared culture.

(continued)

(continued)

FCAT 2.0 Reading Benchmarks
Chapter 4

LA.910.6.1.1 The student will explain how text features (e.g., charts, maps, diagrams, subheadings, captions, illustrations, graphs) aid the reader's understanding.

LA.910.6.2.2 The student will organize, synthesize, analyze, and evaluate the validity and reliability of information from multiple sources (including primary and secondary sources) to draw conclusions using a variety of techniques, and correctly use standardized citations.

FCAT Writing Benchmarks
Chapter 6

LA.910.3.1.1 The student will prewrite by generating ideas from multiple sources (e.g., brainstorming, notes, journals, discussion, research materials or other reliable sources) based upon teacher-directed topics and personal interests.

LA.910.3.1.2 The student will prewrite by making a plan for writing that addresses purpose, audience, a controlling idea, logical sequence, and time frame for completion.

LA.910.3.1.3 The student will prewrite by using organizational strategies and tools (e.g., technology, spreadsheet, outline, chart, table, graph, Venn diagram, web, story map, plot pyramid) to develop a personal organizational style.

LA.910.3.2.1 The student will draft writing by developing ideas from the prewriting plan using primary and secondary sources appropriate to the purpose and audience.

LA.910.3.2.2 The student will draft writing by establishing a logical organizational pattern with supporting details that are substantial, specific, and relevant.

LA.910.3.2.3 The student will draft writing by analyzing language techniques of professional authors (e.g., figurative language, denotation, connotation) to establish a personal style, demonstrating a command of language with confidence of expression.

Chapter 7

LA.910.3.3.1 The student will revise by evaluating the draft for development of ideas and content, logical organization, voice, point of view, word choice, and sentence variation.

LA.910.3.3.2 The student will revise by creating clarity and logic by maintaining central theme, idea, or unifying point and developing meaningful relationships among ideas.

(continued)

(continued)

FCAT 2.0 Reading Benchmarks
Chapter 7

LA.910.3.3.3 The student will revise by creating precision and interest by elaborating ideas through supporting details (e.g., facts, statistics, expert opinions, anecdotes), a variety of sentence structures, creative language devices, and modifying word choices using resources and reference materials (e.g., dictionary, thesaurus) to select more effective and precise language.

LA.910.3.3.4 The student will revise by applying appropriate tools or strategies to evaluate and refine the draft (e.g., peer review, checklists, rubrics).

LA.910.3.4.1 The student will edit for correct use of spelling, using spelling rules, orthographic patterns, generalizations, knowledge of root words, prefixes, suffixes, knowledge of Greek, Latin, and Anglo-Saxon root words, and knowledge of foreign words commonly used in English *(laissez faire, croissant)*.

LA.910.3.4.2 The student will edit for correct use of capitalization, including names of academic courses and proper adjectives.

LA.910.3.4.3 The student will edit for correct use of punctuation, including commas, colons, semicolons, apostrophes, dashes, quotation marks, and underlining or italics.

LA.910.3.4.4 The student will edit for correct use of possessives, subject/verb agreement, comparative and superlative adjectives and adverbs, and noun/pronoun agreement.

LA.910.3.4.5 The student will edit for correct use of sentence formation, including absolutes and absolute phrases, infinitives and infinitive phrases, and use of fragments for effect.

Chapter 8

LA.910.4.1.1 The student will write in a variety of expressive and reflective forms that use a range of appropriate strategies and specific narrative techniques, employ literary devices, and sensory descriptions.

LA.910.4.1.2 The student will incorporate figurative language, emotions, gestures, rhythm, dialogue, characterization, plot, and appropriate format.

LA.910.4.2.1 The student will write in a variety of informational/expository forms, including a variety of technical documents (e.g., how-to manuals, procedures, assembly directions).

(continued)

(continued)

FCAT 2.0 Reading Benchmarks
Chapter 8

LA.910.4.2.2 The student will record information and ideas from primary and/or secondary sources accurately and coherently, noting the validity and reliability of these sources and attributing sources of information.

LA.910.4.2.3 The student will write informational/expository essays that speculate on the causes and effects of a situation, establish the connection between the postulated causes or effects, offer evidence supporting the validity of the proposed causes or effects, and include introductory, body, and concluding paragraphs.

LA.910.4.2.4 The student will write a business letter and/or memo that presents information purposefully and succinctly to meet the needs of the intended audience following a conventional format (e.g., block, modified block, memo, email).

LA.910.4.2.5 The student will write detailed travel directions and design an accompanying graphic using the cardinal and ordinal directions, landmarks, streets and highways, and distances.

LA.910.4.2.6 The student will write a work-related document (e.g., application, résumé, meeting minutes, memo, cover letter, letter of application, speaker introduction, letter of recommendation).

LA.910.4.3.1 The student will write essays that state a position or claim, present detailed evidence, examples, and reasoning to support effective arguments and emotional appeals, and acknowledge and refute opposing arguments.

LA.910.4.3.2 The student will include persuasive techniques.

Section 1
Reading Process

Chapter 1

Fluency and Vocabulary Development

You can be sure that the FCAT 2.0 Reading test will include plenty of questions about vocabulary. Most of these questions will be about context clues, multiple meanings, and word relationships in a passage. The more you read, the more you develop your vocabulary and your ability to determine a word's meaning. Try keeping a list of new words that you encounter each day and review your list periodically. This will help you prepare for the FCAT 2.0 and its questions about unfamiliar or difficult words.

Reading Rate

Benchmark

> • **LA.910.1.5.1** The student will adjust reading rate based on purpose, text difficulty, form, and style.

Reading rate is how fast you read something. The FCAT 2.0 doesn't directly test you on reading rate, but it is an important skill to help you do well on the test. You should adjust your reading rate depending on your purpose for reading and the difficulty of the text. For example, if you are reading a detective story for enjoyment you will probably read very rapidly. Your main goal is to find out what happens next. However, if you are reading an assigned chapter in a biology textbook, you should read more slowly and carefully, taking note of each detail.

The form and style of a text can also affect your reading rate. If the detective story you're reading is a Sherlock Holmes tale by Sir Arthur Conan Doyle, which was written in a dense Victorian style, you might have to read more slowly than usual to understand. In the same way, you should read a poem more slowly to appreciate its verbal effects.

New Vocabulary

Benchmarks

- **LA.910.1.6.1** The student will use new vocabulary that is introduced and taught directly.
- **LA.910.1.6.2** The student will listen to, read, and discuss familiar and conceptually challenging text.
- **LA.910.1.6.4** The student will categorize key vocabulary and identify salient features.
- **LA.910.1.6.5** The student will relate new vocabulary to familiar words.

FCAT Reading 2.0 places special emphasis on dealing with new and unfamiliar vocabulary. There will be plenty of questions about vocabulary on the test. A good way to build your vocabulary and be prepared for these questions is to keep a list of new words as you read. Also, try to read as much as possible, in both fiction and nonfiction. Not only will you expand your vocabulary, you also will develop skills at decoding new words.

The benchmarks here focus on relating new words to words you already know. For example, the word *fortress* may be unfamiliar to you. However, it is similar to the word *fort,* which you might recognize from history books or movies. It is a structure that is built to protect the people inside from attack.

The key vocabulary benchmark is included to help ESL students develop essential vocabulary skills in English. Key vocabulary includes words that you use in everyday contexts, such as for asking directions, ordering from a menu, or applying for a license.

Context Clues

Benchmark

- **LA.910.1.6.3** The student will use context clues to determine meanings of unfamiliar words.

Many vocabulary questions on the FCAT 2.0 will ask you to define a word used in a passage. You can often figure out a word's meaning by looking at its context — that is, the words and sentences around it. Consider this example:

> *Restitution* **was slow in coming, but finally the judge ordered that the sculpture be returned to the person from whom it was stolen.**

From the other words in the sentence, you can tell that *restitution* means "restore to the rightful owner." Context clues may also be found in a longer passage:

> **Kirk was a huge hunk of a dog. When standing upright on his hind legs, he could easily rest his front paws on a man's shoulders. His enormous presence scared most passersby when Kirk strolled in the park on his daily walk on the leash. Other dogs, too, shunned Kirk, fearing death or severe injury should Kirk decide to clamp down on their flesh with his crushing jaws. No one had reason to worry, however. Terrified of squirrels and distrustful of robins and butterflies, Kirk was the most *docile* dog in the world.**

Use the context of this passage to determine the meaning of *docile*. Write the meaning on the line below.

_____

In the passage above, *docile* means "gentle." On the FCAT 2.0 you might also be asked to identify the meaning of a phrase or clause in a passage. Always look at the context of the phrase or clause.

Denotative and Connotative Meanings

Benchmark

• **LA.910.1.6.6** The student will distinguish denotative and connotative meanings of words.

On the FCAT 2.0, you will be asked to determine not only the denotative but also the connotative meaning of a word. The denotative meaning is the basic dictionary meaning of a word. The word *house* means "a structure one lives in" or "a residence."

Words can also have connotative meanings, or subtle shades of meaning that call up certain associations. A *mansion* is a house, but it includes the idea of being very large or expensive. A *hut* is also a house, but one thinks of it as being small and made of simple materials.

Connotative meanings may also be positive or negative. Think of words that mean "a smell." Can you think of one with a negative connotation and one with a positive connotation? Write them on the lines below.

Negative: _____   **Positive:** _____

See how the words summon different reactions? A *fragrance* or *aroma* sounds like a pleasant smell, while a *stink* or *stench* is just the opposite.

Prefixes, Suffixes, and Root Words

Benchmark

• **LA.910.1.6.7** The student will identify and understand the meaning of conceptually advanced prefixes, suffixes, and root words.

On the FCAT 2.0, you will see questions about word parts and how they affect a word's meaning. Understanding the meaning of a word's parts can help you determine its overall meaning. Many words have some or all of these parts:

- Prefix
- Root
- Suffix

The **root of a word** is its most basic part. The word *desire* is a root word. It does not have a prefix or suffix added to it; it is simply a root. *Desire* means "to want." A word part added to the beginning of a word is called a **prefix.** A word part at the end of a word is called a **suffix.** (See the tables in this section for some common prefixes and suffixes.) If you add the prefix *un-* to *desire* and the suffix *-able,* you create the word *undesirable,* which means "not desirable" or "not wanted." In this way, a prefix and/or a suffix changes the meaning of the root word.

If you know the meaning of a word's prefix, root, or suffix, you can often determine the meaning of the word. Consider this example:

I go for a walk each day after lunch. Getting some exercise helps rejuvenate my mind and body.

What does the word *rejuvenate* mean?

   A. keep safe

   B. make fresh

   C. keep healthy

   D. relax

If you know that the prefix *re-* means "again," it can help you figure out the meaning of *rejuvenate* — "to revive or make fresh again." Choice B is the best answer.

Make flashcards to help you study the word parts in the following tables. Knowing the meanings of these word parts will help you answer FCAT 2.0 vocabulary questions correctly.

Common Prefixes

Prefix	Meaning
anti-	against
anthro-	man
arch-	main
auto-	self
bi-	two
bio-	life
circum-	around
de-	not
dis-	not
im-	not
mal-	bad
mis-	bad
pre-	before
pro-	for; in favor of
sub-	below
super-	above; better
tele-	far; away
trans-	across
un-	not
uni-	one
via-	by way of

Common Suffixes

Suffix	Meaning
-able	able to
-er	doer
-ful	full of
-logy	the study of
-ly	like
-ment	state
-ness	state of being
-ous	full of or made of

Advanced Word/Phrase Relationships

Benchmark

• **LA.910.1.6.8** The student will identify advanced word/phrase relationships and their meanings.

On the FCAT 2.0 Reading test, you will be asked to identify words and phrases that are similar in meaning. Read the following passage and then look at the question.

> **The evening wind made such a disturbance just now, among some tall old elm-trees at the bottom of the garden, that neither my mother nor Miss Betsey could forbear glancing that way. As the elms bent to one another, like giants who were whispering secrets, and after a few seconds of such repose, fell into a violent flurry, tossing their wild arms about, as if their late confidences were really too wicked for their peace of mind, some weatherbeaten ragged old rooks'-nest burdening their higher branches, swung like wrecks upon a stormy sea.**

> **From** *David Copperfield* **by Charles Dickens**

Which pair of words from the selection are most similar in meaning?

    A. disturbance and repose

    B. secrets and confidences

    C. wicked and weatherbeaten

    D. ragged and stormy

You may be able to use your own vocabulary to answer the question. Or you might use clues in the passage to find the pair of words that have similar meanings. In this passage, the elms are "like giants whispering secrets," and they toss their branches "as if their late confidences were really too wicked for their peace of mind." Here, *secrets* and *confidences* have basically the same meaning. The correct answer is B.

Multiple Meanings

Benchmark

• **LA.910.1.6.9** The student will determine the correct meaning of words with multiple meanings in context.

Vocabulary questions on the FCAT 2.0 test you on words with multiple meanings. These words are called **homonyms** or **homophones**. Again, you can use context clues to decide which meaning of a word the author intends.

Read the following sentence.

After two warm weeks in March, we were surprised by a cold snap that made us shiver in April.

What does the word *snap* mean in this sentence?

    A. break in two

    B. utter sharp words

    C. something that is easy

    D. sudden spell of weather

Each answer represents a meaning of the word *snap*. However, the sentence describes "a cold snap that made us shiver in April." It is obviously referring to the meaning in answer D, "sudden spell of weather." To answer such questions correctly, try each answer in place of the key word in the sentence or passage. Then you can tell which meaning best fits the context.

Dictionary, Thesaurus, and Digital Tools

Benchmark

- **LA.910.1.6.10** The student will determine meanings of words, pronunciations, parts of speech, etymologies, and alternate word choices by using a dictionary, thesaurus, and digital tools.

Since you will not have access to a dictionary or thesaurus for the FCAT 2.0, you will not be tested on actual word entries. Nevertheless, you should use these tools in your own reading to build a stronger vocabulary.

Words and Phrases from Other Languages

Benchmark

- **LA.910.1.6.11** The student will identify the meaning of words and phrases from other languages commonly used by writers of English (e.g., *ad hoc, ex post facto, RSVP*).

In the course of your reading, you have probably learned many foreign words and phrases that English writers use. French words such as *chef, gourmet,* and *rendezvous* have become part of the English language. The FCAT 2.0 Reading test will not test you directly on the meanings of foreign words, but it may ask you to define a foreign word or phrase using context clues.

Passage 1

Read the following passage. Then answer the questions that follow. Use the Tip below each question to help you choose the correct answer. When you finish, read the answer explanations at the end of this chapter.

Excerpt from *Wuthering Heights*
by Emily Brontë

Yesterday afternoon set in misty and cold. I had half a mind to spend it by my study fire, instead of wading through heath and mud to Wuthering Heights. On coming up from dinner, however, (N.B.—I dine between twelve and one o'clock; the housekeeper, a matronly lady, taken as a fixture along with the house, could not, or would not, comprehend my request that I might be served at five)—on mounting the stairs with this lazy intention, and stepping into the room, I saw a servant-girl on her knees surrounded by brushes and coal-scuttles, and raising an infernal dust as she extinguished the flames with heaps of cinders. This spectacle drove me back immediately; I took my hat, and, after a four-miles' walk, arrived at Heathcliff's garden-gate just in time to escape the first feathery flakes of a snow-shower.

On that bleak hill-top the earth was hard with a black frost, and the air made me shiver through every limb. Being unable to remove the chain, I jumped over, and, running up the flagged causeway bordered with straggling gooseberry-bushes, knocked vainly for admittance, till my knuckles tingled and the dogs howled.

"Wretched inmates!" I ejaculated, mentally, "you deserve perpetual isolation from your species for your churlish inhospitality. At least, I would not keep my doors barred in the day-time. I don't care—I will get in!"

Questions

1   What does the narrator mean when she says the housekeeper "was taken as a fixture along with the house"?

　　A. The housekeeper was no more useful that the furniture in the house.

　　B. The housekeeper was lazy and rarely moved inside the house.

　　C. The housekeeper worked there before the narrator moved into the house.

　　D. The housekeeper had established a routine for running the house.

Tip

Think about the setting. Are the narrator's surroundings new to her? Also, consider the word *fixture* and the way it is used here. A fixture is something that is set permanently in place. In this context, it means something so familiar to the house that it is, in a sense, part of the house.

2   Read this excerpt from the passage.

On that bleak hill-top the earth was hard with a black frost, and the air made me shiver through every limb.

What does *bleak* mean?

　　F. black

　　G. comforting

　　H. dreary

　　I. foul-smelling

Tip

Carefully consider each answer choice. Notice that the details of the hill-top don't seem very comforting. The word *black* is used elsewhere to describe the frost. How did the narrator feel at the sight of the hill-top?

3   Read this sentence from the passage.

"Wretched inmates!" I ejaculated, mentally, "you deserve perpetual isolation from your species for your churlish inhospitality."

What does *inhospitality* mean?

A. meanness

B. unfriendliness

C. foolishness

D. fearfulness

 Tip

Think of the situation the narrator is in. How is she being treated? Then notice the word parts in *inhospitality*. The root is *hospitality*. What does that word mean? How does the prefix *in-* change its meaning?

Passage 2

Read the following passage. Then answer the questions that follow. Use the Tip below each question to help you choose the correct answer. When you finish, read the answer explanations at the end of this chapter.

The Hemingway House and Museum

According to legend, Pulitzer Prize-winning author Ernest Hemingway and his wife first arrived in Key West from Havana, Cuba, to claim a new Ford Roadster his wife's uncle had purchased for them. To their dismay, however, the car was delayed in transit. The managers of the Ford dealership tried to console the disheartened couple by offering them rent-free shelter in an apartment above the dealership, where they could stay until their new car arrived.

Hemingway had begun writing a war story during his journey to Key West, and he quickly established a routine of writing in the mornings, when it was cooler, and then exploring his new surroundings in the afternoon. He befriended a man named Charles Thomson, who ran the local hardware store and introduced Hemingway to deep-sea fishing for giant marlin and tuna. It was a sport that Hemingway, an avid outdoorsman, grew to love.

Hemingway's wife, Pauline, and Thomson's wife, Lorine, also forged a special friendship, and the two couples frequently socialized. In time Pauline's uncle purchased a Spanish-colo-

nial home for her and her husband on Whitehead Street in Key West, where the couple lived for ten years until they divorced and Hemingway returned to Cuba. Hemingway lived in the house long enough to complete his "war story," the critically acclaimed classic *A Farewell to Arms,* a novel based on his experiences as an ambulance driver during the Spanish Civil War. Hemingway also finished several other short stories and novels during his time in the house.

The home is now called the Hemingway House and Museum and is open to the public. Visitors can admire many of the couple's European furnishings, such as Pauline's chandelier collection, as well as Hemingway's typewriter and Cuban cigar maker's chair. The swimming pool in back of the house, installed in the late 1930s, was the first in Key West. The sixty-five-foot-long pool is still the largest. The $20,000 cost to install the pool was so enormous that when Hemingway pressed a penny into the surrounding concrete, he quipped, "Here, take the last penny I've got!"

The Hemingway House is still inhabited—but not by Hemingway or Pauline. An old tale tells of Hemingway admiring a sea captain's six-toed cat. The captain is said to have given the cat to Hemingway, who took it home to live with him on Whitehead Street. Today the house is inhabited by about sixty cats, some of which are polydactyls—six toed—and descendants of Hemingway's original. The cats are cared for by veterinarians and only allowed to breed occasionally to continue their lineage.

(?) Questions

4   Read this sentence from the passage.

He befriended a man named Charles Thomson, who ran the local hardware store and introduced Hemingway to deep-sea fishing for giant marlin and tuna.

What does *befriended* mean?

F.   discovered nearby

G.   reunited with

H.   introduced a friend to

I.   made friends with

 Tip

Find the root of the word. What does it mean? The answer choice you choose should incorporate the meaning of the root.

5   In the second-to-last paragraph, the author says that Hemingway "quipped," which means
     that he

     A. joked.

     B. praised.

     C. wished.

     D. yelled.

 Tip

Reread the second-to-last paragraph. Do you think that Hemingway was serious when he said
that it was his last penny?

6   Which pair of words from the last paragraph are most similar in meaning?

     F. descendants and lineage

     G. captain's and veterinarians

     H. original and breed

     I. admiring and allowed

 Tip

Think about the topic of the last paragraph, which is the group of six-toed cats that still in-
habits the Hemingway House. The cats have passed on this trait (having six toes) down the
line to the present day. Is there one pair of words that both address this topic in a similar way?

Passage 3

Read the following passage. Then answer the questions that follow. Use the Tip below each question to help you choose the correct answer. When you finish, read the answer explanations at the end of this chapter.

The Six Nations of the Iroquois

Long before the United States of America was created, a group of American Indians known as the Iroquois formed a united government of their own. Their government was known as the Six Nations of the Iroquois. It was so fair and effective that it helped to inspire the creation of the United States in 1776.

The history of the Iroquois reaches back thousands of years. Since ancient times, many American Indian tribes lived in the lands around New York State. Among these groups were the Mohawk, Seneca, Onondaga, Oneida, and Cayuga. These five groups had been at odds with one another for many years. A mysterious man arrived in their lands with a plan for peace. Representatives of the five tribes met and listened to the words of their eloquent visitor. After that, they decided to make peace and unite into a single government. (Later, a sixth tribe, the Tuscarora, joined the group.)

The Six Nations government immediately proved its worth. The six tribes no longer had to waste time and energy fighting with one another. Instead, they could advance their cultures and defend themselves against common enemies. Between them, the Six Nations controlled much of the land of the northeast. They referred to their shared lands as their Longhouse. They stationed powerful tribes to guard each end of it. By the 1600s, the Six Nations was a force to be reckoned with.

Colonists from Britain and France began gathering in North America. The Iroquois were pressed into making treaties and agreements with them. Although strictly honest in their dealings, the Iroquois understandably felt no deep loyalty to either side. Both sides were frequently unfair and often brutal to the American Indians and took much of their lands. The Iroquois created a kind of survival technique that involved playing the British and French against one another. By keeping the Europeans angry with one another, the Iroquois could gain benefits and keep more of their power.

However, the Iroquois could not maintain their "catbird seat" between the European competitors for long. As the British and French began to fight one another, the Iroquois were drawn in and forced to choose sides. Later, during the Revolutionary War, they were again forced to choose. That time they had to decide whether to join the British or the Americans. The Six Nations became desegregated during those wars. By around 1800, the power of the Iroquois had been broken.

Although the newcomers to the continent, the Americans, claimed control over the land, the Iroquois people never died out. Descendants of some of the Iroquois groups that had supported the Americans in the Revolution live today as U.S. citizens. They mostly live on reservations in New York State, Oklahoma, and Wisconsin. Many thousands of other Iroquois people currently live in Canada. These people are the descendants of Iroquois who supported the British.

The original lands once owned by the Iroquois are now used by non-Indian citizens. These lands have been changed greatly from their natural state. Today they are largely covered in highways, railroads, reservoirs, power lines, and other technologies. Ironically, most modern Iroquois reservations have not been given the benefits of such helpful projects. Because of this, the standard of living on Iroquois reservations is usually lower than the communities around them.

Nevertheless, Iroquois reservations are not crude or primitive places. Like most communities, they respect the symbols and customs of their ancestors, but they have not been "left behind" in the past. Most reservations today are fully modernized. Some visitors expect to see ancient shelters like teepees and wigwams still in use. These visitors are surprised to realize that most modern Iroquois live in frame or manufactured housing.

Many reservations are full of small businesses. These include markets, mills, repair shops, and gas stations. The communities also support banks, libraries, sports arenas, museums, cultural centers, and places of worship. Gaming is a major industry among some Indian groups. Tourists from all over the United States visit reservations to try their luck at casinos and bingo halls.

The other major industry, one that provides a link between modern Iroquois and their ancient ancestry, is art. The crafts of the Iroquois are unique and of increasing interest as the world becomes more and more reliant on bland manufactured items. Craftspeople among the American Indians carry on long, proud traditions and skills. They are masters of beadwork, basket and doll making, and pottery.

Tourists purchase much of this art, which helps the economy of the reservations. It also enables Iroquois artists to spread their talents to other communities. Iroquois artwork is featured in many museums and at cultural festivals. Other forms of art, including music, dancing, and storytelling, are also popular among modern Indians.

Despite the great changes and sufferings among the Iroquois, the Six Nations is still very much alive. Today Iroquois communities still select chiefs to represent them at the ongoing meetings of the Iroquois Counsel. The Six Nations government considers itself independent and free from the control of the U.S. or Canadian governments. The leaders and citizens of the Six Nations continue to work hard to benefit their people and preserve their customs.

Questions

7 What does the author mean by saying, "These five groups had been at odds with one another for many years"?

   A. The groups had not gotten along for many years.

   B. The groups did not meet together for many years.

   C. The groups worked together peacefully for many years.

   D. The groups were not aware of each other for many years.

 Tip

Read the sentences around the key sentence for context clues.

8 The word *eloquent* in the second paragraph has a positive connotation. Which of the following synonyms has a negative connotation?

   F. articulate

   G. expressive

   H. long-winded

   I. well-spoken

 Tip

Replace *eloquent* with each of the answer words. Which one gives a negative impression of the visitor's style of speaking?

9 Read this sentence from the passage.

By the 1600s, the Six Nations was a force to be reckoned with.

The phrase *a force to be reckoned with* indicates that the Iroquois were

A. cruel to their enemies.

B. feared by other people.

C. very strong.

D. known to everyone.

 Tip

The word *force* in this sentence offers a clue to the meaning of the phrase in context. "To reckon with" something is to deal with it or take it into account.

10 The word *reservations* has several meanings. Which of the following fits the way it is used in the article?

F. specific objections

G. agreements to hold something for later use

H. conditions that limit a contract

I. lands set aside for a certain group's use

 Tip

Think of how *reservations* is used in this article. Compare that usage to each meaning above. Which one applies to this article?

Passage 4

Read the following passage. Then answer the questions that follow. Use the Tip below each question to help you choose the correct answer. When you finish, read the answer explanations at the end of this chapter.

Twins

"Vanessa, can you answer the question?"

My head snaps up from the notebook I've been doodling in. A picture of a strong, black stallion fills the page where my notes should be. My history teacher, Mrs. Vasquez, stares at me intently, anticipating my answer. I wrack my brain, trying to figure out what we've been discussing for the past half an hour. This semester's unit, unfortunately, has been all about the Revolutionary War, but any knowledge of today's lesson eludes me.

I fidget nervously with my pencil as I desperately try to think of something clever to say. After a few moments, I decide that it's time to admit defeat.

"I'm sorry, could you repeat the question?"

Again, Mrs. Vasquez asks for the date of the Boston Tea Party, hoping someone a little more attentive will volunteer an answer. A hand quickly shoots up in the front row and our teacher calls on a student who is, obviously, more prepared than I am.

"1773," says a student in a tone of supreme confidence.

"Very good, Victor. It's too bad your sister doesn't share your aptitude for remembering dates."

I cringe at her words and feel my face redden as a few students chuckle. Before I have an opportunity to keel over and die from embarrassment, the bell rings, signaling the end of a less-than-enlightening academic session. I sigh as I fight my way toward my locker through the throng of students who filter into the halls.

I try not to make a habit of daydreaming in class. It's just that I don't find the Revolutionary War all that stimulating. During most of fifth-period history, I either draw or stare out the window at the courtyard while Mrs. Vasquez drones on and on about Paul Revere, the British, and the battle of Bunker Hill. The 1700s just don't pique my interest as much as a lesson on abstract art might.

As I try to repress any memory of the previous class, my twin brother approaches me. The horde that has invaded the halls of West Palm Beach High School seems to part, allowing Victor to make his way effortlessly, whereas I was nearly crushed by several upperclassmen.

Of course, Victor's extremely popular, a star athlete, and one of the most intelligent people I know. It's little wonder that the student body would make way for the big man on campus.

His perfection is a little hard to deal with sometimes. Albeit, I have a decent grade point average and a group of steadfast friends, but I'm not quite as beloved as Victor. Usually, I'm okay with this.

However, I tend to find comments like the one Mrs. Vasquez made this morning especially irksome. People think that just because Victor and I are twins that they can constantly compare us to one another. Why can't they recognize the fact that we're individuals with our own interests, flaws, and strengths?

Of course, like any brother and sister, we have a few similarities. We both like those campy horror movies that air late at night on the science fiction network, and we like to go surfing in the early morning while all the tourists are still asleep in their overpriced hotel rooms. We both detest strawberry ice cream and those ridiculous bumper stickers that tell you to honk if you love scuba diving or Jack Russell terriers. Nevertheless, the similarities seem to end there. Victor is the ambitious, outgoing one who is never home on a Saturday night, and I'm the quiet, introspective one who'd rather paint a masterpiece . . . or at least attempt to paint a masterpiece.

Victor smiles while I shove my history textbook into my already cramped locker. He kindly informs me that I'd better come up with a stringent study schedule if I plan on passing Mrs. Vasquez's midterm exam next week.

Laughing wryly, I ask him if he really thinks he's being witty.

Victor shrugs his shoulders and then offers his academic assistance this weekend—that is, after he makes some crucial appearances at all the hippest places.

I tell him I'll think about it as the bell rings, causing students to scurry to their next classes.

Later that night, after completing my homework, I decide to work on a painting I'd started earlier in the week. The canvas is almost completely blank, except for the outline of an old, warped-looking tree. While I rummage through my art supplies, searching for a particular shade of green, I hear the sound of the front door opening. It must be my parents, home from yet another one of my brother's football games. As I start shading in a few leaves, the noise from downstairs increases and becomes rather raucous, forcing me to go investigate the source of all the commotion.

Downstairs I find my parents, brother, and a dozen of his teammates. They admonish me for missing the most incredible game ever, during which Victor scored the winning touchdown, ensuring the team a trip to the playoffs. My dad orders a few celebratory pizzas, and my mom dashes to the convenience store to pick up some soda. I offer Victor and his friends my most enthusiastic congratulations, but I'm fairly certain that a twinge of annoyance is visible in my eyes. I can't help but feel a little slighted by my parents' reaction to my brother's big night. I highly doubt that they'd be throwing me an impromptu pizza party for a dozen of my friends on a school night if I'd won first place in an art exhibition.

They would be proud of me and try to do something special, like make my favorite meal, but I don't think they would be as elated about a prize-winning water color as they are about a game-winning play. Despite feeling slightly miffed, I help my dad empty bags of chips and pretzels into plastic bowls as the boys exchange exuberant high-fives.

After everyone's gone home and we've finished helping my parents tidy up, Victor and I watch TV in the den. Just before the show we're watching comes back from a commercial break, our dad storms into the room. He's mad at me because I forgot to take out the trash, and now we've missed the weekly pickup. I tell him I'm sorry that I forgot, but he's pretty aggravated and complains that he'll have to take it all to the waste station after work tomorrow. I apologize again, but it doesn't seem to be enough.

"Victor remembered to put the trash out last week when it was his turn, why couldn't you," he asks.

At that moment, something inside me snaps.

"Well, we all can't be perfect like Victor," I shriek before making a mad dash for my room.

I slam the door loudly, hoping to take some of my frustration out on the wooden frame. It seems to shake the entire house, but I could really care less. I flop down on my bed and feel sorry for myself. I usually don't let this sort of thing bother me, but today has been too much. It's like everywhere I go all I hear about is how studious, responsible, and generally wonderful my brother is. If you ask me, it's enough to make any girl have a bit of a hysterical breakdown.

After spending about fifteen minutes wallowing in self-pity, I hear a knock on my door. I tell whomever it is to go away, but the knocking persists. After a third attempt at gaining admittance, the person ignores my pleas to be left alone and lets himself in. It's Victor. I groan and tell him I want to be left alone. He sits on the edge of my bed and asks me why I'm so upset.

I laugh a little bitterly. "Isn't it obvious?"

"Not really. Why don't you try explaining it to me," he replies.

But how do I do that? It doesn't seem fair to tell him that I'm irrationally jealous of the admiration people shower on him daily. It's not right to fault him simply because he's smart and talented. Of course, my brain isn't working in the most logical manner at the moment, and I tell him how I truly feel.

"I'm upset because it seems like you can do no wrong, and everyone seems to think I'm a complete failure. The bad twin!" I exclaim.

Victor laughs loudly at this and then looks at me like some alien life form has taken possession of my body.

"Are you crazy?"

"First there was Mrs. Vasquez's remark this morning, then there was the party, and finally Dad yelling at me. . . . they all think you're perfect and that I don't measure up."

"Come on, Vanessa. I make just as many mistakes as you do."

Victor explains that just today he'd forgotten to compose an original haiku for English class and received an incomplete. He also admits to missing the ball in the first half of tonight's game and says if he hadn't made that final play, his football coach would have been furious and blamed Victor for losing the game. And, he reminds me, Dad was more than a little upset last week when Victor forgot to fill up his car after borrowing it and Dad ran out of gas on his way to work the next morning.

I consider all this for a few moments. It was true that our dad had been pretty irate about the whole car situation, but I still feel like everyone is comparing the two of us and that I just don't measure up.

After I inform Victor of this, he just laughs again.

"I get compared to you all the time, you know. I hate going to art class now because all Mr. Johnson talks about is how talented my sister is and how he can't believe that one twin got all the artistic ability and the other can barely draw a stick figure."

My mouth gapes open as Victor continues.

"He's right though—you're a really amazing artist. I've always been a little jealous of your talent. I can't even draw a straight line."

My infallible brother is jealous of me? I stare at him a little stunned.

"The way I see it, everyone's always going to compare us. The best we can do is appreciate our differences," he wisely observes.

I give him a smile and he puts his arm around my shoulder.

"Of course, you do know that if you ever mention this conversation to anyone I'll have to disavow any knowledge of it," Victor says.

I laugh a little and start to feel better than I have all day.

? Questions

11 Read this sentence from the selection.

This semester's unit, unfortunately, has been all about the Revolutionary War, but any knowledge of today's lesson eludes me.

In which sentence does *unit* have the same meaning as in the sentence above?

A. The soldier returned to his unit after a week's leave.

B. Tomorrow's test covers the last unit and two additional chapters.

C. Her room was still cool, despite the fact that the window unit was unplugged.

D. The degree is the unit of measurement for temperatures.

 Tip

Notice that the word *unit* in the sentence from the selection is "all about the Revolutionary War." What does this tell you about how the word is being used?

12 Read this sentence from the selection.

I highly doubt that they'd be throwing me an impromptu pizza party for a dozen of my friends on a school night if I'd won first place in an art exhibition.

This sentence contains the word *impromptu,* which is borrowed from the French language. The word means

F. expected.

G. leisurely.

H. rapid.

I. unplanned.

 Tip

Reread the passage that precedes the sentence above. Notice how the narrator's parents prepare for the pizza party.

13 Read this sentence from the passage.

He kindly informs me that I'd better come up with a stringent study schedule if I plan on passing Mrs. Vasquez's midterm exam next week.

What does *stringent* mean?

A. approved

B. daily

C. flexible

D. tough

 Tip

Keep in mind that the narrator needs to spend a lot of time studying.

14 Read this sentence from the passage.

Victor is the ambitious, outgoing one who is never home on a Saturday night, and I'm the quiet, introspective one who'd rather paint a masterpiece . . . or at least attempt to paint a masterpiece.

What does *introspective* mean?

F. backward

G. peaceful

H. thoughtful

I. unknown

 Tip

What kind of person would spend a lot of time painting?

Turn the page for the answers to the questions in this chapter.

✓ Answers

1   C

The narrator has just moved to the house. When she says the housekeeper was a fixture that came with the house, she means that the housekeeper was like a permanent part of the house. Students may recognize the word *fixture* and use its ordinary meaning to figure out how it is used here.

Benchmark: LA.910.1.6.5 The student will relate new vocabulary to familiar words.

2   H

The description of the hill-top does not seem comforting and there is no mention of a foul smell. The details do seem dreary, however.

Benchmark: LA.910.1.6.3 The student will use context clues to determine meanings of unfamiliar words.

3   B

Students should recognize that the prefix *in-* means "not." The inmates are not hospitable; they are unfriendly.

Benchmark: LA.910.1.6.7 The student will identify and understand the meaning of conceptually advanced prefixes, suffixes, and root words.

4   I

The word *befriended* means "to make friends with." Hemingway made friends with Charles Thomson.

Benchmark: LA.910.1.6.7 The student will identify and understand the meaning of conceptually advanced prefixes, suffixes, and root words.

5   A

Hemingway is being sarcastic and making a joke when he says that the pool might as well take his last penny.

Benchmark: LA.910.1.6.1 The student will use new vocabulary that is introduced and taught directly.

6   F

The words *descendants* and *lineage* both have to do with a line of generations in which traits are passed on. This is the topic of the last paragraph.

Benchmark: LA.910.1.6.8 The student will identify advanced word/phrase relationships and their meanings.

7   A

When you are "at odds" with someone, you are not getting along. The context of this phrase is a clue to the correct answer. The next sentence says that a mysterious man arrived to make peace between the five groups, so you can conclude that they were not getting along before the man came.

Benchmark: LA.910.1.6.3 The student will use context clues to determine meanings of unfamiliar words.

8   H

The word *long-winded* is a negative way of saying that a person uses lots of words. It gives the impression that a person is boring, and so has the most negative connotation of the answer choices.

Benchmark: LA.910.1.6.6 The student will distinguish denotative and connotative meanings of words.

9   C

The phrase "a force to be reckoned with" means that they were powerful and could not be ignored. The context of the phrase is a clue to the correct answer.

Benchmark: LA.910.1.6.3 The student will use context clues to determine meanings of unfamiliar words.

10   I

The article indicates that Iroquois reservations are lands set aside for them in place of their original lands.

Benchmark: LA.910.1.6.9 The student will determine the correct meaning of words with multiple meanings in context.

11   B

In the sentence from the selection, the word *unit* means a section of a textbook. The context clue about the Revolutionary War indicates it is a history book. Answer B uses *unit* in the same way.

Benchmark: LA.910.1.6.9 The student will determine the correct meaning of words with multiple meanings in context.

12   I

The pizza party is unplanned, since it occurs on the spur of the moment and the parents have to rush to get the pizzas and drinks. Students might look for word parts in *impromptu* such as *im-* and *prompt,* but should be reminded that it is a foreign word and cannot be analyzed for parts exactly like an English word.

Benchmark: LA.910.1.6.11 The student will identify the meaning of words and phrases from other languages commonly used by writers of English (e.g., *ad hoc, ex post facto, RSVP*).

13 D

A *stringent* study schedule is a strict or tough schedule. Vanessa needs to study very hard to pass the midterm exam.

Benchmark: LA.910.1.6.3 The student will use context clues to determine meanings of unfamiliar words.

14 H

Vanessa is introspective, or "thoughtful." We do not know that she is especially shy nor is there any indication that she's backward, but we do know that she likes to spend time thinking about her art.

Benchmark: LA.910.1.6.2 The student will listen to, read, and discuss familiar and conceptually challenging text.

Chapter 2

Reading Comprehension

The FCAT 2.0 Reading test will feature many questions on reading comprehension. In other words, you'll be asked to show that you understand what you have just read. You may be asked about the main idea of a passage, the author's attitude towards the material, or the cause or effect of a particular event. For these types of questions, make sure that you first read the passage carefully. You might also refer back to the passage to check an important fact or detail.

Prereading Strategies

Benchmark

- **LA.910.1.7.1** The student will use background knowledge of subject and related content areas, prereading strategies (e.g., previewing, discussing, generating questions), text features, and text structure to make and confirm complex predictions of content, purpose, and organization of a reading selection.

Before you read a selection, it is a good idea to preview the material and think about its topic, structure, and special features, if any. These prereading strategies can help you understand what you read. The FCAT 2.0 does not test you directly on these strategies, since you will have already read each selection before you begin answering questions about it. Nevertheless, you can use them to improve your comprehension, which in turn will help you answer questions about the author's purpose, main idea, and text structure.

Author's Purpose

Benchmark

- **LA.910.1.7.2** The student will analyze the author's purpose and/or perspective in a variety of texts and understand how they affect meaning.

Authors write for various reasons. Some write short stories, novels, plays, or poems to entertain their readers. Other authors write articles or nonfiction books to inform or describe something to readers. Still others write political essays, editorial opinion pieces, or letters to editors to persuade readers to think and act as they do about certain issues.

The FCAT 2.0 includes several questions about author's purpose. Some questions will ask you to identify the purpose of a text—to inform, persuade, entertain, or describe. Others will ask you about an author's opinion or point of view. For example, you might have to determine how an author feels about his or her subject. In addition, you might have to determine why an author writes in a certain style or uses a particular form. For example, you might be asked why an author asks a question at the beginning of an essay. Another type of question you are likely to see on the FCAT 2.0 will ask you to identify a statement that an author would agree with. To answer correctly, you must determine the author's opinion of the topic at hand.

Main Idea or Essential Message

Benchmark

- **LA.910.1.7.3** The student will determine the main idea or essential message in grade-level or higher texts through inferring, paraphrasing, summarizing, and identifying relevant details.

Many questions on the FCAT 2.0 will ask you to find the main idea of a passage or selection. The **main idea** of a passage is its primary focus or what it is mostly about. You might also be asked to choose the best summary of a passage. In a nonfiction passage, the main idea or thesis is often given in the introduction or first paragraph. Sometimes the title also offers a clue to the main idea. In most instances, however, the exact answer to a question about main idea will NOT be found in the passage. You will have to read the passage carefully and decide what it is about or its most important points. In a fiction piece, such as a story or poem, you must infer the main idea or essential message. Choose the answer option that tells what the entire passage is about.

Some questions will ask you to identify the main idea of only part of a passage. You may have to choose the best subheading or summary for a part of the passage.

Several questions will ask you about relevant details that support the main idea of a passage. For most questions on supporting details, you can look back at the passage to find the correct answer.

Cause and Effect

Benchmarks

- **LA.910.1.7.4** The student will identify cause-and-effect relationships in text.

- **LA.910.1.7.5** The student will analyze a variety of text structures (e.g., comparison/contrast, cause/effect, chronological order, argument/support, lists) and text features (main headings with subheadings) and explain their impact on meaning in text.

You will have to answer cause-and-effect questions on the FCAT 2.0. A **cause** is the reason for something happening. An **effect** is what happens as the result of the cause. For example, suppose your school bus ran over a nail this morning and one of its tires went flat. Running over a nail is the cause; the flat tire is the effect. Perhaps you were also late for school—that is another effect. Similarly, if you received an "A" on an exam because you studied very hard, your grade—the "A"—is the effect. And the cause? Your hard work, of course. Cause-and-effect questions often begin with the word *why*.

Often you can find the answer to a cause-and-effect question right in the passage. Whenever you are unsure of an answer, it is a good idea to go back and reread the relevant part of the passage to find the cause or effect. Also, you may be asked questions about cause-and-effect as a text structure. For example, a science article may show how one breakthrough is the cause for other discoveries by later scientists.

Similar Themes and Topics

Benchmark

- **LA.910.1.7.6** The student will analyze and evaluate similar themes or topics by different authors across a variety of fiction and nonfiction selections.

Certain questions on the FCAT 2.0 may ask you to analyze the theme of a nonfiction passage, or compare the themes or topics of different nonfiction selections. For example, two selections may approach a topic such as environmentalism from different angles. One might describe how government agencies make rules to reduce air pollution, while another might detail how automobile companies have refined their engines to produce cleaner emissions. As in finding the main idea, you should look for the author's overall approach to the topic and analyze the theme that runs through each article. Be prepared to identify the key details that contribute to the theme and help the author present the topic clearly and concisely.

Comparison/Contrast

Benchmarks

- **LA.910.1.7.7** The student will compare and contrast elements in multiple texts.

- **LA.910.1.7.5** The student will analyze a variety of text structures (e.g., comparison/ contrast, cause/effect, chronological order, argument/support, lists) and text features (main headings with subheadings) and explain their impact on meaning in text.

When you compare and contrast, you identify how things are alike and different. **Comparison questions** ask how two things (or more) are alike. **Contrast questions** ask how two things are different.

While you'll often be able to find the answer to this type of question in the text, sometimes you will have to synthesize or analyze details to find the correct answer. Compare-and-contrast questions usually include words and phrases such as *alike, different, like, similar, the major advantage/disadvantage, the major similarity with/difference between,* and *the most important similarity with/difference between.*

For fiction passages on the FCAT 2.0, you may be asked to compare or contrast two characters in a short story or in two different stories or poems. You might also be asked to compare and contrast settings, tones, or topics of two works of fiction. Some questions might ask why the author compares things, ideas, or people.

For nonfiction passages, you might be asked to compare and contrast the main idea, author's purpose, or author's point of view. You might also have to compare and contrast supporting details, such as how one thing is the same as or different from something else. Often (but not always) compare and contrast questions will be on paired passages, or two shorter passages about a similar subject. You might also be asked to analyze how an author uses a compare-and-contrast text structure to organize a passage.

Chronological Order

Benchmark

- **LA.910.1.7.5** The student will analyze a variety of text structures (e.g., comparison/contrast, cause/effect, chronological order, argument/support, lists) and text features (main headings with subheadings) and explain their impact on meaning in text.

On the FCAT 2.0, you may be asked about the **chronological order of a series of events** in a passage. This means the time order, or what happens from first to last. For example, you might be asked, "Which of the following events happened first?" Most fiction is written with events in chronological order. Nonfiction articles such as historical writing are also usually in time order.

Argument/Support

Benchmark

- **LA.910.1.7.5** The student will analyze a variety of text structures (e.g., comparison/contrast, cause/effect, chronological order, argument/support, lists) and text features (main headings with subheadings) and explain their impact on meaning in text.

The **argument/support text structure** is closely related to presenting the main idea and then supporting details. This structure is often used in nonfiction text. The author might begin with a statement such as, "Our city should build a new sports arena downtown." Then she will support her main contention with facts and reasons to persuade the reader. On the FCAT 2.0, you may be asked to identify supporting facts and details, or choose the detail that does not support the main statement.

Lists and Text Features

Benchmark

- **LA.910.1.7.5** The student will analyze a variety of text structures (e.g., comparison/ contrast, cause/effect, chronological order, argument/support, lists) and text features (main headings with subheadings) and explain their impact on meaning in text.

Sometimes nonfiction text is organized into lists of short topics that explain a larger topic. This structure may also include main headings and subheadings to introduce each section. You may be asked why an author uses this text structure. You may also see questions about the difference between a main heading and a subheading.

Self-Monitoring

Benchmark

- **LA.910.1.7.8** The student will use strategies to repair comprehension of grade-appropriate text when self-monitoring indicates confusion, including but not limited to rereading, checking context clues, predicting, note-making, summarizing, using graphic and semantic organizers, questioning, and clarifying by checking other sources.

Self-monitoring is a reading strategy to improve your comprehension of a text that you did not fully understand on a first reading. You might reread the text, or the parts that you failed to understand. You might look more closely for context clues that will explain difficult terms or confusing events. You can even draw your own graphic organizers to deal with the text. Self-monitoring is not tested on the FCAT 2.0, but it is a useful strategy for checking your own comprehension of a passage. You might use one or more of its tools to help you answer the questions on the FCAT 2.0.

Passage 1

Read the following passage. Then answer the questions that follow. Use the Tip below each question to help you choose the correct answer. When you finish, read the answer explanations at the end of this chapter.

Safe at Sixteen? Why We Should Raise the Legal Driving Age
by Eliot Golden

To many teens, turning sixteen is a rite of passage. In most states, this is the age when young people become eligible for a driver's license. Adolescents see this as the beginning of freedom and independence, but many adults feel that this is a dangerous and deadly time for many teenage drivers. Statistics show that young drivers are more likely to speed, run red lights, and behave recklessly behind the wheel than more mature, experienced drivers. Many experts agree that this kind of behavior accounts for the thousands of teens killed every year in automobile accidents. In fact, according to the National Center for Injury Prevention and Control, teens are four times more likely to crash than are older drivers. This has caused many to question what can be done to keep teen drivers safe.

A growing number of people feel that the only way to truly prevent tragedy is to raise the legal driving age. Most teens, and even some parents, scoff at this idea, but many people feel that such action is necessary, and their concerns are being heard by our nation's lawmakers. A number of states have already raised the minimum age a teen must be to acquire a full, unrestricted license, meaning that many young drivers must be accompanied by a licensed adult when they hit the roads. These states use graduated licensing programs that put limitations on young drivers. The programs restrict teens from driving late at night or carrying other teenage passengers until they have logged a certain number of hours driving under the supervision of a parent or guardian. Safety experts point out that more supervised experience makes safer drivers and reduces the risk of fatal accidents among teens. But are these programs doing enough to keep kids safe?

Researchers also note that maturity plays a major role in safety on the roads. Many young drivers are overconfident in their abilities and do not think about the risks associated with getting behind the wheel. Studies show that of all age groups, teens are the most likely to drive while under the influence of alcohol or drugs, drive without wearing a seat belt, and underestimate hazardous road conditions. Some argue that making mature decisions about driving is something that can only come with age, despite the number of hours spent practicing.

Keeping all this in mind, the only logical and responsible solution to this problem is to raise the legal driving age. Many teens will argue that their freedom is being taken from them, and many parents might be inconvenienced by having to drive their kids to school, work, or practice, but the alternative is far worse. Turning sixteen is an important milestone in any young person's life, but it doesn't necessarily mean that they are ready to drive. By raising the legal driving age and giving teens more time and experience behind the wheel, we can help make sure that turning seventeen, eighteen, and nineteen is just as exciting and safe for teens.

 **Questions**

1   The author's main purpose for writing this article was to

    A. inform readers about changes in the minimum driving age.

    B. convince readers that the legal driving age should be raised.

    C. describe what it is like to drive at sixteen years old.

    D. explain why young drivers are overconfident in their abilities.

 Tip

Think about what the author hopes to accomplish with this essay. What effect does he intend to have on his readers?

2   According to the article, what is the main reason that the minimum driving age should be raised?

    F. Driving gives adolescents too much freedom and independence.

    G. Not all teenagers have parents or guardians to supervise their driving.

    H. Teenagers never wear seatbelts and always misjudge hazardous road conditions.

    I. Statistics show that teenagers are much more likely to crash or drive recklessly than older drivers.

 Tip

Reread the title of this article. Also, notice what information the author uses to support his opinion about teenage driving.

3　To organize the ideas in this article, the author mostly used which of the following text structures?

    A.　argument/support

    B.　comparison/contrast

    C.　chronological order

    D.　cause/effect

 Tip

Think of how ideas are presented in each of the text structures in the answer choices. Is the author mainly comparing two or more things? Does he use chronological order? Is he most interested in how something causes something else to happen?

Passages 2 and 3

Read the following passages. Then answer the questions that follow. Use the Tip below each question to help you choose the correct answer. When you finish, read the answer explanations at the end of this chapter.

Passage 2

The Yangtze River

The Yangtze River stretches about 6,380 kilometers (3,964 miles) across the middle of China, making it the longest river in Asia and the third-longest river in the world. It flows west to east, beginning in a glacier in the western Dangla Mountains and drawing water from many lakes and over 700 tributaries along the way. It virtually divides the country in half horizontally before emptying into the East China Sea at Shanghai. It is so long that it is known by different names throughout the nine provinces it occupies. For instance, it is called the Dangqu at its point of origin and the Jinsha near its center.

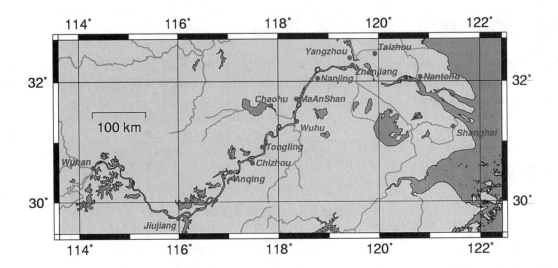

One reason the Yangtze River is so important is that it serves as a major Chinese shipping route, connecting far western inland China to the country's coast in the east. Almost 800 million tons of various cargoes are shipped across its waters each year, entering and leaving the country through ports in Shanghai. It also facilitates irrigation across the country, watering and nourishing crops such as rice and wheat. While controlled amounts of water have been beneficial to Chinese lands for many years, the river has overflowed and flooded China many times since the country's ancient past.

Another beneficial purpose of the river is its capacity to produce the hydroelectric power used throughout China. The Three Gorges Dam, completed in 2008, is 600 feet tall and 1.5 miles long and creates a 400-mile-long reservoir that holds 5 trillion gallons of water. The dam is responsible for providing one-ninth of China's citizens with power, because it is able to produce electrical output equivalent to that of eighteen nuclear power plants. The dam is also intended to control some of the flooding problems suffered by those in the riverside towns and cities.

Passage 3

China's Huang He

The Huang He is the second-longest river in China, stretching for 4,700 kilometers (2,920 miles). Its literal translation from the Chinese is "Yellow River," so named for its yellow color, created by the massive amounts of ochre-colored silt that it carries. The Huang He carries approximately 1.6 billion tons of silt every year, depositing about 1.4 billion tons into the Bohai Sea, an arm of the Yellow Sea. Silt that does not make it out to sea settles in the riverbeds, causing them to rise. The Huang He carries the most silt of any river in the world, making it a nutrient-rich irrigation source. Because it nourishes the land so well, it has often been referred to as "China's Pride." On the other hand, one aspect of it has also earned the nickname

"China's Sorrow." Like other rivers in China, the Huang He sometimes floods. However, it cannot simply be harnessed by dams. While dams have been built in an attempt to hold back the Huang He's waters, the river's heavy silt wears away at the dams very quickly, eventually making them useless.

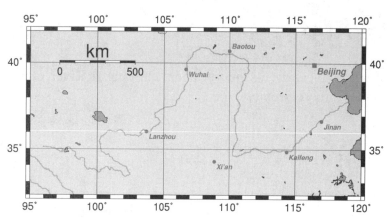

One interesting thing about this river is that its lower portion sometimes runs dry because of overuse—especially by industries—during dry spells. It provides water to 12 percent of China's citizens and is used extensively for irrigation purposes, especially during March through June, when crops are being cultivated. In 1997, the Huang He went dry for more than two hundred days—more than half a year. When the river dries up, farmers cannot water and enrich their crops, and agricultural production drops dramatically. Because the great majority of the world's rice is produced in China, the drying up of the river can have disastrous consequences for the Chinese people.

Scientists and environmentalists are now creating and implementing water conservation plans to reduce the amount of water drawn from the river for agricultural and industrial uses, to prevent depletion of the yellow waters of the mighty Huang He.

Questions

4   Which of the following is NOT one of the major benefits that the Yangtze River provides for the Chinese people?

   F.   It serves as a major Chinese shipping route.

   G.   It virtually divides the land of China in two.

   H.   It helps to produce hydroelectric power that is used throughout China.

   I.   It provides irrigation across China for crops such as rice and wheat.

 Tip

While all these details are true about the Yangtze River, one of them is of no particular benefit to the Chinese people.

5   According to the articles, the Huang He is different from the Yangtze because it

   A.   flows from west to east.

   B.   nourishes crops and helps them grow.

   C.   extends for a much greater distance.

   D.   contains massive amounts of silt that give it a yellowish color.

Tip

Reread the main points of the two articles to compare features between the two rivers. What is the main difference?

6   What causes dams to be ineffective in holding back the waters of the Huang He?

    F.   The floodwaters of the Huang He are too powerful to be controlled by dams.

    G. Chinese engineers have not figured out how to build huge dams.

    H. The Huang He changes course too often for dams to be effective.

    I.   Heavy silt in the Huang He wears away at dams and makes them useless.

 Tip

Think of the cause-effect relationship that answers this question.

Passage 4

Read the following passage. Then answer the questions that follow. Use the Tip below each question to help you choose the correct answer. When you finish, read the answer explanations at the end of this chapter.

A Superstition Mission
by Mark Smith

"The exam will be on Monday," announced Mrs. Keenan, the science teacher. "You'll have the entire weekend, so there is no excuse for forgetting to prepare!"

Pete squirmed in his seat, his mind reeling with considerations of all of the tasks he'd need to perform before the exam. The exam would cover the first five chapters in their massive textbook—chapters that covered topics ranging from earth science to space exploration. He found the material difficult and knew he'd have to really make an effort in order to get a decent grade.

Mentally reviewing his schedule for the weekend, Pete knew right away he'd need to dedicate most of his time over the next few days to preparing for Mrs. Keenan's test. He was going to start preparing immediately after school, but he remembered that it was Friday the thirteenth. Not wanting to jinx himself, Pete instead resolved to start preparing bright and early on Saturday morning. On Friday night, he placed his textbook on the head of his bed, and stacked next to it a pile of science handout sheets.

"Here's everything I need to absorb by Monday afternoon," he thought, plopping a pillow on top of it all. "So I'll start by sleeping on it so maybe the information will soak up into my brain."

Pete rested his tired head on the pillow. Though the pillow was lumpy from all the papers underneath, Pete knew his discomfort was necessary. He didn't want a single thing to go wrong with his preparation routine.

Pete woke up at nine o'clock on Saturday, since nine was his lucky number. He'd spent the night dreaming of the flood of science topics he needed to master by Monday. He realized now more than ever that he needed some special preparations. For breakfast he ate some cereal with marshmallows shaped like traditional good-luck charms like horseshoes and four-leaf clovers. "This'll fill me up with good luck," he thought as he scanned through the topics of his textbook.

Each time he saw a new chapter heading in his book, he thought of an appropriate activity to help him absorb its information. For the chapter on the revolutions of planets, he spun his textbook around three times—three was his personal lucky number. Then he spun his chair around, too, for good measure. When he saw information about the winds that blew across Earth, he remembered a good-luck ritual of blowing on his hands.

"Maybe that'll help my hands write down the correct answers on Monday," Pete thought hopefully.

Again, he slept with the textbook and handouts under his pillow, and all day Sunday he observed every superstitious ritual he could think of. He didn't step on any cracks in the sidewalk, he entered and exited his house through the same door, and he kept well away from any roving black cats. Then, on Sunday night, Pete carefully chose his lucky sweatshirt, his lucky socks, and his lucky baseball cap. He even accessorized with a lucky charm that his grandmother had given him years ago.

Pete was feeling confident as he swaggered into class, feeling assured that his weekend of preparation would pay off. Mrs. Keenan passed out the exams, and Pete grabbed his enthusiastically, gripping his old, chewed-up lucky pencil.

The next day, Pete found out that he'd failed the test. He shook his head in amazement. "I did everything I could to prepare," he said. "Who'd have thought I'd forget to read the book?"

⑦ Questions

7   Which of the following best describes the organization of this selection?

   A. a general idea followed by specific events to prove a point

   B. events presented to show cause and effect

   C. events presented in chronological order

   D. events in one person's life compared to those in another person's life

 Tip

Think about how the author relates the events in the story.

8   With which statement would the author of this selection most likely agree?

    F. It is fine to be superstitious but not to get carried away.

    G. It is a good idea to avoid superstitions and work hard.

    H. Children are more likely to be superstitious than adults.

    I. Teachers should spend more time teaching kids to study.

 Tip

Think about the ending of the story. What was Pete's mistake that led to his failing the test?

9   Why did the author write this passage?

    A. to entertain readers with a story about a superstitious boy

    B. to teach readers about a wide variety of superstitions

    C. to reveal the scientific facts about superstitions

    D. to persuade readers not to bother with superstitions

 Tip

Is this passage fiction or nonfiction? What is the usual purpose for this kind of writing?

Passage 5

Read the following passage. Then answer the questions that follow. Use the Tip below each question to help you choose the correct answer. When you finish, read the answer explanations at the end of this chapter.

The Truth about Year-Round Education
by Rebecca Simonson

No More Teachers, No More Books

Summer. For many students, summer means vacations with their families, time to relax with their friends, or opportunities to make extra money at summer jobs. But believe it or not, summer still means school for some students. These kids aren't attending classes because of poor grades or to try to get ahead but because their school districts run on a year-round schedule.

The traditional ten-month school schedule that most students are accustomed to was formed at a time when many Americans lived on farms. During the summer, children were needed to help their families work the fields and prepare for the fall harvest. Even after farming declined, many schools stuck with the original schedule because many felt that it was too hot to keep students cooped up inside all day when many schools lacked air-conditioning systems. However, in recent years there has been a movement to institute year-round education in school districts throughout the United States.

How Year-Round Education Really Works

Despite what many people think, many students who go to school year-round don't spend more days in class than children that attend traditional schools. Besides the extended school-day program, which considerably lengthens the time that children spend in school, most students in year-round programs spend the traditional 170 to 180 days in class, but their vacation time is broken up throughout the year.

Some schools use a single-track system. This means that all students and faculty are in session and take breaks at the same time. This system has several subsystems, including a flexible all-year calendar that allows students and teachers to take short breaks when it is convenient for them. Modified schedules are also used in this system. Some schools will have forty-five days of instruction followed by a fifteen-day break, while others keep students and teachers in class for ninety days and then break for thirty days.

Multitrack systems are also used in year-round education, usually by schools that have overcrowding issues. Multitrack systems usually have three to five tracks, and each student is assigned to a specific track. While students in certain tracks are in school, one or two other tracks will be on vacation. This is generally used so that a district can educate more students without having to build new schools or shipping students to other districts.

Benefits

Besides allowing school districts to accommodate an ever-growing number of students, year-round education is thought to have many more benefits. Some argue that cutting out the long summer break decreases the amount of information students lose while not receiving instruction. This allows teachers to focus more on new material rather than wasting time reviewing at the beginning of the year.

Others feel that more frequent breaks mean that both students and teachers will be absent less often because this schedule allows for time to rest and relax during the school year. Another appealing aspect of the system is that the program not only helps to alleviate overcrowding but also would save taxpayers' money that would need to be spent creating new schools and hiring more faculty. Supporters of the system also argue that year-round education is used throughout the world in many countries where students perform better academically than their U.S. counterparts.

Drawbacks

Of course, there are those who believe that a year-round school system is not the answer to America's educational problems. Critics argue that doing away with summer vacation will greatly disrupt many families' social schedules. Parents of young children will have to find someone to watch their kids during these short breaks because they cannot attend camps or day care usually offered during the summer months. Also, many feel that extracurricular activities would suffer under the year-round education system. Sports and music events often require interaction among school districts. If one school is year-round and another is not, scheduling a time for mutual activities could be very difficult.

The most important argument against the system is that there is no statistically significant evidence showing that year-round education improves students' academic abilities or increases standardized test scores. Supporters argue that this is not the case, but critics point to several studies that show only minor improvements among students participating in year-round education.

So Long, Summer?

According to the National Association for Year-Round Education, 3,181 American schools had adopted this alternative educational system by the 2002–2003 school year. Does this mean that students should live in fear of the day when their summers are no longer their own? Well, let's just say that they shouldn't throw in their beach towels just yet. Between fall 2004 through spring 2008, Miami-Dade public schools tried a year-round school but dropped the program because there was no difference in test scores between the targeted schools and the control group.

Parents, teachers, and students across the United States continue to debate the positive and negative aspects of the program. The topic remains a controversial one, and many school districts have opposed a switch. But the truth is, American students continue to lag behind children in Europe and Asia academically. Perhaps a little less fun in the sun and a little more time in the classroom might be just what students need to help them get ahead.

 Questions

10 Read these sentences from the article.

> **The traditional ten-month school schedule that most students are accustomed to was formed at a time when many Americans lived on farms. During the summer, children were needed to help their families work the fields and prepare for the fall harvest.**

The author includes these sentences in order to show that

F. schools provided better education to students years ago.

G. the old ten-month school schedule should still be used everywhere.

H. the reasoning behind the ten-month school schedule is out of date.

I. the traditional ten-month school schedule is unfair to city children

 Tip

Think of what these sentences tell us about the old school schedule. Do these conditions still exist?

11 One positive effect of the multitrack system in year-round education is that

    A. families can still take long summer vacations if they choose.

    B. all students and faculty are in session and take breaks at the same time.

    C. teachers can focus more on new material rather than on reviewing at the beginning of the year.

    D. school districts can educate more students without building more schools.

 Tip

Reread the paragraph on multitrack systems in the second section of the article. Which answer choice fits the information in this paragraph?

12 In this article, the author includes subheadings mainly to

    F. introduce the topic of the section that follows.

    G. make humorous comments on her topic.

    H. make the selection look easier to read.

    I. encourage readers to skip ahead to more interesting sections.

 Tip

Reread the subheadings and think about how they relate to the sections of the article.

13 Read the following sentences from the article.

Does this mean that students should live in fear of the day when their summers are no longer their own? Well, let's just say that they shouldn't throw in their beach towels just yet.

Which of the following is the best paraphrase of the idea in these sentences?

A. Students who want to can still spend their summers away from school as long as they agree to do extra work.

B. Students need not worry that year-round schools are coming to their area anytime soon.

C. Students are so fearful of losing their summers off from school that they will support almost any other compromise.

D. Students might as well forget the idea of spending the entire summer out of school.

 Tip

Think about the play on words that the author is using to make her point.

14 What is the author's point of view in this article?

F. She thinks all schools would be better off on a multitrack system.

G. She thinks more schools should consider year-round education.

H. She thinks a single-track system is better than a multitrack system.

I. She thinks that schools in warm climates should have the summer off.

 Tip

Think about why the author wrote this article. How does she feel about her subject matter? What important point does she want to make to her readers?

Passage 6

Read the following passage. Then answer the questions that follow. Use the Tip below each question to help you choose the correct answer. When you finish, read the answer explanations at the end of this chapter.

Blah, Blah, Blog

A shortened form of *weblog*, *blog* is the name given to a kind of online journal that is updated frequently. Blogs can include original text, photos, links to other Web sites and blogs, and pretty much anything else.

Blogging (the act of creating or posting to a blog) developed from technically adept Internet surfers who kept logs of what was worth viewing on the Internet. Readers could come back every day to see what wonderful Web content the blogger had most recently found. Bloggers posted their findings in an easy-to-update, easy-to-read format from which they could link their readers to the sites they mentioned.

Today's blogs offer places for readers to comment and places for readers and writers to comment on comments, so that blogs are more like conversations than traditional forms of writing. Posts on blogs are listed in reverse chronological order so that the newest post is always at the top of the blog, where readers can easily find it. Older posts are archived and organized in an easy-to-navigate list so that readers can quickly search for all posts about a specific subject.

According to recent research, about 4 percent of people who spend time online read blogs, but the number is increasing. Because most search engines direct people to blogs, many new people join the blogosphere every day. Anyone who reads should be reading a blog because blogs discuss every subject under the sun, and blogs often have the most up-to-the-minute information. The surge in the popularity of reality TV programs suggests that people find real life and real problems worthy of their attention. According to one blog directory, there are more than 20 million blogs in the United States alone. Blogging is still a very new phenomenon but one that is gaining recognition quickly.

People write blogs because they have something to say about a number of topics. There are blogs about politics and news, fashion blogs, and blogs about TV and movies. Families use blogs to share personal photos, keep in touch with each other, and plan reunions. Some people have personal blogs, sort of like diaries, where they post their innermost feelings, and they don't allow their posts to be viewed by the public. Some people keep anonymous diaries that they do allow the public to read. Perhaps the best reason to write a blog is because you have something original to say about something people are interested in.

Creating your own blog is not difficult. Use a search engine to find one of the free blogging sites. These sites walk users through the setup process, helping first-timers post photos and text and design a unifying motif for their blog. Some sites even let bloggers call in audio files that will post immediately to their blog. Because they are fairly easy for the novice and they are free, these sites are invaluable to beginners. Once you get established, you might want to look into the companies that host blogs for a charge. The fee is small, and the sites offer bloggers more control over the appearance of their blogs as well as more storage space.

Before you initiate your search for the precise site to host your blog, you'll want to consider a couple of factors. First, ask yourself what your blog will be about. Blogs usually have catchy titles and memorable taglines that describe the blogs' contents. Also, because nothing is more daunting than a blank page, you should brainstorm on a topic for your first entry so you don't get hung up waiting for inspiration.

As with everything else you want people to know about, you need to advertise your blog; however, that does not entail booking a commercial slot during the Super Bowl. The best way to increase readership is to read and post to plenty of other people's blogs, making sure to include a link to your blog in your comments. Include a blogroll on your site so that readers can visit the blogs that you find entertaining. Bloggers pay attention to being listed on others' sites, and they may even return the favor. In the blogosphere, what goes around comes around!

Blogulary

blog: a frequently updated online journal.

blogger: a person who writes a blog.

blogging: the act of writing a blog.

permalink: each blog entry gets a permalink (short for *permanent link*), so that readers can find a specific post quickly and easily.

post: when you add a new entry or a comment to a blog, you are posting.

comments: readers can post their comments to entries.

Bloggies: every year, the Weblog Awards, or Bloggies for short, are bestowed on the most read, enjoyed, and respected blogs on the Internet. The Bloggies are grouped into 30 award categories, and the award winners are chosen by the public.

blogosphere: the world of bloggers and blog readers.

RSS: stands for Rich Site Summary. Um, what? Well, say you find a new blog that you really like, but you keep checking back and nothing new has been added. If you sign up for the blog's RSS, you will be notified whenever a new entry has been posted.

blogroll: a list of other blogs that a blogger likes, respects, or just wants to advertise. Most people who write, read. Most people who play music listen to music. Most people who blog maintain a blogroll of blogs they admire.

Questions

15 Which of the following best describes how the author organized the information in this article?

   A. The author presents a history of blogging in chronological order.

   B. The author compares and contrasts blogging with other forms of communication.

   C. The author first explains what blogging is and then how to set up a blog.

   D. The author presents questions about blogging and then answers them.

 Tip

Skim the article and think about how its information is presented. Is there an overall pattern of organization from start to finish or does the first half differ from the second half?

16 Read these sentences from the article.

> **Include a blogroll on your site so that readers can visit the blogs that you find entertaining. Bloggers pay attention to being listed on others' sites, and they may even return the favor. In the blogosphere, what goes around comes around!**

By including this passage, the author wants to show that

   F. blogging is a cooperative effort among many writers.

   G. blogging is difficult and best left to expert writers.

   H. blogging involves stealing the work of other writers.

   I. blogging is much like a popularity contest.

Tip

Reread the passage and think about its main point. What does the author mean by "what goes around comes around"?

17 How does the Blogulary box help readers understand the article?

   A. It teaches readers step by step how to start their own blogs.

   B. It provides terms and definitions associated with blogging.

   C. It lists all the software and equipment needed to start a blog.

   D. It gives definitions of important terms from the article.

 Tip

Think about the title of the box. What word is the title playing on?

18 The author's main purpose in writing this article is to

   F. entertain readers with humorous stories about writers who become obsessed with blogging.

   G. inform readers about how the most popular blogs were started.

   H. encourage readers to read blogs and perhaps start blogs of their own.

   I. caution readers about the problems associated with starting a blog.

 Tip

What is the author trying to accomplish with the advice and details that are provided in the article?

 Answers

1 B

The author intends to convince readers that the legal minimum driving age should be raised. He indicates his intention in the second part of the title: *Why We Should Raise the Legal Driving Age.*

Benchmark: LA.910.1.7.2 The student will analyze the author's purpose and/or perspective in a variety of texts and understand how they affect meaning.

2 I

The author's main concern is the safety of young drivers and of other drivers. Again, the title gives a clue: *Safe at Sixteen*. He does not object to teenagers having freedom or focus on teenagers who don't have parents or guardians. He doesn't say that teenagers never wear seatbelts and always misjudge road conditions.

Benchmark: LA.910.1.7.3 The student will determine the main idea or essential message in grade-level or higher texts through inferring, paraphrasing, summarizing, and identifying relevant details.

3 A

The author organizes his article by providing details that support his argument that the driving age should be raised.

Benchmark: LA.910.1.7.5 The student will analyze a variety of text structures (e.g., comparison/contrast, cause/effect, chronological order, argument/support, lists) and text features (main headings with subheadings) and explain their impact on meaning in text.

4 G

All the choices are benefits that the Yangtze provides except for answer G. The fact that the river divides the country in half is of no particular benefit to the people compared with the other items.

Benchmark: LA.910.1.7.3 The student will determine the main idea or essential message in grade-level or higher texts through inferring, paraphrasing, summarizing, and identifying relevant details.

5   D

Both rivers flow from west to east, as the maps indicate. Both rivers also nourish crops with their waters. The Huang He is actually shorter than the Yangtze River. The major difference is that the Huang He contains huge amounts of yellowish silt.

Benchmark: LA.910.1.7.7 The student will compare and contrast elements in multiple texts.

6   I

According to the second article, "the river's heavy silt wears away at the dams very quickly, eventually making them useless."

Benchmark: LA.910.1.7.4 The student will identify cause-and-effect relationships in text.

7   C

The author relates the events of the story in time order, from Friday until Monday.

Benchmark: LA.910.1.7.5 The student will analyze a variety of text structures (e.g., comparison/contrast, cause/effect, chronological order, argument/support, lists) and text features (main headings with subheadings) and explain their impact on meaning in text.

8   G

The point of the story is that the superstitions did not help Pete and that he should have studied harder.

Benchmark: LA.910.17.3 The student will determine the main idea or essential message in grade-level or higher texts through inferring, paraphrasing, summarizing, and identifying relevant details.

9   A

Since this is a fiction passage, the author's main purpose is to entertain. If the story also persuades readers to abandon superstitions, that is a secondary purpose.

Benchmark: LA.910.1.7.2 The student will analyze the author's purpose and/or perspective in a variety of texts and understand how they affect meaning.

10 H

The author includes these sentences to show that conditions have changed and the old ten-month school schedule is no longer necessary to help farmers.

Benchmark: LA.910.1.7.3 The student will determine the main idea or essential message in grade-level or higher texts through inferring, paraphrasing, summarizing, and identifying relevant details.

11 D

According to the article, under multitrack systems "a district can educate more students without having to build new schools or ship students to other districts."

Benchmark: LA.910.1.7.4 The student will identify cause-and-effect relationships in text.

12 F

Each subheading briefly introduces the topic of the section that it begins.

Benchmark: LA.910.1.7.5 The student will analyze a variety of text structures (e.g., comparison/contrast, cause/effect, chronological order, argument/support, lists) and text features (main headings with subheadings) and explain their impact on meaning in text.

13 B

The idiom *throw in the towel* comes from boxing and means "to give up." Since the author says that students shouldn't "throw in their beach towels just yet," she is saying that students don't need to give up on spending their summers out of school. Many districts have opposed the switch to full-time schools.

Benchmark: LA.910.1.7.3 The student will determine the main idea or essential message in grade-level or higher texts through inferring, paraphrasing, summarizing, and identifying relevant details.

14 G

The author doesn't indicate that all schools should adopt a year-round education system because it has drawbacks as well as benefits, but she believes the system is something they should consider.

Benchmark: LA.910.1.7.2 The student will analyze the author's purpose and/or perspective in a variety of texts and understand how they affect meaning.

15 C

In the first half of the article, the author explains what blogging is, and in the second half the author describes how a person can begin a blog. The article does not have one organizational pattern from start to finish.

Benchmark: LA.910.1.7.5 The student will analyze a variety of text structures (e.g., comparison/contrast, cause/effect, chronological order, argument/support, lists) and text features (main headings with subheadings) and explain their impact on meaning in text.

16 F

The main point of the passage is that bloggers work together to increase their readership by linking to other blogs. The author describes this process as "what goes around comes around," or, in other words, returning the favor of linking to other blogs.

Benchmark: LA.910.1.7.3 The student will determine the main idea or essential message in grade-level or higher texts through inferring, paraphrasing, summarizing, and identifying relevant details.

17 B

The box serves as a glossary for the article and for the topic of blogging. It contains blog-related terms and their definitions. The title *Blogulary* is a play on the word "vocabulary." Notice that answer choice D is incorrect because some of the words in the Blogulary do not appear in the article but are connected to the topic of blogging.

Benchmark: LA.910.1.7.5 The student will analyze a variety of text structures (e.g., comparison/contrast, cause/effect, chronological order, argument/support, lists) and text features (main headings with subheadings) and explain their impact on meaning in text.

18 H

The author mainly wants to get readers interested in blogs and blogging, perhaps to the point of starting their own blogs. That is why the author explains in detail how to start a blog and increase its readership.

Benchmark: LA.910.1.7.2 The student will analyze the author's purpose and/or perspective in a variety of texts and understand how they affect meaning.

Chapter 3
Fiction

Fiction includes novels, stories, and plays that are made up by the author. Fiction may be realistic, like Stephen Crane's Civil War novel *The Red Badge of Courage,* or fantastical, like Shakespeare's *A Midsummer Night's Dream.* On the FCAT 2.0 Reading test, you will read passages from stories, plays, and poems and answer questions about elements in them. This chapter reviews some of the tools you will need to answer these questions correctly.

Major Genres and Literary Devices

Benchmarks

- **LA.910.2.1.1** The student will analyze and compare historically and culturally significant works of literature, identifying the relationships among the major genres (e.g., poetry, fiction, nonfiction, short story, dramatic literature, essay) and the literary devices unique to each, and analyze how they support and enhance the theme and main ideas of the text.

- **LA.910.2.1.8** The student will explain how ideas, values, and themes of a literary work often reflect the historical period in which it was written.

- **LA.910.2.1.10** The student will select a variety of age- and ability-appropriate fiction materials to read based on knowledge of author's styles, themes, and genres to expand the core foundation of knowledge necessary to connect topics and function as a fully literate member of a shared culture.

A **literary genre** is a category of literature with its own style, form, and content. Questions on the FCAT 2.0 will cover several different genres, including novels, short stories, memoirs, essays, poems, and plays. You should be able to analyze these genres and recognize what features they have in common and what features are unique to each. For example, a short story and a play both can present characters and tell a story. Yet they look different on the page, and a short story usually focuses on a single incident while a play often presents a series of events. You may be asked to identify the characteristic features of different genres and explain how an author uses them to get certain effects.

Each genre has its own literary devices. A **poem** may feature rhyme, meter, and figurative language. A **play** is written in dialogue form, and usually is based on a certain conflict between characters. A **short story** may contain devices such as foreshadowing or flashback. You will be tested on your ability to recognize these devices and understand how they are used to create effects or enhance the author's theme.

Different periods of history have seen genres become very popular or almost die away. In Elizabethan England, plays written in blank verse (such as those by Shakespeare) were extremely popular. In the early 1900s, dozens of magazines printed short stories in every issue. Today, however, plays are written in prose and few short stories appear each month. On the FCAT 2.0, you may be asked why a certain feature of a genre seems old-fashioned now, or how an author's period of history may have affected his or her writing.

Narrative Elements

Benchmark

- **LA.910.2.1.2** The student will analyze and compare a variety of traditional, classical, and contemporary literary works, and identify the literary elements of each (e.g., setting, plot, characterization, conflict).

The FCAT 2.0 will ask you to read and answer questions about prose fiction and plays. These items may be excerpts from novels or plays or entire short stories. You will be asked to identify tools that the author uses to develop a story, such as setting, plot, characterization, point of view, and conflict. Be prepared to analyze how these elements help to create the author's effects and present the theme.

- **Setting** is the time and place of a story's action. The setting can be in the past, present, or future. The setting may also be a specific location, such as Yankee Stadium or the Grand Canyon, or a vague location such as a house in the woods. The setting in a play is presented in stage directions, while the setting of a short story may be described by the narrator or suggested with specific details. The FCAT 2.0 may include questions about how the setting of a story or play affects its plot.

- **Plot** is the series of events in a story from beginning to end. A plot usually has a beginning, rising action, a climax, falling action, and a resolution. On the FCAT 2.0, you will be asked about the events that make up a plot and how they fit together. You may also be asked how the beginning of a story foreshadows its ending, or why the ending of a story is ironic.

- **Characterization** is how the characters in a fictional work are presented. Characters are people or animals in a story or play. An author may use actions, dialogue, physical descriptions, and styles of speaking to show what characters are like. In a novel or short story, characters are described; in a play, their words bring out their personalities. On the FCAT 2.0, you might be asked to choose which word or phrase best describes a character.

- **Point of view** is how the author chooses to tell a story. It may be a first-person story, which is told by one of the characters. The narrator in a first-person story has a limited point of view and cannot know everything that is going on. The story may be told in the third-person. This is sometimes called an **omniscient narrator,** or one that can tell everything that is happening including the characters' thoughts. Some stories feature both first-person and third-person points of view. The FCAT 2.0 may include questions about why an author used a certain point of view in a story.

- **Conflict** is the opposition between people or forces that creates dramatic interest in a plot. A character may be in conflict with another character, with society and its values, with him/herself, or even with nature. Conflict is usually presented as a problem that the main character must solve or overcome. On the FCAT 2.0, you may be asked to identify the conflict between two characters, or explain why a character has an inner conflict.

Features of Poetry

Benchmark

- **LA.910.2.1.3** The student will explain how meaning is enhanced through various features of poetry, including sound (e.g., rhythm, repetition, alliteration, consonance, assonance), structure (e.g., meter, rhyme scheme), and graphic elements (e.g., line length, punctuation, word position).

On the FCAT 2.0, you may be asked to analyze a poem. For example, you might see a question like this:

Read the following lines from Robert Frost's poem "Birches."

> **They click upon themselves**
>
> **As the breeze rises, and turn many-colored**
>
> **As the stir cracks and crazes their enamel.**

What literary device does the poet use in the last line above?

A. repetition

B. alliteration

C. personification

D. consonance

Notice that *cracks and crazes* is an example of alliteration, or repeating the beginning sounds of words. The correct answer is B. You may also be asked about the structure of a poem, such as its line lengths, stanzas, and punctuation. You might have to analyze how a poet uses imagery to express a theme.

You will find more about literary devices used in poetry in the section "Literary Elements and Figurative Language" below.

Universal Themes and Symbols

Benchmark

- **LA.910.2.1.4** The student will identify and analyze universal themes and symbols across genres and historical periods, and explain their significance.

The **theme** of a short story, play, or poem is the underlying message about life that its author seeks to convey. Certain themes such as "love conquers all" or "money is the root of all evil" have been used for centuries. Themes can sometimes be summed up in familiar maxims, such as "Don't judge a book by its cover" or "You reap what you sow." On the FCAT 2.0, you might be asked to identify the theme in a literary work and how the author explores it.

A **symbol** is a literary device in which a person or thing represents an emotion or abstract idea. For example, a dried flower pressed in a book might represent the love that an older woman once felt as a teenager. A growing crack in a wall might stand for the tension in an unhappy family. The Russian playwright Anton Chekhov famously used a dead seagull as a symbol for a young girl who had been mistreated and abandoned by others. On the FCAT 2.0, you may be asked to identify a symbol or what it represents.

Literary Elements and Figurative Language

Benchmarks

• **LA.910.2.1.5** The student will analyze and develop an interpretation of a literary work by describing an author's use of literary elements (e.g., theme, point of view, characterization, setting, plot), and explain and analyze different elements of figurative language (e.g., simile, metaphor, personification, hyperbole, symbolism, allusion, imagery).

• **LA.910.2.1.7** The student will analyze, interpret, and evaluate an author's use of descriptive language (e.g., tone, irony, mood, imagery, pun, alliteration, onomatopoeia, allusion), figurative language (e.g., symbolism, metaphor, personification, hyperbole), common idioms, and mythological and literary allusions, and explain how they impact meaning in a variety of texts.

We've already discussed the narrative tools that authors use in fiction. On the FCAT 2.0, you might also be asked about figurative language in a short story, play, or poem. This is language used to create an image or to compare things in an imaginative way. Examples of figurative language include the following.

- A **simile** compares two unlike things using the words *like* or *as*. Robert Frost uses this simile: "a moth/ like a piece of rigid satin cloth."

- A **metaphor** compares two unlike things directly, without *like* or *as*. Emily Dickinson uses this metaphor: "Hope is the thing with feathers."

- **Personification** describes something nonhuman as if it were a person: "After I tripped over the footstool, it stood there with a straight face, trying not to laugh."

- **Hyperbole** is an extreme exaggeration to make a point: "It was so hot outside that the birds were panting instead of singing."

- An **allusion** is a reference to a person, place, or thing from literature or mythology. Literary allusion: "She was ready to fall in love like Juliet, but had yet to find her Romeo." Mythological allusion: "I don't think Hercules could loosen the lug nuts on that wheel."

- **Imagery** is the use of language to appeal to one or more of the senses: "The splashing sounds, the smell of chlorine, and the patter of children's feet on wet concrete brought back memories of poolside vacations."

- **Tone** is the attitude or feeling towards the characters or subject that an author expresses with language. The tone of a comic story is lighthearted, while a tragic tale has a more solemn tone.

- **Mood** is the overall feeling that a short story or poem conveys. For example, a detective story may contain words such as *deceptive, baffling,* and *shrouded* to create a mood of mystery.

- **Irony** can refer to verbal irony, situational irony, or dramatic irony. **Verbal irony** is saying one thing and meaning the opposite: "I hope you're feeling good about breaking my vase." **Situational irony** is when an occurrence is the opposite of what was expected: "I bought a book called *Bad Luck* and found a hundred dollar bill inside!" **Dramatic irony** is when the reader or the audience knows more about a situation than the characters in a story or play.

- A **pun** is a play on words: "Trying to write with a broken pencil is pointless."

- **Onomatopoeia** is the use of words that sound like what they mean: *sizzle, creak, plop.*

- An **idiom** is a phrase whose meaning is different from that of its separate words: "I will take heart even though I've fallen on hard times."

Time and Sequence

Benchmark

- **LA.910.2.1.6** The student will create a complex, multi-genre response to the reading of two or more literary works, describing and analyzing an author's use of literary elements (e.g., theme, point of view, characterization, setting, plot), figurative language (e.g., simile, metaphor, personification, hyperbole, symbolism, allusion, imagery), and analyzing an author's development of time and sequence through the use of complex literary devices such as foreshadowing and flashback.

On the FCAT 2.0, you may be asked about how an author uses foreshadowing and flashback to provide plot information or emphasize a theme. These literary devices interrupt the time sequence of a story to give extra information. **Foreshadowing** is used by an author to provide a glimpse of later events or clues to what will happen at the end of a story. A **flashback** is a description of earlier events that helps explain what happens in a story and why it happened.

Multi-Genre Response

Benchmark

• **LA.910.2.1.6** The student will create a complex, multi-genre response to the reading of two or more literary works, describing and analyzing an author's use of literary elements (e.g., theme, point of view, characterization, setting, plot), figurative language (e.g., simile, metaphor, personification, hyperbole, symbolism, allusion, imagery), and analyzing an author's development of time and sequence through the use of complex literary devices such as foreshadowing and flashback.

For some questions on the FCAT 2.0, you will have to gather information from more than one source and draw a conclusion. You might have to read two passages by different authors about the same subject. You might compare excerpts from a novel and a play on the same topic. You might even read a passage and look at a map and draw a conclusion based on the two. When answering questions about multiple genres or passages, you first should eliminate answer choices that are untrue or that apply to only one genre or passage.

English Language Patterns and Vocabulary

Benchmark

• **LA.910.2.1.9** The student will identify, analyze, and compare the differences in English language patterns and vocabulary choices of contemporary and historical texts.

On the FCAT 2.0, you may be asked about English words or phrases that had a different meaning or tone years ago than they do today. Be prepared to choose the word or words that define or are the equivalent of older words and phrases.

Passage 1

Read the following passage. Then answer the questions that follow. Use the Tip below each question to help you choose the correct answer. When you finish, read the answer explanations at the end of this chapter.

Excerpt from *Ripe Figs*
by Kate Chopin

Maman-Nainaine said that when the figs were ripe Babette might go to visit her cousins down on Bayou-Boeuf, where the sugar cane grows. Not that the ripening of figs had the least thing to do with it, but that is the way Maman-Nainaine was.

It seemed to Babette a very long time to wait; for the leaves upon the trees were tender yet, and the figs were like little hard, green marbles.

But warm rains came along and plenty of strong sunshine; and though Maman-Nainaine was as patient as the statue of la Madone, and Babette as restless as a humming-bird, the first thing they both knew it was hot summer-time. Every day Babette danced out to where the fig-trees were in a long line against the fence. She walked slowly beneath them, carefully peering between the gnarled, spreading branches. But each time she came disconsolate away again. What she saw there finally was something that made her sing and dance the whole day long.

When Maman-Nainaine sat down in her stately way to breakfast, the following morning, her muslin cap standing like an aureole about her white, placid face, Babette approached. She bore a dainty porcelain platter, which she set down before her godmother. It contained a dozen purple figs, fringed around with their rich, green leaves.

"Ah," said Maman-Nainaine, arching her eyebrows, "how early the figs have ripened this year!"

"Oh," said Babette, "I think they have ripened very late."

"Babette," continued Maman-Nainaine, as she peeled the very plumpest figs with her pointed silver fruit-knife, "you will carry my love to them all down on Bayou-Boeuf. And tell your tante Frosine I shall look for her at Toussaint—when the chrysanthemums are in bloom."

❓ Questions

1   Read the following sentences from the passage.

Maman-Nainaine said that when the figs were ripe Babette might go to visit her cousins down on Bayou-Boeuf, where the sugar cane grows. Not that the ripening of figs had the least thing to do with it, but that is the way Maman-Nainaine was.

These sentences serve to show that Maman-Nainaine is

A. cruel.

B. confused.

C. inscrutable.

D. cautious.

 Tip

Remember that Maman-Nainaine thinks the figs have ripened early and Babette thinks they have ripened very late.

2   When the author writes that Babette was "as restless as a humming bird," she is using

F. personification.

G. symbolism.

H. metaphor.

I. simile.

 Tip

What kind of literary device uses comparison?

3   Which sentence best describes the main idea of the passage?

    A. Some people are more patient than others.

    B. The young and old view time differently.

    C. Planning an important trip takes time.

    D. Waiting for figs to ripen can be frustrating.

 Tip

Consider what the entire passage is about. What causes the conflict between Maman-Nainaine and Babette?

Passage 2

Read the following passage. Then answer the questions that follow. Use the Tip below each question to help you choose the correct answer. When you finish, read the answer explanations at the end of this chapter.

If You Were Coming in the Fall
by Emily Dickinson

If you were coming in the fall,

I'd brush the summer by

With half a smile and half a spurn,

As housewives do a fly.

If I could see you in a year,

I'd wind the months in balls,

And put them each in separate drawers,

Until their time befalls.

If only centuries delayed,

I'd count them on my hand,

Subtracting till my fingers dropped

Into Van Diemen's land.[1]

If certain, when this life was out,

That yours and mine should be,

I'd toss it yonder like a rind,

And taste eternity.

But now, all ignorant of the length

Of time's uncertain wing,

It goads me, like the goblin bee,

That will not state its sting.

1. Van Diemen's land: Tasmania, an island off the coast of Australia.

 **Questions**

4   What is the speaker's problem in this poem?

   F.   She is uncertain where she will spend eternity.

   G.   She is angry because a special person refuses to see her again.

   H.   She is uncertain when she will be reunited with someone she loves.

   I.   She is fearful that time is passing too quickly.

 Tip

The poem is mostly about the passage of time. Why is time a problem for the speaker?

5   What is the speaker's tone in the poem?

   A.   weary

   B.   reflective

   C.   resentful

   D.   humorous

 Tip

Eliminate answer choices that are obviously incorrect. Choose the one that best describes how the speaker communicates her feelings.

6   Which word best describes the speaker's feelings in the last stanza?

   F.   frightened

   G.   bothered

   H.   outraged

   I.   resigned

 Tip

Think about what the speaker describes in the last two lines of the poem. What kind of feelings might result from this?

7   Read the following stanza from the poem.

   If only centuries delayed,

   I'd count them on my hand,

   Subtracting till my fingers dropped

   Into Van Diemen's land.

   These lines contain an example of what literary device?

   A. onomatopoeia

   B. personification

   C. hyperbole

   D. symbolism

 Tip

What literary device would refer to a delay of "only centuries" and "subtracting till my fingers dropped"?

8   For the structure of her poem, the author uses all of the following EXCEPT

   F. regular rhythm.

   G. repetition of phrases.

   H. rhyming words.

   I. punctuation.

 Tip

Think about the features of poetry that contribute to a poem's structure.

Passage 3

Read the following passage. Then answer the questions that follow. Use the Tip below each question to help you choose the correct answer. When you finish, read the answer explanations at the end of this chapter.

Excerpt from Act I of *The Importance of Being Earnest*
by Oscar Wilde

Jack Worthing is the adopted son of the late Thomas Cardew and inherited the Cardew estate in the English countryside. There, as the owner of a large tract of land, Jack has several tenant farmers and a large house full of servants who depend on him. But there is another side to Jack. To his friends and family in the country, he pretends to have an irresponsible brother named Ernest who lives in London and is always getting into trouble, forcing Jack to rush to his aid. In fact, Ernest and Jack are one and the same. Jack's phantom double allows him to abandon his responsibilities for days at a time. In London, where Jack is known only as Ernest Worthing, he engages in the very sort of behavior he pretends to disapprove of in his imaginary brother.

Scene: Morning-room in Algernon's flat in Half-Moon Street. The room is luxuriously and artistically furnished.

ALGERNON: How are you, my dear Ernest? What brings you up to town?

JACK: Oh, pleasure, pleasure! What else should bring one anywhere? Eating as usual, I see, Algy!

ALGERNON: [*Stiffly.*] I believe it is customary in good society to take some slight refreshment at five o'clock. Where have you been since last Thursday?

JACK: [*Sitting down on the sofa.*] In the country.

ALGERNON: What on earth do you do there?

JACK: [*Pulling off his gloves.*] When one is in town one amuses oneself. When one is in the country one amuses other people. It is excessively boring.

ALGERNON: And who are the people you amuse?

JACK: [*Airily.*] Oh, neighbours, neighbours.

ALGERNON: Got nice neighbours in your part of Shropshire?

JACK: Perfectly horrid! Never speak to one of them.

ALGERNON: How immensely you must amuse them! [*Goes over and takes sandwich.*] By the way, Shropshire is your county, is it not?

JACK: Eh? Shropshire? Yes, of course. Hallo! Why all these cups? Why cucumber sandwiches? Why such reckless extravagance in one so young? Who is coming to tea?

ALGERNON: Oh! merely Aunt Augusta and Gwendolen.

JACK: How perfectly delightful!

ALGERNON: Yes, that is all very well; but I am afraid Aunt Augusta won't quite approve of your being here.

JACK: May I ask why?

ALGERNON: My dear fellow, the way you flirt with Gwendolen is perfectly disgraceful. It is almost as bad as the way Gwendolen flirts with you.

JACK: I am in love with Gwendolen. I have come up to town expressly to propose to her.

ALGERNON: I thought you had come up for pleasure? . . . I call that business.

JACK: How utterly unromantic you are!

ALGERNON: I really don't see anything romantic in proposing. It is very romantic to be in love. But there is nothing romantic about a definite proposal. Why, one may be accepted. One usually is, I believe. Then the excitement is all over. The very essence of romance is uncertainty. If ever I get married, I'll certainly try to forget the fact.

JACK: I have no doubt about that, dear Algy. The Divorce Court was specially invented for people whose memories are so curiously constituted.

ALGERNON: Oh! there is no use speculating on that subject. Divorces are made in Heaven— [*JACK puts out his hand to take a sandwich. ALGERNON at once interferes.*] Please don't touch the cucumber sandwiches. They are ordered specially for Aunt Augusta. [*Takes one and eats it.*]

JACK: Well, you have been eating them all the time.

ALGERNON: That is quite a different matter. She is my aunt. [*Takes plate from below.*] Have some bread and butter. The bread and butter is for Gwendolen. Gwendolen is devoted to bread and butter.

JACK: [*Advancing to table and helping himself.*] And very good bread and butter it is too.

ALGERNON: Well, my dear fellow, you need not eat as if you were going to eat it all. You behave as if you were married to her already. You are not married to her already, and I don't think you ever will be.

JACK: Why on earth do you say that?

ALGERNON: Well, in the first place girls never marry the men they flirt with. Girls don't think it right.

JACK: Oh, that is nonsense!

ALGERNON: It isn't. It is a great truth. It accounts for the extraordinary number of bachelors that one sees all over the place. In the second place, I don't give my consent.

JACK: Your consent!

ALGERNON: My dear fellow, Gwendolen is my first cousin. And before I allow you to marry her, you will have to clear up the whole question of Cecily. [*Rings bell.*]

JACK: Cecily! What on earth do you mean? What do you mean, Algy, by Cecily! I don't know any one of the name of Cecily.

[*Enter LANE.*]

ALGERNON: Bring me that cigarette case Mr. Worthing left in the smoking-room the last time he dined here.

LANE: Yes, sir. [*LANE goes out.*]

JACK: Do you mean to say you have had my cigarette case all this time? I wish to goodness you had let me know. I have been writing frantic letters to Scotland Yard about it. I was very nearly offering a large reward.

ALGERNON: Well, I wish you would offer one. I happen to be more than usually hard up.

JACK: There is no good offering a large reward now that the thing is found.

[*Enter LANE with the cigarette case on a salver. ALGERNON takes it at once. LANE goes out.*]

ALGERNON: I think that is rather mean of you, Ernest, I must say. [*Opens case and examines it.*] However, it makes no matter, for, now that I look at the inscription inside, I find that the thing isn't yours after all.

JACK: Of course it's mine. [*Moving to him.*] You have seen me with it a hundred times, and you have no right whatsoever to read what is written inside. It is a very ungentlemanly thing to read a private cigarette case.

ALGERNON: Oh! it is absurd to have a hard and fast rule about what one should read and what one shouldn't. More than half of modern culture depends on what one shouldn't read.

JACK: I am quite aware of the fact, and I don't propose to discuss modern culture. It isn't the sort of thing one should talk of in private. I simply want my cigarette case back.

ALGERNON: Yes; but this isn't your cigarette case. This cigarette case is a present from some one of the name of Cecily, and you said you didn't know any one of that name.

 Questions

9   What is the central conflict of this excerpt?

   A. the social conventions of the city versus those of the country

   B. the relationship between Jack and Gwendolen

   C. the rivalry between two old friends

   D. the sincerity of Jack's love for Gwendolen

 Tip

Think about why Algernon does not want Jack to marry Gwendolyn.

10 Which pair of words best describes Algernon?

   F. witty and imaginative

   G. controlling and deceitful

   H. intelligent and manipulative

   I. insightful and cruel

 Tip

Reread the excerpt, paying close attention to Algernon's words and actions. Then choose the answer choice that describes him best.

11 Read the following lines from the play.

JACK: I was very nearly offering a large reward.

ALGERNON: Well, I wish you would offer one. I happen to be more than usually hard up.

In this excerpt, the phrase "hard up" means

A. busy.

B. lacking money.

C. in debt.

D. greedy.

 Tip

To find the meaning of the idiom, think about the context of the phrase.

12 Oscar Wilde wrote this play in 1895. Which element of the play would be least likely to be used in a modern play?

F. the style of speech

G. the comic tone

H. the romantic plot

I. the London setting

 Tip

Think about the different elements of this play. Did one of the elements in the answer choices strike you as somewhat outdated?

Passage 4

Read the following passage. Then answer the questions that follow. Use the Tip below each question to help you choose the correct answer. When you finish, read the answer explanations at the end of this chapter.

Logan's Lesson

Logan slammed the passenger door of his father's pickup truck and gazed warily at the main entrance of the Oceanside Nursing Home. He groaned inwardly and trudged toward the door, each step feeling heavier than the previous one.

Inside, Logan was greeted by a receptionist with a smile the size of the Florida panhandle and more perkiness in her greeting than Logan had been able to muster in his entire life. Her name tag said Suzanne. "You must be Logan," she chirped. "I can't *wait* for you to meet our residents."

Suzanne motioned for Logan to follow her, and he struggled to maintain the Olympic pace she set as she sped down a long corridor toward a set of double doors. A sign near the doors indicated that he was standing outside the Recreation Room. Peering through the window, Logan spied about a dozen silver-haired men and women in the room. Two men played a game of checkers in the corner, while another maneuvered a small scooter toward a rack of magazines. A few women sat in a circle of rocking chairs around a television watching a news program. One of them held yarn and knitting needles in her lap. On the far side of the room, one elderly man with white hair sat at a table by himself carving something from a small scrap of wood.

"That's Hector. I think you two will get along quite nicely," said Suzanne, pointing to the man at the far table.

Suzanne's pager began to beep, and after glancing at the numbers, she sprinted down the corridor. "I'm afraid you're on your own, Logan. I've got to get back to the reception area," she explained as she disappeared around the corner.

Logan sighed, shifted his backpack to his left shoulder, and shuffled toward Hector's table. As Logan extended his hand to introduce himself, Hector spoke. "Troublemaker, eh?"

Logan stepped back and withdrew his hand, the puzzled look on his face prompting Hector to continue.

"They always send me the troublemakers," he said, turning back to his wooden sculpture. "That, and your black eye gave you away."

Logan raised his hand to touch the painful bruise near his right eye. Hector's insights were correct. Logan's punishment for getting into a fight at school was to spend at least one hour every day at the nursing home until the end of the semester. Mr. Weatherby, the principal at Logan's high school, thought that spending time with some of the elderly residents at Ocean-side would help him learn to care about others' thoughts and feelings.

Logan settled into the chair across from Hector. He watched silently as sawdust and shavings fell from the scrap of wood in Hector's wrinkled hands, until finally Hector set down his carving knife and placed the finished sculpture on the table. Logan carefully examined the petite form, amazed by the intricate details etched into the wood. It was a boxer wearing a helmet and boxing gloves, his feet slightly separated and his arms in a position indicating that he was ready to fight.

Logan glanced at Hector. "A fighter for a fighter," said the old man. With that, he lifted himself from his chair and moved toward the door.

"Wait," said Logan. "Aren't we supposed to talk or something?"

Hector turned around and winked, then disappeared through the double doors. Glancing at his watch, Logan realized that an hour had already passed and that his father would be waiting for him. He scooped the wooden figurine off the table, wrapped it in a tissue, and placed it in the zippered pouch of his backpack.

Logan remained quiet on the way home, thinking about the unusual events of the afternoon. Hector had called him a troublemaker and a fighter. It was a fitting description, but Logan had never intended to be either. It just seemed that sometimes, when someone or something made him angry or upset, he felt the need to release his anger, and the easiest way to do that was to punch, kick, or break something.

That night, Logan rummaged through his backpack until he found the boxer statue. Placing it on his desk, he stared at it for a long time. When he finally crawled into bed, he knew what he could discuss with Hector.

The next day, Logan looked for Hector in the Recreation Room, but he was nowhere to be found. Returning to the reception area, Logan ask Suzanne for directions to Hector's living quarters, but she informed him that Hector was on the balcony outside the craft room on the second floor. At the top of the steps, Logan made a left as Suzanne had instructed and walked the length of a blue hallway. He opened a door on the left and entered a room lined with shelves and overflowing with cans of paint, bottles of glue, stacks of paper, and a mishmash of other art supplies. Through the sliding door, Logan could see Hector standing at an easel, and beyond him, a magnificent view of the Atlantic Ocean.

"You paint, too," said Logan as he stepped outside.

Hector turned toward Logan, revealing a painting so similar to the ocean view Logan had just admired that the boy wondered if he was looking through an empty frame.

"What else do you do?" Logan asked.

Hector thought for a moment, and then explained that his numerous creative activities corresponded to how he felt at a particular point in time. When feeling happy or peaceful, he painted, and when feeling lonely or sad, he wrote poetry. When nervous, such as when he's about to meet someone new, he liked to whittle away at a piece of wood. Logan smiled, thinking of the wooden boxer. He was amazed by Hector's artistic abilities—poetry, paintings, drawings, sculptures, and carvings—each chosen to convey a certain mood, thought, or feeling.

"What do you do when you're angry?" asked Logan.

This time it was Hector who smiled. "I build things. Whether it's a chair, a table, or a simple puzzle, building things helps me release my anger *con*structively, rather than *destruc*tively," he explained.

Hector went inside to rinse his paintbrushes, and Logan contemplated what the old man had told him. A few minutes later, Logan joined Hector at the sink. "How do you release your emotions if you have no artistic abilities?" he asked. Like the day before, Hector winked and left Logan standing alone, filled with questions.

When Logan arrived home, his mother yelled at him for forgetting to take the trash out. Later, his father grounded him because of Logan's poor showing on his history exam. Retiring to his room for the night, Logan then noticed that his sister's hamster had chewed a hole through one of his new sneakers. Logan could feel his anger building, but just as he was about to explode, he caught a glimpse of the wooden figurine on his desk.

Taking a deep breath, Logan thought of Hector. *Do something constructive, not destructive,* he said to himself. Looking around his room, Logan spied his guitar in the corner. He hadn't touched it in years, but something inside told him to pick it up and play. Sitting on the corner of his bed, he rested the guitar on his lap and began plucking the strings. Instantly, the storm that had been building inside him dissipated, and his shoulders relaxed.

Logan played cards with Hector in the Recreation Room the next day, and they exchanged stories about their families and friends. At the end of the hour, Logan hoisted his backpack and guitar case onto his shoulders, said goodbye, and started to walk away. When he reached the door, he turned around and winked at Hector.

"Thanks," he said.

 **Questions**

13 Why is the setting at the beginning of the story important?

    A. It helps explain why Logan is uneasy and reluctant.

    B. It shows that Logan is a generous person.

    C. It provides a contrast with Logan's school.

    D. It provides a clue to why Logan gets so angry.

 Tip

Do you think Logan has been in this setting before? How does he feel there?

14 Why does Hector think that Logan is a troublemaker?

    F. He sees Logan carrying a backpack.

    G. He finds out that Logan plays the guitar.

    H. He knows why kids come to the nursing home after school.

    I. He sees Logan's black eye.

 Tip

Scan the story and find the section where the word *troublemaker* appears. Which answer choice fits what happens in this section?

15 Which of the following best expresses the theme of this story?

    A. "How do you release your emotions if you have no artistic abilities?"

    B. "A fighter for a fighter."

    C. *Do something constructive, not destructive.*

    D. When feeling happy or peaceful, he painted.

 Tip

Think about the main point the author is making in this story.

✔ Answers

1 C

The sentences indicate that Maman-Nainaine sets the time for the trip for no particular reason — "but that is the way Maman-Nainaine was." Thus, she is *inscrutable,* or difficult to pin down as to the reasons for her behavior.

Benchmark: LA.910.2.1.2 The student will analyze and compare a variety of traditional, classical, and contemporary literary works, and identify the literary elements of each (e.g., setting, plot, characterization, conflict).

2 I

The phrase "as restless as a humming-bird" uses the word *as* to compare two unlike things, so it is a simile.

Benchmark: LA.910.2.1.5 The student will analyze and develop an interpretation of a literary work by describing an author's use of literary elements (e.g., theme, point of view, characterization, setting, plot), and explain and analyze different elements of figurative language (e.g., simile, metaphor, personification, hyperbole, symbolism, allusion, imagery).

3 B

The passage implies that patience is something that is learned with age. Waiting is harder for the young.

Benchmark: LA.910.2.1.4 The student will identify and analyze universal themes and symbols across genres and historical periods, and explain their significance.

4 H

The speaker doesn't know when she will see a certain person again and the uncertainty is nettling her. She does expect to see the person again apparently. But her overall concern is not about eternity or love and marriage.

Benchmark: LA.910.2.1.2 The student will analyze and compare a variety of traditional, classical, and contemporary literary works, and identify the literary elements of each (e.g., setting, plot, characterization, conflict).

5 B

The speaker spends a lot of time reflecting on, or thinking about, the time that may pass before she sees this person again.

Benchmark: LA.910.2.1.7 The student will analyze, interpret, and evaluate an author's use of descriptive language (e.g., tone, irony, mood, imagery, pun, alliteration, onomatopoeia, allusion), figurative language (e.g., symbolism, metaphor, personification, hyperbole), common idioms, and mythological and literary allusions, and explain how they impact meaning in a variety of texts.

6 H

The speaker says the situation "goads" her, or provokes her. She is obviously bothered by her lover's uncertain return.

Benchmark: LA.910.2.1.2 The student will analyze and compare a variety of traditional, classical, and contemporary literary works, and identify the literary elements of each (e.g., setting, plot, characterization, conflict).

7 C

Since the speaker exaggerates a delay of "only" centuries and imagines subtracting centuries till her fingers drop off, she is using hyperbole.

Benchmark: LA.910.2.1.5 The student will analyze and develop an interpretation of a literary work by describing an author's use of literary elements (e.g., theme, point of view, characterization, setting, plot), and explain and analyze different elements of figurative language (e.g., simile, metaphor, personification, hyperbole, symbolism, allusion, imagery).

8 G

The author does not repeat phrases in the poem, so G is the correct answer.

Benchmark: LA.910.2.1.3 The student will explain how meaning is enhanced through various features of poetry, including sound (e.g., rhythm, repetition, alliteration, consonance, assonance), structure (e.g., meter, rhyme scheme), and graphic elements (e.g., line length, punctuation, word position).

9   D

Although answer choice B might seem correct, the main conflict is whether Jack is telling the truth. If he is lying to Algernon, he may not be honest to Gwendolen either. Answer choice D is the best answer.

Benchmark: LA.910.2.1.2 The student will analyze and compare a variety of traditional, classical, and contemporary literary works, and identify the literary elements of each (e.g., setting, plot, characterization, conflict).

10 H

While many of the words describe Algernon, answer choice H is best because Algernon shows that he is intelligent not only with his clever words but also by tricking Jack into revealing the truth.

Benchmark: LA.910.2.1.5 The student will analyze and develop an interpretation of a literary work by describing an author's use of literary elements (e.g., theme, point of view, characterization, setting, plot), and explain and analyze different elements of figurative language (e.g., simile, metaphor, personification, hyperbole, symbolism, allusion, imagery).

11 B

When Jack mentions a reward, Algernon says he is "more than usually hard up." This means he could use the money because he doesn't have as much as usual.

Benchmark: LA.910.2.1.7 The student will analyze, interpret, and evaluate an author's use of descriptive language (e.g., tone, irony, mood, imagery, pun, alliteration, onomato-poeia, allusion), figurative language (e.g., symbolism, metaphor, personification, hyper-bole), common idioms, and mythological and literary allusions, and explain how they impact meaning in a variety of texts.

12 F

The elaborate style of speech in this play would probably not be used in a modern drama. Today's plays and movies tend to have simpler, more colloquial dialogue — that is, dialogue that is like everyday speech.

Benchmark: LA.910.2.1.8 The student will explain how ideas, values, and themes of a literary work often reflect the historical period in which it was written.

13 A

The setting, which is a nursing home, is evidently new and unappealing to Logan, since he trudges his way toward the door. A nursing home is not a usual place for a teenager to visit.

Benchmark: LA.910.2.1.2 The student will analyze and compare a variety of traditional, classical, and contemporary literary works, and identify the literary elements of each (e.g., setting, plot, characterization, conflict).

14 I

Hector tells Logan that the troublemakers are always sent to him, and he sees Logan's black eye.

Benchmark: LA.910.2.1.2 The student will analyze and compare a variety of traditional, classical, and contemporary literary works, and identify the literary elements of each (e.g., setting, plot, characterization, conflict).

15 C

Hector tells Logan that doing something creative helps him release his anger constructively, not destructively. It is the main lesson that he teaches Logan.

Benchmark: LA.910.2.1.4 The student will identify and analyze universal themes and symbols across genres and historical periods, and explain their significance.

Chapter 4

Nonfiction and Informational Text

Nonfiction is fact-based text that deals with the real world. Most of the nonfiction you'll encounter on the FCAT 2.0 is informational text. While these passages present facts, they may also be written so as to emphasize the author's opinions or point of view. You may see questions about magazine articles, autobiographies, letters to the editor, travel guidebooks, or user's manuals.

Text Features

Benchmarks
- **LA.910.2.2.1** The student will analyze and evaluate information from text features (e.g., transitional devices, table of contents, glossary, index, bold or italicized text, headings, charts and graphs, illustrations, subheadings).
- **LA.910.6.1.1** The student will explain how text features (e.g., charts, maps, diagrams, subheadings, captions, illustrations, graphs) aid the reader's understanding.

On the FCAT 2.0, you will be questioned about text features in informational text. These are features that help you understand an article by presenting extra information. You might be asked about photographs and illustrations, footnotes, subheadings, diagrams, charts and graphs — anything that adds to the meaning of the article.

To answer questions about text features, look carefully at all parts of the article. Think about how each text feature supports the article's main idea. For example, a bar graph showing a rise in movie ticket prices might accompany an article on how movie attendance has changed over the years. There might also be a caption to explain the purpose of the bar graph. Be prepared to explain the purpose of the bar graph or analyze how it supports the main idea of the article.

Use Information

Benchmark

- **LA.910.2.2.2** The student will use information from the text to answer questions or to state the main idea or provide relevant details.

The FCAT 2.0 will ask you to find details in informational text to answer questions. Often you will be asked to find the main idea of a section or of the entire article. You may also be required to identify the detail that supports a particular idea or point of view. Always read each question carefully, so that you understand exactly what information is needed for the answer.

Organize Information

Benchmark

- **LA.910.2.2.3** The student will organize information to show understanding of relationships among facts, ideas, and events (e.g., representing key points within text through charting, mapping, paraphrasing, summarizing, comparing, contrasting, or outlining).

This benchmark tests you on your ability to see how facts and ideas fit together in informational text. Needless to say, you won't have to draw a map or chart or even make an outline on the FCAT 2.0. Still, you may have to analyze the text using one of the kinds of graphic organizers for important facts. Mainly, you will have to organize facts and ideas according to their importance or how they relate to each other. For example, facts may be organized by cause and effect or in chronological order.

Evaluate Information

Benchmark

- **LA.910.6.2.2** The student will organize, synthesize, analyze, and evaluate the validity and reliability of information from multiple sources (including primary and secondary sources) to draw conclusions using a variety of techniques, and correctly use standardized citations.

To answer questions on the FCAT 2.0 that assess this benchmark, you'll need to read the passages carefully and show that you understand them. You might have to analyze or synthesize information. When you synthesize information, you process it, which means that you understand it so completely that you can use it in a different situation or context.

On the FCAT 2.0, you may also be asked to compare two or more texts to decide which is more reliable as a source of information. In particular, you might compare a primary source, which is written in a person's own words, to a secondary source, which is written about the person by someone else. For example, a personal letter written by Eleanor Roosevelt would be a more reliable source about an incident in her life than a newspaper article written by a reporter.

In the same way, some texts are more valid — or carry more weight — than others. Suppose you are doing research for a school report about types of bridges. You find two essays in the library. One is written by an architect who has designed bridges, including the Dames Point Bridge in Jacksonville, Florida. The other essay is written by a student and gives her personal opinions on what types of bridges are the most beautiful. Which essay would you read first? The one by the architect, of course! The information in that essay is more likely to be valid and reliable.

Characteristics of a Variety of Types of Text

Benchmark

 • **LA.910.2.2.4** The student will identify and analyze the characteristics of a variety of types of text (e.g., references, reports, technical manuals, articles, editorials, primary source historical documents, periodicals, job-related materials, practical/functional text).

On the FCAT 2.0, you will see questions about several kinds of informational text. Most of the passages will be nonfiction articles on various topics. You will also see technical manuals, job-related handbooks, and other practical kinds of text. You might be questioned about part of a manual for operating a flat-screen television or a cell phone. Other questions might address an on-the-job safety handbook for employees at a fast-food restaurant. Treat these passages as you would any other kind of text. Read them carefully and look for any special features or illustrations that are included.

Reading Nonfiction Materials

Benchmark

• **LA.910.2.2.5** The student will select a variety of age and ability appropriate nonfiction materials (e.g., biographies and topical areas, such as science, music, art, history, sports, current events) to expand the core knowledge necessary to connect topics and function as a fully literate member of a shared culture.

You won't be tested on this benchmark on the FCAT 2.0. However, just as it is important for you to read a variety of fiction and poetry, you should also read many kinds of nonfiction texts. Seek out books and magazines on science topics or about famous explorers or inventors. Find websites that investigate historical subjects or discuss new breakthroughs in technology. This kind of wide-ranging reading will help you handle the FCAT 2.0 articles more easily.

To help get you going, on the following pages we have given you five passages that cover nonfiction topics.

Passage 1

Read the following passage. Then answer the questions that follow. Use the Tip below each question to help you choose the correct answer. When you finish, read the answer explanations at the end of this chapter.

Carbohydrate Craze

Carb-Free Is Unhealthy

by Dr. Rubina Gad

The American public's obsession with dieting has led to one of the most dangerous health misconceptions of all time. Many television ads, sitcoms, movies, magazine articles, and diet-food product labels would have consumers believe that carbohydrates are bad for the human body and that those who eat them will quickly become overweight. We are advised to avoid foods such as pasta, potatoes, rice, and white bread and opt for meats and vegetables instead. Some companies promote this idea to encourage consumers to buy their "carb-free" food products. But the truth is, as I stress to patients who come to our weight-loss clinic, the human body needs carbohydrates to function properly, and a body that is starved of this dietary element is not in good shape after all.

Carbohydrates are macronutrients, meaning they are essential sources of fuel that are necessary for survival. Contrary to popular belief, carbohydrates have many health benefits; however, the key to maintaining a healthy body is to consume these and other macronutrients—such as protein and fat—in appropriate amounts.

Most foods that we consume on a daily basis are loaded with carbohydrates. Many people mistakenly believe that carbohydrates can only be found in filling foods such as potatoes and pastas. In truth, carbohydrates are also naturally found in fruits, vegetables, dairy products, and whole grains. Many of these carbohydrate-containing foods also have essential health benefits; some fight diseases such as high blood pressure and heart disease, and others help to prevent cancer and stroke. Cutting these foods out of your diet may increase your chances of contracting one of these diseases. It also deprives your body of the many health benefits of carbohydrates.

One of the best benefits of carbohydrates is their ability to provide fuel to the muscles and the brain. They also help to maintain the health of our organs, tissues, and cells. Scientific studies have shown that one type of carbohydrate called fiber, also commonly referred to as roughage, reduces the risk of heart disease and diabetes. Carbohydrates also contain antioxidants, which protect the body's cells from harmful particles with the potential to cause cancer.

This does not mean that the human body can survive on a diet composed entirely of carbohydrates. We also need certain percentages of proteins and fats to maintain healthy bodies. But carbohydrates certainly should not be avoided altogether. In fact, the food pyramid, the recommended basis for a healthy diet, shows that a person should consume six to eleven servings of breads, grains, and pastas, as well as three to four servings each of fruits and vegetables—all carbohydrate-containing foods. It is easy to see why cutting carbohydrates out of a person's diet is not a good idea.

The only way to know what is truly healthy for your own body is to talk to a nutritionist or dietitian, who can help you choose foods that are right for you as well as guide you toward a proper exercise program for weight loss, muscle gain, or toning. These professionals will never tell you to cut out carbohydrates entirely. The bottom line: listen to the experts, not the advertisers!

Questions

1 The author appears to be qualified to explain why it is important to eat carbohydrates because she

    A. has talked to many experts and nutritionists.

    B. is a doctor and works at a weight-loss clinic.

    C. has studied the food pyramid.

    D. conducts a lot of research on food.

 Tip

Reread the beginning of the article. What details do you learn about the author?

2 According to the article, the American public mistakenly believes that carbohydrates

    F. can protect the body's cells from cancer-causing agents.

    G. should not be included in a healthy diet.

    H. have many health benefits.

    I. can reduce the risk of heart disease and diabetes.

 Tip

What is the main argument that the author is making about the public's recent views on carbohydrates?

3   The illustration included with this article on page 92 emphasizes the point that

    A.   you should eat many different kinds of food.

    B.   you might get sick without enough protein.

    C.   too many carbohydrates will make you tired.

    D.   carbohydrates are found only in meat and poultry.

 Tip

Look carefully at the illustration. Then eliminate answer choices that are obviously incorrect. What does the illustration seem to be saying?

4   The main purpose of the last paragraph of this article is to

    F.   contrast carbohydrates to other types of food products.

    G.   introduce the effects of adding carbohydrates to your diet.

    H.   paraphrase what advertisers tell the public about carbohydrates.

    I.   summarize the author's views about carbohydrates.

 Tip

Think about how the ideas of this article are presented. What usually comes last in an article that is making an argument?

Passage 2

Read the following passage. Then answer the questions that follow. Use the Tip below each question to help you choose the correct answer. When you finish, read the answer explanations at the end of this chapter.

Comets, Meteors, and Asteroids . . . Oh My!

It is a crystal clear night without a cloud in the sky, and you and your friends have set up camp in the backyard to view some of the solar system's extraordinary phenomena. As you lie on your back staring into the sky, you can see millions of twinkling stars, a few constellations, and, of course, the bright glow of the moon. Suddenly, a streak of light shoots across the sky and disappears. At the same time, you and your friends cry out with multiple explanations for what you saw: a meteor, a comet, a shooting star, a meteorite, an asteroid. Which one of you is correct? What was that momentary streak of light that you and your friends witnessed?

Comets

Comets are objects with a nucleus, or center, composed mostly of ice, frozen gases, and dust that were left over when our solar system formed more than 4 billion years ago. Scientists believe that many comets originate in an area beyond the planet Neptune called the Kuiper Belt and in a region known as the Oort Cloud. Like planets, comets orbit the sun. Some, such as Comet Halley, take as few as seventy-six years to complete an orbit. Others can take millions of years to complete one full orbit. The part of the comet that people can see in the sky is usually the dust tail. As the comet nears the sun, the nucleus warms up and the ice begins to vaporize, releasing gas and dust. The material emanating from the center of the comet forms a cloud around the nucleus called a *coma*. Solar wind pushes the gas and dust in the coma away from the sun, thus forming a long, bright tail.

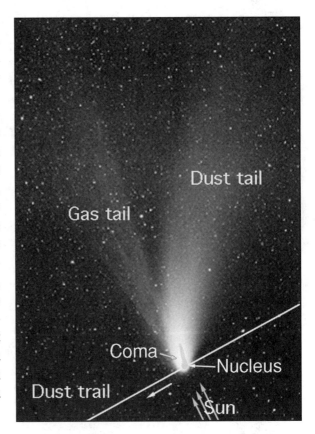

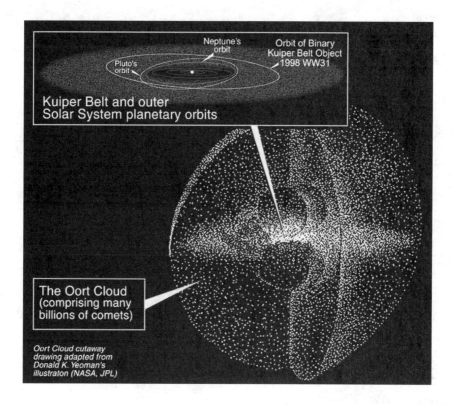

Kuiper Belt and outer
Solar System planetary orbits

Neptune's orbit

Pluto's orbit

Orbit of Binary
Kuiper Belt Object
1998 WW31

The Oort Cloud
(comprising many
billions of comets)

*Oort Cloud cutaway
drawing adapted from
Donald K. Yeoman's
illustraton (NASA, JPL)*

Asteroids

Like comets, asteroids are rocky objects that were left over when the solar system formed. Scientists often compare asteroids' uneven shape to that of a potato. Some asteroids are quite dense, while others are packed more loosely. Asteroids range in size from a half mile to more than 500 miles wide. Many asteroids are found in an area called the Asteroid Belt, or Main Belt, located between Mars and Jupiter. Occasionally, an asteroid gets too close to Mars or Jupiter, spins out of its orbit, and flies into space. There is evidence that stray asteroids have crashed into Earth in the past.

Meteors

To understand meteors, often mistakenly referred to as "shooting stars," you must first understand the difference between a meteoroid, a meteor, and a meteorite. Meteoroids are chunks of material sailing through space. Some scientists believe that meteoroids are pieces of asteroids or comets. When a meteoroid breaks through Earth's atmosphere, it burns up and gives off light, which creates a momentary streak of light in the sky known as a meteor. A meteor shower occurs when many meteors streak through the sky at the same time. Unlike comets, which can often be seen in the sky for several days in a row, meteors last for only a moment. Pieces of a meteor that make it to the surface of Earth are known as meteorites. Meteorites, which often look like ordinary rocks, vary in size, shape, and composition. Scientists study meteorites to learn more about comets and asteroids.

Questions

5   According to the evidence in the article, the Oort Cloud is

   A. the orbit pattern of many different comets.

   B. the dust tail that trails behind the nucleus of a comet.

   C. a region beyond Neptune where many comets are formed.

   D. a region beyond Neptune that is also called the Halley Belt.

Tip

Find the paragraph about comets and skim for information about the Oort Cloud.

6   What is the main purpose of the subheadings in this article?

   F. to introduce the topic of each section of text

   G. to introduce the topic of each illustration or graphic

   H. to emphasize the question-answer structure of the article

   I. to indicate the topics' order of importance

Tip

Look at the subheadings in this article. How does each one relate to what comes after it?

7   What part of a comet is inside the coma?

   A. the tail

   B. the orbit

   C. the nucleus

   D. the dust tail

Tip

One way to answer this question is simply to examine the diagram. However, you can also reread the section about comets.

8 In the diagram on page 97, the main purpose of the small upper box is to

    F. show the orbits of the planets Neptune and Pluto.

    G. show a cutaway drawing of the Oort Cloud.

    H. compare the orbit of the Oort Cloud to that of objects in the Kuiper Belt.

    I. compare the orbit of a comet in the Kuiper Belt to the orbits of Pluto and Neptune.

 Tip

Find the rectangular box at the top of the diagram on page 97. Notice what three things are labeled with arrows.

9 With which of the following statements would the author most likely agree?

    A. The average person probably does not understand the differences among comets, asteroids, and meteors.

    B. Asteroids and meteors are so similar that they can't be distinguished from one another.

    C. Stories that asteroids have crashed into Earth have no basis in scientific fact.

    D. The differences and similarities among comets, asteroids, and meteors are so widely understood that everyone knows them.

 Tip

Think about the author's main purpose in writing this article. What phenomenon does the author describe in the opening paragraph that leads to the discussion of comets, meteors, and asteroids?

Passages 3 and 4

Read the following passages. Then answer the questions that follow. Use the Tip below each question to help you choose the correct answer. When you finish, read the answer explanations at the end of this chapter.

Passage 3

Excerpt from *Narrative of the Life of Frederick Douglass*
by Frederick Douglass

My new mistress proved to be all she appeared when I first met her at the door, — a woman of the kindest heart and finest feelings. She had never had a slave under her control previously to myself, and prior to her marriage she had been dependent upon her own industry for a living. She was by trade a weaver; and by constant application to her business, she had been in a good degree preserved from the blighting and dehumanizing effects of slavery. I was utterly astonished at her goodness. I scarcely knew how to behave towards her. She was entirely unlike any other white woman I had ever seen. I could not approach her as I was accustomed to approach other white ladies. My early instruction was all out of place. The crouching servility, usually so acceptable a quality in a slave, did not answer when manifested toward her. Her favor was not gained by it; she seemed to be disturbed by it. She did not deem it impudent or unmannerly for a slave to look her in the face. The meanest slave was put fully at ease in her presence, and none left without feeling better for having seen her. Her face was made of heavenly smiles, and her voice of tranquil music.

But, alas! this kind heart had but a short time to remain such. The fatal poison of irresponsible power was already in her hands, and soon commenced its infernal work. That cheerful eye, under the influence of slavery, soon became red with rage; that voice, made all of sweet accord, changed to one of harsh and horrid discord; and that angelic face gave place to that of a demon.

Very soon after I went to live with Mr. and Mrs. Auld, she very kindly commenced to teach me the A, B, C. After I had learned this, she assisted me in learning to spell words of three or four letters. Just at this point of my progress, Mr. Auld found out what was going on, and at once forbade Mrs. Auld to instruct me further, telling her, among other things, that it was unlawful, as well as unsafe, to teach a slave to read. . . . He would at once become unmanageable, and of no value to his master. As to himself, it could do him no good, but a great deal of harm. It would make him discontented and unhappy.

These words sank deep into my heart, stirred up sentiments within that lay slumbering, and called into existence an entirely new train of thought. It was a new and special revelation, explaining dark and mysterious things, with which my youthful understanding had struggled, but struggled in vain. I now understood what had been to me a most perplexing difficulty — to wit, the white man's power to enslave the black man. It was a grand achievement, and I prized it highly. From that moment, I understood the pathway from slavery to freedom. It was just what I wanted, and I got it at a time when I the least expected it. Whilst I was saddened by the thought of losing the aid of my kind mistress, I was gladdened by the invaluable instruction which, by the merest accident, I had gained from my master. Though conscious of the difficulty of learning without a teacher, I set out with high hope, and a fixed purpose, at whatever cost of trouble, to learn how to read. The very decided manner with which he spoke, and strove to impress his wife with the evil consequences of giving me instruction served to convince me that he was deeply sensible of the truths he was uttering. It gave me the best assurance that I might rely with the utmost confidence on the results which, he said, would flow from teaching me to read. What he most dreaded, that I most desired. What he most loved, that I most hated. That which to him was a great evil, to be carefully shunned, was to me a great good, to be diligently sought; and the argument which he so warmly urged, against my learning to read, only served to inspire me with a desire and determination to learn. In learning to read, I owe almost as much to the bitter opposition of my master, as to the kindly aid of my mistress. I acknowledge the benefit of both.

Passage 4

Excerpt from *Frederick Douglass*
by Booker T. Washington

When Fred became nine years old, the most important event in his life occurred. His master determined to send him to Baltimore to live with Hugh Auld, a brother of Thomas Auld. Baltimore at this time was little more than a name to young Douglass. When he reached the residence of Mr. and Mrs. Auld and felt the difference between the plantation cabin and this city home, it was to him, for a time, like living in Paradise. Mrs. Auld is described as a lady of great kindness of heart, and of a gentle disposition. She at once took a tender interest in the little servant from the plantation. He was much petted and well fed, permitted to wear boy's clothes and shoes, and for the first time in his life, had a good soft bed to sleep in. His only duty was to take care of and play with Tommy Auld, which he found both an easy and an agreeable task.

Young Douglass yet knew nothing about reading. A book was as much of a mystery to him as the stars at night. When he heard his mistress read aloud from the Bible, his curiosity was aroused. He felt so secure in her kindness that he had the boldness to ask her to teach him. Following her natural impulse to do kindness to others and without, for a moment, thinking of the danger, she at once consented. He quickly learned the alphabet and in a short time could spell words of three syllables. But alas, for his young ambition! When Mr. Auld discovered what his wife had done, he was both surprised and pained. He at once stopped the perilous practice, but it was too late. The precocious young slave had acquired a taste for book-learning. He quickly understood that these mysterious characters called letters were the keys to a vast empire from which he was separated by an enforced ignorance. In discussing the matter with his wife, Mr. Auld said: "If you teach him to read, he will want to know how to write, and with this accomplished, he will be running away with himself." Mr. Douglass, referring to this conversation in later years, said: "This was decidedly the first anti-slavery speech to which I had ever listened. From that moment, I understood the direct pathway from slavery to freedom."

During the subsequent six years that he lived in Baltimore in the home of Mr. Auld, he was more closely watched than he had been before this incident, and his liberty to go and come was considerably curtailed. He declares that he was not allowed to be alone, when this could be helped, lest he would attempt to teach himself. But these were unwise precautions since they but whetted his appetite for learning and incited him to many secret schemes to elude the vigilance of his master and mistress. Everything now contributed to his enlightenment and prepared him for that freedom for which he thirsted. His occasional contact with free colored people, his visit to the wharves where he could watch the vessels going and coming, and his chance acquaintance with white boys on the street, all became a part of his education and were made to serve his plans. He got hold of a blue-back speller and carried it with him all the time. He would ask his little white friends in the street how to spell certain words and the meaning of them. In this way he soon learned to read. The first and most important book owned by him was called the Columbian Orator. He bought it with money secretly earned by blacking boots on the streets. It contained selected passages from such great orators as Lord Chatham, William Pitt, Fox, and Sheridan. These speeches were steeped in the sentiments of liberty, and were full of references to the "rights of man." They gave to young Douglass a larger idea of liberty than was included in his mere dream of freedom for himself, and in addition they increased his vocabulary of words and phrases. The reading of this book unfitted him longer for restraint. He became all ears and all eyes. Everything he saw and read suggested to him a larger world, lying just beyond his reach. . . .

⍰ Questions

10 As a historical document, *The Autobiography of Frederick Douglass* would be considered

   F. a primary source because it was written long ago.

   G. a primary source because it was written by Douglass himself.

   H. a secondary source because it was written by Booker T. Washington.

   I. a secondary source because it deals with a personal story rather than public events.

Tip

Think about what an autobiography is. Also, what makes a document a primary source?

11 Read the following lines from *The Autobiography of Frederick Douglass.*

In learning to read, I owe almost as much to the bitter opposition of my master, as to the kindly aid of my mistress. I acknowledge the benefit of both.

These sentences show that Douglass

A. realized that Mr. Auld actually wanted to help him.

B. hated his master and mistress equally.

C. understood that Mr. Auld's attitude actually made him work harder to succeed.

D. was fooled into thinking that Mr. and Mrs. Auld had both benefited his education.

 Tip

Reread the section about the Aulds' attitude toward teaching Douglass to read. Which answer choice fits the facts as he describes them?

12 A key difference in these two passages is that

F. Douglass describes how he learned to read while Washington focuses on Douglass's escape from slavery.

G. Douglass sugarcoats events while Washington describes the harsh reality of what happened.

H. Douglass relates events without emotion, while Washington focuses more on what Douglass felt.

I. Douglass describes how Mrs. Auld later became harsh and angry, while Washington describes her throughout as tender and kind.

 Tip

Eliminate the answer choices that are obviously wrong. Then skim the appropriate passages to test the answer choices that remain.

Passage 5

Read the following passage. Then answer the questions that follow. Use the Tip below each question to help you choose the correct answer. When you finish, read the answer explanations at the end of this chapter.

Curious Crop Circles

Imagine for a moment that you are a farmer. One morning you awaken to find a large circular pattern in the middle of your fields. Where rows of wheat, soy, or corn stood tall just yesterday, there is now a perfectly shaped circle. For many farmers around the world, this is a baffling reality. This strange phenomenon is known as crop circles, and they are characterized by the symmetrical flattening of crops into a geometric pattern, usually occurring overnight when there are no witnesses. The formations generally appear starting in late spring until early autumn, with most circles discovered during the summer months. The United Kingdom has had the largest number of crop circles over the years, but countries like the United States, Germany, Canada, and the Netherlands have reported an increase in incidents since the late twentieth century.

Crop circles first gained international attention in the media during the early 1980s, when a series of circles was discovered in southern England. However, many argue that the circles have been reported since the early seventeenth century. A tale dating back to 1678 tells of a farmer who refused to pay a laborer to mow a field. That night, the field appeared to be on fire.

When the farmer went to inspect his crops the following morning, instead of finding charred remains, he discovered that the field had indeed been mowed—by whom or what he could not say. Although many dispute the validity of this early incident, others note that farmers have been reporting crop circles for generations.

Of course, the real mystery is who or what is behind the creation of these circles in the middle of the night. Theories explaining the existence of crop circles range from the mundane to the supernatural. Many feel that most crop circles are nothing but elaborate hoaxes perpetrated by people with nothing better to do with their time or looking for their fifteen minutes of fame.

Two of the most famous hoaxers were discovered in England. In 1991, Doug Bower and Dave Chorley claimed they had been staging crop circles for nearly fifteen years, creating more than 200 circles. The men said they would sneak into fields at night and use a wooden plank tied to some string to flatten the crops into circles while the owners of the fields were asleep. Even if Bower and Chorley told the truth, their story does not account for the more than 2,000 other circles reported around the country during the time they supposedly created their circles.

Today the debate over hoaxing continues. Professional circle makers have appeared on numerous television programs, trying to prove that crop circles, even the extremely complex ones, are made by people. Circle makers have created formations for everything from music videos to movies, like the 2002 film *Signs*. Several businesses use computer technology to create circle advertisements in fields where airplane passengers are most likely to spot them.

Still, crop circle researchers note several key differences between artificial and what they call authentic crop circles. First, researchers note that when an artificial pattern is formed, there is usually evidence of a human presence left behind, like footprints in the soil or impressions from the tools that were used. Second, when a genuine formation is found, there is sometimes unexplainable effects on the environment that do not occur when a circle is the work of tricksters.

One especially interesting fact that researchers point out is that crops that are particularly unyielding, like canola plants, tend to snap when they are bent by the tools hoaxers use but inexplicably bend in "legitimate" formations. Other important differences that researchers have noted between what they consider real crop circles and hoaxes are cellular changes in plants, changes in seeds, and dehydrated soil in the "genuine" cases.

The most popular, and the most controversial, theory of the cause of crop circles is that they are the work of extraterrestrial life forms trying to make contact with human beings. Proponents of this idea believe that the formations must be created by an intelligent life form and that the circles are far too intricate for even a small team of humans to create overnight without being caught. To support this claim, many people point to other strange phenomena that sometimes accompany crop circles as evidence of an alien presence. These reports include seeing balls of light and hearing unusual sounds in the areas where the circles are later discovered. Some believe that this theory might also explain the curious effect that some circles have on plants, but so far there is not enough conclusive evidence to link crop circles to an otherworldly force.

The search for a more terrestrial answer to the cause of crop circles continues. Some scientists believe that the Earth itself is the cause of these mysterious events. One argument is that a shift in the Earth's electromagnetic field would be enough to flatten crops without breaking them. Another idea is that changes in weather patterns over the last few centuries could be the source of crop circles. Several other theories conclude that crop circles are probably more natural than supernatural.

Although some crop circle cases have proved to be nothing more than mere pranks, others are not so easy to dismiss. Until there is a clear-cut explanation for the phenomenon, it is likely that these mysterious formations will continue to fascinate researchers and others worldwide for some time to come.

 **Questions**

13 According to the article, which of the following is evidence that a crop circle was created by human beings?

   A. bent plants

   B. impressions from tools

   C. balls of light

   D. dehydrated soil

 Tip

Reread the parts of the article that discuss crop circles created by humans.

14 A caption to the photograph in this article would be MOST helpful if it explained

    F. what crop circles are.

    G. where the crop circles in the photograph are located.

    H. whether the crop circles in the photograph are believed to be human-made or "genuine."

    I. what kind of crops were growing in the field where the crop circles appeared.

 Tip

Think about the main point of debate in this article. Which kind of caption would add important information about this point?

15 Which of the following statements is the best paraphrase of the author's attitude toward the topic of crop circles?

    A. Crop circles are a fascinating phenomenon that shows how gullible people are.

    B. Crop circles are the work of hoaxers, not supernatural forces or extraterrestrials.

    C. While most crop circles are obviously the work of humans, some are just as obviously the signs of aliens trying to communicate with us.

    D. While some crop circles are easily explained as manmade pranks, some are more difficult to account for.

 Tip

Reread the last paragraph of the article and think about what conclusion the author reaches about crop circles.

✔ Answers

1 B

The author is Dr. Rubina Gad, and she refers to patients that come into her weight-loss clinic. These details affirm her qualifications to write about carbohydrates.

Benchmark: LA.910.6.2.2 The student will organize, synthesize, analyze, and evaluate the validity and reliability of information from multiple sources (including primary and secondary sources) to draw conclusions using a variety of techniques, and correctly use standardized citations.

2 G

The author's main point is that the American public mistakenly believes that carbohydrates are bad for a person's diet. She explains all the actual benefits that carbohydrates provide.

Benchmark: LA.910.2.2.2 The student will use information from the text to answer questions or to state the main idea or provide relevant details.

3 A

The author stresses in the article that you should eat a balanced diet with many different kinds of food, and includes the illustration of the food pyramid to reinforce this idea.

Benchmark: LA.910.6.1.1 The student explain how text features (e.g., charts, maps, diagrams, subheadings, captions, illustrations, graphs) aid the reader's understanding.

4 I

The last paragraph summarizes the author's argument. In fact, the last sentence is the "bottom line," or her basic point boiled down to the essential idea. The last paragraph of a persuasive article is often a summary of the author's argument.

Benchmark: LA.910.2.2.3 The student will organize information to show understanding of relationships among facts, ideas, and events (e.g., representing key points within text through charting, mapping, paraphrasing, summarizing, comparing, contrasting, or outlining).

5   C

The second sentence of the section about comets says: *Scientists believe that many comets originate in an area beyond the planet Neptune called the Kuiper Belt and in a region known as the Oort Cloud.* If comets *originate* in the Oort Cloud region, that means they are formed there.

Benchmark: LA.910.2.2.2 The student will use information from the text to answer questions or to state the main idea or provide relevant details.

6   F

The subheadings introduce the topic of each text section. The graphics do not have subheadings. The article doesn't have a question-answer structure and the topics are not presented in any special order of importance.

Benchmark: LA.910.6.1.1 The student will explain how text features (e.g., charts, maps, diagrams, subheadings, captions, illustrations, graphs) aid the reader's understanding.

7   C

In the diagram, you can see that the nucleus is inside the coma. The article also explains that *the material emanating from the center of the comet forms a cloud around the nucleus called a coma.*

Benchmark: LA.910.2.2.2 The student will use information from the text to answer questions or to state the main idea or provide relevant details.

8   I

In the upper rectangular box in the diagram, the orbits of Pluto, Neptune, and a "Binary Kuiper Belt Object" are overlaid for comparison. Answer choice I is correct.

Benchmark: LA.910.2.2.1 The student will analyze and evaluate information from text features (e.g., transitional devices, table of contents, glossary, index, bold or italicized text, headings, charts and graphs, illustrations, subheadings).

9　A

The author begins with the observation that ordinary people looking at the night sky can't decide if a phenomenon of streaking light is a comet, a meteor, or an asteroid. Then the author goes on to describe these things in detail to distinguish them from each other.

Benchmark: LA.910.1.7.2 The student will analyze the author's purpose and/or perspective in a variety of texts and understand how they affect meaning.

10　G

An autobiography is the story of a person's life written by that person. For that reason, it is a primary source.

Benchmark: LA.910.6.2.2 The student will organize, synthesize, analyze, and evaluate the validity and reliability of information from multiple sources (including primary and secondary sources) to draw conclusions using a variety of techniques, and correctly use standardized citations.

11　C

Douglass realizes that Mr. Auld's concerns about his learning to read and opposition to it indicate that reading will make him stronger, and so they inspired him to work harder at it.

Benchmark: LA.910.2.2.2 The student will use information from the text to answer questions or to state the main idea or provide relevant details.

12　I

The second paragraph of this excerpt from Douglass's autobiography describes how Mrs. Auld later became more harsh and hateful. On the other hand, Washington's account of Mrs. Auld portrays her as unfailingly kind.

Benchmark: LA.910.2.2.3 The student will organize information to show understanding of relationships among facts, ideas, and events (e.g., representing key points within text through charting, mapping, paraphrasing, summarizing, comparing, contrasting, or outlining).

13　B

The article says that when a crop circle is created by humans, "there is usually evidence of a human presence left behind, like footprints in the soil or impressions from the tools that were used."

Benchmark: LA.910.2.2.2 The student will use information from the text to answer questions or to state the main idea or provide relevant details.

14 H

Since the main point of debate in the article is whether or not crop circles are sometimes caused by other than human means, the most helpful kind of caption would explain whether the crop circles pictured were believed to be hoaxes or not. It would also be interesting to know where the field in the photograph is located, but that information would be secondary to the main point.

Benchmark: LA.910.6.1.1 The student will explain how text features (e.g., charts, maps, diagrams, subheadings, captions, illustrations, graphs) aid the reader's understanding.

15 D

Answer choice D is a close paraphrase of this sentence from the last paragraph of the article: "Although some crop circle cases have proved to be nothing more than mere pranks, other are not so easy to dismiss."

Benchmark: LA.910.2.2.3 The student will organize information to show understanding of relationships among facts, ideas, and events (e.g., representing key points within text through charting, mapping, paraphrasing, summarizing, comparing, contrasting, or outlining).

Part 2
Writing Process

Chapter 5

The FCAT Writing Test

About the FCAT Writing Test

Section 2 of this book helps you prepare for the FCAT Writing test. For this test, you will be given a writing folder and a prompt. You will have 45 minutes to read the prompt, plan what you want to write, and write your essay. A separate planning sheet will be provided, but you will not be graded on your work on this sheet. The prompt will direct you to write either an expository or a persuasive essay on a certain topic.

Beginning in 2012, the FCAT Writing test is being scored differently than in the past. Students will still be scored mainly on the elements of *focus, organization, support,* and *conventions*. However, increased attention will be paid to scoring in two areas. First, students will be expected to use standard English conventions correctly. In prior years, FCAT scorers were lenient in this area. Now, to earn higher scores students must avoid errors in sentence structure, mechanics, usage, punctuation, and spelling. Second, scorers will focus more on the supporting details in a response. Higher-scored responses must include details that are relevant, logical, and specific. Details should help make the writer's main points clearer, and should be written in unpretentious language.

The new FCAT Writing test no longer features a separate section on mechanics and usage. However, this book includes exercises in these areas to help you prepare for the new emphasis in scoring. The exercises are in the form of multiple-choice questions with three answer choices each.

Expository Prompt

An **expository prompt** asks you to define, explain, or tell how to do something. The following is an example of an expository writing prompt.

Writing Situation

Most people have a favorite season or time of year.

Directions for Writing

Write an essay describing your favorite season. Discuss what makes that season special to you.

Persuasive Prompt

A **persuasive prompt** asks you to convince the reader to accept your opinion or to take a specific action. The following is an example of a persuasive writing prompt.

Writing Situation

To cut back on expenses, your principal has asked the school board for permission to cancel all field trips for the remainder of the year.

Directions for Writing

Think about how you feel about this issue. Some people think this is a good idea because they consider field trips "vacations" from learning and, therefore, an unnecessary expense. Write a letter to the school board explaining your position on the issue. Use facts and examples to develop your argument.

Responding to a Prompt

You should write your response to the prompt neatly and show that you can organize and express your thoughts quickly, clearly, and completely. You will not have a dictionary or any other reference materials. In fact, your only tools will be a couple of pencils — and your imagination!

Unlike the FCAT 2.0 Reading test, the FCAT Writing test is not used as a requirement for graduation. Mainly, it helps your school evaluate your skills as a writer, and decide in which areas you might need reinforcement. No one expects you to write a flawless essay in 45 minutes. Scorers will take into account that your essay is a draft. However, you should be able to produce an organized piece of writing that states its purpose clearly, follows through with supporting details, and ends with a strong conclusion that sums up the topic.

Hints for Taking the FCAT Writing Test

- Read the prompt carefully.
- Plan your writing by organizing your ideas.
- Support your ideas by providing details about each event, reason, or argument.
- Use a variety of sentence structures.
- Choose words that help others understand what you mean.
- Review and edit your writing.

How Essays Are Graded

On the FCAT Writing test, two trained scorers (readers) evaluate an essay for its overall quality and assign each paper a score from 1 to 6 based on specific scoring guidelines. The final score is the average of the two scores. If both scorers give a paper a score of 3, the final score is 3. If one scorer assigns the paper a score of 3 and the other scorer assigns it a score of 2, the final score is 2.5. When making their overall judgments about a piece of writing, scorers consider four elements: focus, organization, support, and conventions.

- **Focus** refers to how clearly the essay presents and maintains the main idea, theme, or unifying point.

- **Organization** refers to the structure or plan of development (beginning, middle, and end) and the relationship of one point to another. Organization also includes the use of transitional devices (terms, phrases, and variations in sentence structure) to signal both the relationship of the supporting ideas to the main idea, theme, or unifying point and the connections between and among sentences.

- **Support** refers to the quality of details used to explain, clarify, or define. The quality of support depends on the choice of words and the specificity, depth, relevance, and thoroughness of the ideas presented in the essay.

- **Conventions** refer to sentence structure, punctuation, capitalization, spelling, and usage.

As mentioned earlier, scorers now place special emphasis on support and conventions.

The following scoring rubric outlines how your essay will be scored:

6   The writing is focused and purposeful, and it reflects insight into the writing situation. The organizational pattern provides for a logical progression of ideas. Effective use of transitional devices contributes to a sense of completeness. The development of the support is substantial, specific, relevant, and concrete. The writer shows commitment to and involvement with the subject and may use creative writing strategies. The writing demonstrates a mature command of language with freshness of expression. Sentence structure is varied, and few, if any, convention errors occur in mechanics, usage, punctuation, and spelling.

5   The writing is focused on the topic, and its organizational pattern provides for a logical progression of ideas. Effective use of transitional devices contributes to a sense of completeness. The support is developed through ample use of specific details and examples. The writing demonstrates a mature command of language, and there is variation in sentence structure. The response generally follows the conventions of mechanics, usage, punctuation, and spelling.

4   The writing is focused on the topic and includes few, if any, loosely related ideas. An organizational pattern is apparent, and it is strengthened by the use of transitional devices. The support is consistently developed, but it may lack specificity. Word choice is adequate, and variation in sentence structure is demonstrated. The response generally follows the conventions of mechanics, usage, punctuation, and spelling.

3 The writing is focused but may contain ideas that are loosely connected to the topic. An organizational pattern is demonstrated, but the response may lack a logical progression of ideas. Development of support may be uneven. Word choice is adequate, and some variation in sentence structure is demonstrated. The response generally follows the conventions of mechanics, usage, punctuation, and spelling.

2 The writing addresses the topic but may lose focus by including extraneous or loosely related ideas. The organizational pattern usually includes a beginning, middle, and ending, but these elements may be brief. The development of the support may be erratic and nonspecific, and ideas may be repeated. Word choice may be limited, predictable, or vague. Errors may occur in the basic conventions of sentence structure, mechanics, usage, and punctuation, but commonly used words are usually spelled correctly.

1 The writing addresses the topic but may lose focus by including extraneous or loosely related ideas. The response may have an organizational pattern, but it may lack a sense of completeness or closure. There is little, if any, development of the supporting ideas, and the support may consist of generalizations or fragmentary lists. Limited or inappropriate word choice may obscure meaning. Frequent and blatant errors may occur in the basic conventions of sentence structure, mechanics, usage, and punctuation, and commonly used words may be misspelled.

U Most writing that is unscorable is unrelated to the assigned topic or cannot be read.

Chapter 6
Prewriting and Drafting

As you begin the FCAT Writing test, remember the three stages of writing: prewriting, drafting, and revising. Whether you are responding to an expository prompt or a persuasive prompt, you should always begin to develop your essay by prewriting. Once you have plan for your essay in mind, you can begin the drafting stage. The sections below will lead you through the benchmarks for the prewriting and drafting stages on the FCAT writing test. The following chapter will address the revising stage.

Generating Ideas from Multiple Sources

Benchmark

• **LA.910.3.1.1** The student will prewrite by generating ideas from multiple sources (e.g., brainstorming, notes, journals, discussion, research materials or other reliable sources) based upon teacher-directed topics and personal interests.

As noted above, you will not have any reference materials when you take the FCAT Writing test. Nevertheless, once you read the prompt, you should immediately try to think of ideas to use that might come from several different sources.

For example, you might be given the following prompt: How would your life be different if you were a famous film star? At once you might brainstorm ideas about what it would be like to be a star in Hollywood. (**Brainstorming** consists of jotting down ideas quickly as they occur to you.) Then you might recall articles you have read that describe the real lives of movie stars, including the hard work and long hours they must put in to be successful. Next, you might think of stories about a friend or relative who actually made a career as an actor, or think about actors' stories from talk shows on TV. Finally, you would compare these details to your present life — for the prompt asks how your life would be different. See how you can generate plenty of ideas by looking at the topic in different ways?

Making a Plan for Writing

Benchmark

- **LA.910.3.1.2** The student will prewrite by making a plan for writing that addresses purpose, audience, a controlling idea, logical sequence, and time frame for completion.

Since you have only 45 minutes to complete your essay on the FCAT Writing test, you do not have time to make an elaborate plan for your writing. First, read the prompt carefully. Then, focus on the essentials: What is your purpose for writing? Who is your audience? (Probably your teacher or an independent grader.) What is the main point you want to make? What other ideas can you include? How can you sum up your description or opinion? Are your ideas appropriate for the amount of time you have to write?

You will be given a writing folder that includes a sheet for jotting down ideas. You could write sentences or phrases that answer the above questions. Or you could use other tools to organize your ideas, as in the next section.

Using Organizational Strategies and Tools

Benchmark

- **LA.910.3.1.3** The student will prewrite by using organizational strategies and tools (e.g., technology, spreadsheet, outline, chart, table, graph, Venn diagram, web, story map, plot pyramid) to develop a personal organizational style.

Again, with a limited amount of time to draft your essay, you shouldn't spend too much time charting your ideas. However, you might benefit from using a graphic organizer. A **word web** is a good tool for brainstorming key details about topics. For example, this student used a word web (see page 121) to arrange some ideas about her favorite animal, the manatee:

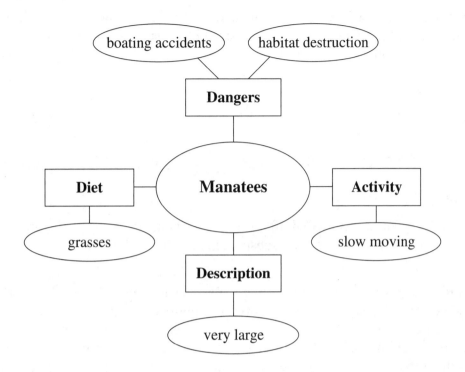

Another kind of graphic organizer could be used for ideas in a compare/contrast essay about tennis and ping pong. A **Venn diagram** consists of two overlapping ovals with labels inside. Qualities that are unique to tennis or to ping pong are written in the left or right oval. Ways in which these games are alike are written in the overlapping section of the diagram.

For a persuasive essay, you might create a table with two columns. In the left column you could write arguments in favor of a proposition and in the right column arguments against it.

Developing Ideas from the Prewriting Plan

Benchmark
- **LA.910.3.2.1** The student will draft writing by developing ideas from the prewriting plan using primary and secondary sources appropriate to the purpose and audience.

Once you've determined your central idea and jotted down some supporting material, you are ready to begin drafting your essay. In this stage, you will write a rough draft of your work. Remember that the most important thing when writing a draft is to briskly get your ideas down on paper. Your writing at this stage doesn't have to be perfect. Any mistakes you make in organizing your ideas or in grammar and usage can be fixed when you revise and edit your work.

Try to frame your essay with strong opening and closing ideas. Make sure that you have addressed the topic in the prompt and that you have clearly stated a main idea and a variety of supporting details. Don't simply repeat the same idea over and over in different words.

Establishing a Logical Organizational Pattern

Benchmark

- **LA.910.3.2.2** The student will draft writing by establishing a logical organizational pattern with supporting details that are substantial, specific, and relevant.

As you draft your essay, focus on presenting your ideas in a logical progression. Begin with a strong statement of your main idea or overall argument. Then follow it with supporting subtopics and details that are clear, specific, and relevant to your main point. Your transitions from one idea to the next should be smooth and logical, not abrupt or choppy. When ideas flow smoothly in a piece of writing, the reader finds it easier to follow the argument the writer is making.

For example, you might draft a persuasive piece in the form of a letter to the editor. Your main point is that your city needs to build a new multi-purpose arena downtown. After stating this main idea, you would follow it with supporting details such as the economic benefits of the arena, the need for more entertainment options downtown, the possibility of attracting a professional team to the city, etc. You might then present two or three possible arguments against the idea, with your responses to these arguments. Then you could conclude by restating your main point and summarizing your most important ideas.

Analyzing Language of Professional Authors

Benchmark

- **LA.910.3.2.3** The student will draft writing by analyzing language techniques of professional authors (e.g., figurative language, denotation, connotation) to establish a personal style, demonstrating a command of language with confidence of expression.

This benchmark is only indirectly helpful on the FCAT Writing test. One way to improve your writing skills is by noting how professional authors express themselves in a strong personal style. Pay particular attention to an author's use of figurative language and words and phrases that carry positive or negative connotations. Don't copy any one author's style. Instead, try to pick up stylistic pointers from several of your favorite writers.

? Prewriting and Drafting Exercises

Exercise 1

Morris created the writing plan below to organize ideas for an essay. Use his writing plan to answer questions 1 through 3.

Morris's Writing Plan

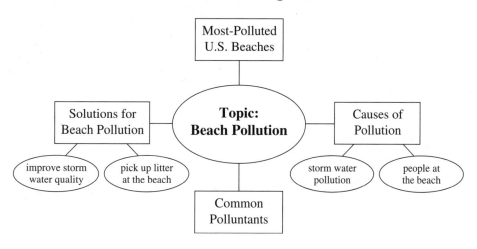

1   Under which subtopic should Morris add information about toxic household cleaning products?

   A. Solutions for Beach Pollution

   B. Common Pollutants

   C. Most-Polluted U.S. Beaches

   D. Causes of Pollution

2   Based on the information in the writing plan, what type of essay is Morris planning to write?

   F.   an informative essay about how storm water becomes polluted

   G. a descriptive essay about forming a beach-raking crew

   H. a persuasive essay about keeping beaches clean

   I.   an expository essay about how to find polluted beaches

3   Which detail focuses on the subtopic "Solutions for Beach Pollution"?

    A. oil from recreational and commercial boats

    B. detergents from driveway car washing

    C. minimal use of chemicals in home gardens

    D. wastewater from sewage treatment plants

Exercise 2

Cynthia created the writing plan below to organize ideas for an essay. Use her writing plan to answer questions 4 through 6.

Cynthia's Writing Plan

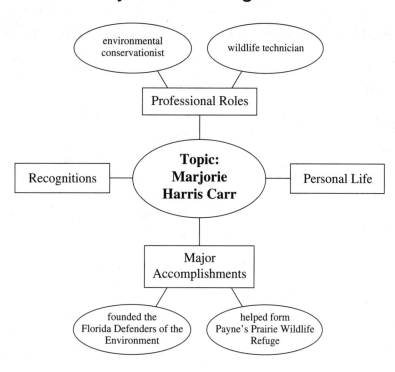

4   Based on the information in the writing plan, what type of essay is Cynthia planning to write?

F.   an expository essay about steps for starting an environmental conservation organization

G.   a persuasive essay about protecting Florida's wildlife

H.   a descriptive essay about Payne's Prairie Wildlife Refuge

I.   an informative essay about the life and work of a Florida conservationist

5   Which detail adds information to the subtopic "Recognitions"?

    A. stopped damaging construction of the Cross Florida Barge Canal

    B. married Archie Carr in 1937

    C. became a member of the Florida Women's Hall of Fame

    D. studied zoology as an undergraduate

6   Under which subtopic should Cynthia add information about Carr's five children?

    F. Major Accomplishments

    G. Personal Life

    H. Professional Roles

    I. Recognitions

Exercise 3

Julia is writing notes about the life of the novelist Charles Dickens. Read the notes to answer questions 7 through 9.

Julia's Notes

1. Charles John Huffman Dickens was born on February 7, 1812, in Portsmouth, Hampshire, England.

2. Charles attended a private school until the age of twelve, when his father was jailed for unpaid debts.

3. *The Pickwick Papers*, Dickens's first novel, was published in 1836.

4. Also in 1836, Dickens married Catherine Thompson Hogarth. The couple had ten children from 1837 to 1852.

5. Dickens served as the editor of *Bentley's Miscellany*, a popular publication in Victorian times, for three years.

6. In 1870, Dickens gave his first public reading in New York City.

7. On June 9, 1870, Dickens passed away at the age of fifty-eight. He was buried in the Poets' Corner of Westminster Abbey.

---

7   Based on the organization of the notes, which sentence should Julia add to the list after sentence 2?

A. After leaving school, Dickens had to work in a boot-blacking factory to support his family.

B. Dickens's first son, born on January 6, 1837, was named Charles Culliford Boz Dickens.

C. In 1400, Engish writer Geoffrey Chaucer was the first person to be buried in Westminster Abbey.

D. Not many schools today require students to read *The Pickwick Papers*.

8   Julia wants to add the following detail to the notes.

Dickens began his second novel, *Oliver Twist,* **in 1837. The work reveals the dark and hidden world of child labor in Victorian England.**

Based on the organization of the notes, after which number on the list should Julia add this detail?

F.   after sentence 1

G.   after sentence 4

H.   after sentence 5

I.   after sentence 7

9   Based on the information in the notes, what kind of paper is Julia planning to write?

A.   She will describe for the reader what it was like to work in a boot-blacking factory.

B.   She will tell the reader about Dickens's vacation spots in England.

C.   She will persuade the reader to read *The Pickwick Papers*.

D.   She will inform the reader about events in the life of Charles Dickens.

Exercise 4

Kelvin has written notes about ancient Egypt. Read the notes to answer questions 10 through 12.

Kelvin's Notes

1. The Egyptian state was founded in the Late Predynastic Period—the same time that the earliest hieroglyphs were created.

2. People buried their dead in the sand until the first pyramid was created during the Early Dynastic Period, when King Narmer came to power, creating the first dynasty.

3. During the ninth to eleventh dynasties, Egypt split, creating a northern state and a southern state.

4. Egypt was reunited by King Mentuhotep at the end of the eleventh dynasty.

5. The first female pharaoh, Hatshepsut, became the eighteenth-dynasty ruler of Egypt after the death of her husband.

6. In the Late Period, Egypt was conquered by Persia before quickly regaining its independence.

7. Cleopatra became the last pharaoh before Egypt was finally conquered by the Roman Empire.

---

10 Kelvin wants to add the following detail to the notes.

Twelfth-dynasty kings began building pyramids out of mud-brick instead of stone.

Based on the organization of the notes, after which sentence in the list should Kelvin add this detail?

F. after sentence 3

G. after sentence 4

H. after sentence 5

I. after sentence 6

11 Based on the information in the notes, what kind of paper is Kelvin planning to write?

   A. He will tell the reader about events in the history of ancient Egypt.

   B. He will persuade readers to study further about the ancient Egyptians.

   C. He will describe for the reader how step pyramids were constructed.

   D. He will inform the reader about the clothing worn by female pharaohs of ancient Egypt.

12 Based on the organization of the notes, which sentence should Kelvin add to the list?

   F. Cleopatra was the most interesting of all ancient Egyptian rulers.

   G. The year of King Narmer's birth is not known.

   H. The art and literature of ancient Egypt thrived during the Middle Kingdom.

   I. Tourists can visit some of the pyramids in Egypt today.

 Answers

1   B

The word *toxic* suggests that this type of household cleaning product can be a pollutant. Details about this pollutant should be placed under the subtopic "Common Pollutants."

Benchmark: LA.910.3.1.1 The student will prewrite by generating ideas from multiple sources (e.g., brainstorming, notes, journals, discussion, research materials or other reliable sources) based upon teacher-directed topics and personal interests.

2   H

The essay will include facts about beach pollution, but it will also include information on solutions to beach pollution. This information is included to persuade readers to adopt these actions.

Benchmark: LA.910.3.1.2 The student will prewrite by making a plan for writing that addresses purpose, audience, a controlling idea, logical sequence, and time frame for completion.

3   C

The detail "minimal use of chemicals in home gardens" focuses on the subtopic "Solutions for Beach Pollution." It should be written in a balloon connected to that subtopic in the idea web. The other items contain causes, not solutions, for the pollution.

Benchmark: LA.910.3.1.3 The student will prewrite by using organizational strategies and tools (e.g., technology, spreadsheet, outline, chart, table, graph, Venn diagram, web, story map, plot pyramid) to develop a personal organizational style.

4   I

Based on the information in the writing plan, Cynthia's essay will contain factual information about Marjorie Harris Carr's life and work.

Benchmark: LA.910.3.1.2 The student will prewrite by making a plan for writing that addresses purpose, audience, a controlling idea, logical sequence, and time frame for completion.

5 C

This detail focuses on the subtopic "Recognitions." It is apparent that people recognized Marjorie and her great work when she was included in the Florida Women's Hall of Fame.

Benchmark: LA.910.3.1.3 The student will prewrite by using organizational strategies and tools (e.g., technology, spreadsheet, outline, chart, table, graph, Venn diagram, web, story map, plot pyramid) to develop a personal organizational style.

6 G

This detail relates to Marjorie's personal life.

Benchmark: LA.910.3.1.1 The student will prewrite by generating ideas from multiple sources (e.g., brainstorming, notes, journals, discussion, research materials or other reliable sources) based upon teacher-directed topics and personal interests.

7 A

Based on the chronological organization of Julia's notes, a detail about what Dickens did after leaving school should follow sentence 2, which says he attended private school until the age of twelve.

Benchmark: LA.910.3.2.2 The student will draft writing by establishing a logical organizational pattern with supporting details that are substantial, specific, and relevant.

8 G

Based on the date and the reference to Dickens's second novel, this note would fit after sentence 4.

Benchmark: LA.910.2.1.3 The student will explain how meaning is enhanced through various features of poetry, including souwill draft writing by establishing a logical organizational pattern with supporting details that are substantial, specific, and relevant.

9 D

Julia's notes contain many details about events in the life of Charles Dickens. She has included these details with the intention of informing readers about these events.

Benchmark: LA.910.3.2.1 The student will draft writing by developing ideas from the prewriting plan using primary and secondary sources appropriate to the purpose and audience.

10 G

A note referring to the twelfth dynasty would fit here because the notes are arranged in chronological order.

Benchmark: LA.910.3.2.2 The student will draft writing by establishing a logical organizational pattern with supporting details that are substantial, specific, and relevant.

11 A

It is apparent from his notes that Kelvin intends to inform readers about events in the history of ancient Egypt.

Benchmark: LA.910.3.2.1 The student will draft writing by developing ideas from the prewriting plan using primary and secondary sources appropriate to the purpose and audience.

12 H

This is the only choice that is relevant to the topics presented in the notes.

Benchmark: LA.910.3.2.2 The student will draft writing by establishing a logical organizational pattern with supporting details that are substantial, specific, and relevant.

Chapter 7

Revising and Editing

Once you have created a rough draft for the FCAT Writing test, you must revise and edit your writing. The sections below will instruct you about how to use the editing process to make your writing stronger in both content and usage. Remember, you are not expected to write a perfect essay on demand — just a well-organized, grammatical essay that displays your skills as a writer.

Evaluating the Draft

Benchmarks
- **LA.910.3.3.1** The student will revise by evaluating the draft for development of ideas and content, logical organization, voice, point of view, word choice, and sentence variation.
- **LA.910.3.3.4** The student will revise by applying appropriate tools or strategies to evaluate and refine the draft (e.g., peer review, checklists, rubrics).

The first step in evaluating your draft is to reread what you have written with a critical eye. Here are some things you should look for.

- Is your main idea or key argument presented clearly towards the beginning of your essay?

- Did you develop your essay by presenting your ideas in a logical sequence?

- Is your "voice," or the personal style of your writing, consistent throughout the essay? For a formal piece of writing, you probably shouldn't use slang or colloquial turns of phrase.

- Is your point of view consistent throughout? If you begin writing in the first-person point of view, don't change to third-person in the middle of your essay.

- Are there certain words or phrases that you used that could be changed to improve clarity or bring in a subtler shade of thought?

- Are your sentences varied in style and length, including simple declarative sentences, compound sentences, and complex sentences? You might also include questions and exclamations in your writing.

The following sections will examine your revising and editing tools in detail.

Creating Clarity

Benchmark

- **LA.910.3.3.2** The student will revise by creating clarity and logic by maintaining central theme, idea, or unifying point and developing meaningful relationships among ideas.

As you revise your essay for the FCAT Writing test, check to see that your central theme and supporting ideas are presented clearly and logically. Since you only have 45 minutes to complete your essay, make sure that every sentence adds something important to your main idea. If a sentence wanders off the topic, cross the sentence out. Also, try to see your writing from an outside reader's point of view. Your plan of organization — how the ideas in your essay fit together — should be easy for the reader to follow.

As you revise your writing, look for connecting words that join sentences or ideas in a logical way. For example, words such as *similarly* and *therefore* can show how ideas are alike or fit together logically:

> **My father taught me how to use carpenter's tools from an early age; therefore, it was easy for me to help Mr. Thompson repair his garage door.**

Words such as *however* or *nevertheless* can show the contrast between ideas:

> **Heavy rains were predicted for this afternoon. Nevertheless, our soccer game began on time and with a large crowd in the stands.**

Finally, avoid stilted or overly complicated writing. Try to present your ideas in a straightforward way, without jargon or unnecessary words. Look at the samples from a humorous essay below. Example A uses stilted, clotted language that is hard to read, while Example B is clear and to the point.

Example A

The family of which I am a member has never utilized the best strategy for ensuring that all family members have reasonable access to the bathroom facilities in the morning before school or before work. Therefore, to correct this deficiency, I am presenting my own well-thought-out strategy.

Example B

My family does not have a plan for fair and equal bathroom use on weekday mornings. To solve this problem, I suggest the following arrangement.

Creating Precision and Interest

Benchmark

- **LA.910.3.3.3** The student will revise by creating precision and interest by elaborating ideas through supporting details (e.g., facts, statistics, expert opinions, anecdotes), a variety of sentence structures, creative language devices, and modifying word choices using resources and reference materials (e.g., dictionary, thesaurus) to select more effective and precise language.

On the FCAT Writing test, you will be scored on the precision of your writing. Precise writing means using the exact words necessary to get across one's meaning. A precise writer avoids words such as *thing, stuff,* or *kind of.* In revising, a precise writer changes general words to more specific ones: *elm* instead of *tree, duplex* instead of *house, carpenter* instead of *worker.* Another way to be precise in your writing is to include facts and statistics to support your main idea. However, on the FCAT Writing test you won't have access to outside sources of information.

As you revise your essay, check to see that you have used a variety of sentence lengths and structures. If all your sentences are short or very long, your writing will be monotonous. A short declarative sentence that introduces or sums up a passage with longer sentences can be very effective.

Editing Spelling, Capitalization, and Punctuation

Benchmarks

- **LA.910.3.4.1** The student will edit for correct use of spelling, using spelling rules, orthographic patterns, generalizations, knowledge of root words, prefixes, suffixes, knowledge of Greek, Latin, and Anglo-Saxon root words, and knowledge of foreign words commonly used in English *(laissez faire, croissant)*.
- **LA.910.3.4.2** The student will edit for correct use of capitalization, including names of academic courses and proper adjectives.
- **LA.910.3.4.3** The student will edit for correct use of punctuation, including commas, colons, semicolons, apostrophes, dashes, quotation marks, and underlining or italics.

On the FCAT Writing test, you will also be scored on mechanics or conventions. This is your use of spelling, capitalization, and punctuation in your writing. As you revise your essay, look for misspelled words and proper nouns and adjectives that need to be capitalized. Also check to see that every sentence begins with a capital letter and ends with the correct punctuation mark. Make sure you have used commas, semicolons, apostrophes, and quotation marks correctly throughout.

Editing Grammar

Benchmark

- **LA.910.3.4.4** The student will edit for correct use of possessives, subject/verb agreement, comparative and superlative adjectives and adverbs, and noun/pronoun agreement.

As you revise your essay for the FCAT Writing test, look for errors in grammar and usage. Be sure to check that you have used correct verb tenses and agreements. For example, if you are writing about something that happened in the past, be sure that all the verbs you use to describe the past event are in the past tense. Check for agreement of nouns and pronouns. Make sure you have used possessives correctly. Watch for mistakes in comparative and superlative adjectives (the better of the two, the best of the three). Avoid double negatives.

As mentioned in the introduction to Chapter 5, FCAT scorers are not going to be as lenient about errors in mechanics and usage as they have been in the past. Remember to check your writing carefully for errors before you submit it.

Editing Sentence Formation

Benchmark

• **LA.910.3.4.5** The student will edit for correct use of sentence formation, including absolutes and absolute phrases, infinitives and infinitive phrases, and use of fragments for effect.

On the FCAT Writing test, you might use more complex sentence structures to show your writing skill. If so, make sure you use these sentence forms correctly. For example, you might use absolute phrases to go from a description of a person or thing to its parts. Here is an example from John Steinbeck's story "The Red Pony." The absolute phrases are in italics:

> **"Six boys came over the hill half an hour early that afternoon, running hard,** *their heads down, their forearms working, their breath whistling."*

You might also use infinitive phrases, as Mark Twain does in a famous quote:

> **"It is better** *to keep* **your mouth closed and let people think you are a fool than** *to open* **it and remove all doubt."**

In general, you should avoid sentence fragments in formal writing. However, a sentence fragment might occasionally be used for a strong effect, as novelist Charles Portis does here:

> **"There are tigers in Korea, but I never saw one. Nor had I ever caught a glimpse of a jaguar here in the Petén forest.** *Pumas, ocelots, margays, but not one tiger."*

Finally, check for run-on sentences and rewrite them either as compound or complex sentences or as two separate sentences.

⑦ Revising and Editing Exercises

Exercise 1

The following article is a first draft that Derek wrote for his teacher. The article contains errors. Read the article to answer questions 1 through 5.

College-Bound Turnaround

[1] I never imagined that I would want to attend college. [2] Until this school year, I thought that I would want to start working at a full-time job as soon as I graduated from high school. [3] Then, after I gained some experience, I thought I might move up to a managerial position. [4] My parents always wanted me to go to college. [5] They gave me the freedom to make my own choices.

[6] Then my sister Adrian came home to stay with us over winter break. [7] She is an art major at Bruni University. [8] Over dinner, she told the family stuff about being at school. [9] She also told us how much she likes her classes and how she was eager to return to school after break. [10] Our cousin Becky is the same way. [11] Before Adrian left, she asked me if I wanted to come for a visit. [12] Since I was still on break from school, I followed her back to the university. [13] I never thought that short trip would change my mind about college.

[14] Adrian took me on a tour of the campus, and I was very impressed. [15] The buildings were old and unique, and the campus was full of trees and quiet, sunny spots to study. [16] While we were walking around, I met some of Adrian's friends. [17] They were all very nice to me, and I could tell that they thought my sister was a talented artist. [18] She

introduced me as a great writer, which embarrassed me, but it made me think about my own talents. [19] When we got back to her apartment, I started looking at the university's catalogue. [20] I saw that they offered a lot of different writing classes that sounded fun and interesting.

[21] I have decided to go to college after graduation. [22] I am even going to take a writing workshop this summer. [23] I would say I owe it all to my sister, but really the change came from inside of me. [24] Maybe that's what getting older is all about.

1   Which transition should be added to the beginning of sentence 5 to show a connection to the previous sentence?

   A. Similarly

   B. Therefore

   C. However

   D. For example

2   Read sentence 8 from the essay.

Over dinner, she told the family stuff about being at school.

Which words should replace the word *stuff* so that the reader knows specifically what was being told?

   F.   some things

   G. interesting words

   H. funny stories

   I.   different reports

3   Which sentence should be added after sentence 14 to support the ideas in the paragraph?

   A. There were so many things about Adrian's school that I found appealing.

   B. She walked so fast that I quickly got tired and wanted to go home.

   C. I asked Adrian not to tell anyone that I liked to write, but she never listens to me.

   D. She reminded me that I am also good at sketching still-life scenes.

4   Which sentence is off-topic and should be removed from the second paragraph?

   F. sentence 10

   G. sentence 11

   H. sentence 12

   I. sentence 13

5   Which sentence should be added to the first paragraph to help support the topic?

   A. They tried to make me apply to the local community college, but I didn't want to.

   B. My sister went to college last year.

   C. I thought that I could start by washing cars or working as a waiter at a popular restaurant.

   D. My friends all want to go to different colleges across the country.

Exercise 2

Pamela wrote the following letter to her pen pal in France. The letter contains errors. Read the letter to answer questions 6 through 9.

57 North Shore Rd.
Ft. Lauderdale, FL 33314
April 17, 2006

Dear Aimée,

[1] Bonjour! [2] I haven't heard from you in a long time, and I was wondering how you are. [3] I hope you are doing well.

[4] I have been having a fun time here in the states. [5] My family and I recently took a great trip to Miami for the weekend. [6] If you don't know, Miami is a large city with lots of shopping, dining, beaches, and other attractions. [7] We have relatives who live there—my Uncle Ramon and Aunt Norma—so we went to visit them. [8] My eighteen-year-old cousin Marisa lives there, too. [9] I had a lot of fun spending time with her. [10] She showed me many of the things in Miami that are really fun to do.

[11] First Marisa took me to the Miami Metrozoo, where I got to see many different animals. [12] The chimpanzees were my favorite animals because they were showing off for us. [13] They imitated everything that we did—it was so funny. [14] When Marisa lifted her arms in the air or when I jumped up and down, so did the chimps! [15] I also really like the tigers, especially the white ones, because they were sleek and graceful. [16] They reminded me of my cat, Remie. [17] After that I wanted to see Coral Castle, where there was a garden of intricate coral sculptures. [18] I've never seen anything like it.

[19] Saturday night we all went out for dinner at a restaurant on the ocean. [20] I ordered alligator bites, but I didn't like them, so Marisa finished them for me. [21] The next day, Marisa took me to the Miami Seaquarium, where we watched a dolphin show. [22] Marisa started clowning around in the aquarium's playground, which was funny until the kids got scared and started crying, so we left really fast. [23] When we got back to Marisa's house, it was time to go home. [24] I was sad to leave, but I made plans to come back in the summer. [25] If you come to the states this summer, you should come with me! [26] I hope you are having a good time in France.

Sincerely,
Pamela

6   How does Pamela show that she is writing to inform?

    F.   She argues that Miami is the best city in the world.

    G.   She presents many details about her visit to Miami.

    H.   She states opinions about the people who live in Miami.

    I.   She contrasts positive and negative aspects of Miami.

7   Read sentence 10 from the letter.

She showed me many of the things in Miami that are really fun to do.

Which revision of the sentence provides the most specific word choices?

    A.   Marisa took me to some fun places that were in the city of Miami.

    B.   She showed me some of Miami's most exciting and interesting attractions.

    C.   We, Marisa and I, saw lots of interesting stuff during our weekend in Miami.

    D.   She and I did lots of activities and saw many different details.

8   Which kind of detail should Pamela add to help support the topic of the third paragaph?

    F.   a sentence about other places that Pamela wants to visit

    G.   a definition of *funny*

    H.   an example of the types of sculptures at Coral Castle

    I.   a detail about the visit to the Miami Metrozoo

9   Which sentence contains the word choices suitable for Pamela's letter to Aimée?

    A.   In closing, I would like to extend an offer for you to vacation in my home.

    B.   I really hope we can meet in person someday soon.

    C.   It would super cool to see ya.

    D.   Please consider embarking on a journey to visit America.

Exercise 3

Read the article "Bird Brains." Choose the word or words that correctly complete questions 10 through 13. Then find the correct sentences in questions 14 through 19.

Bird Brains

Do animals have the capacity to retain as much information as human beings? This question has been __(16)__ by scientists for many years. To properly answer it, one scientist decided to ask an animal with speech capabilities: the African gray parrot.

In the late 1970s, research scientist Irene Pepperberg set out to prove that African gray parrots have cognitive abilities. Dr. Pepperberg has worked with a specific parrot named Alex for more than twenty-eight years. Her research has sparked much debate __(17)__ the scientific community.

Alex can name more than fifty different objects when they are presented to him. He can express certain desires and accept or refuse the __(18)__ of others. Alex can answer questions about the colors, shapes, and materials of different objects with __(19)__ 80 percent accuracy. He can make comparisons and sort items by type. Alex can also count up to six and find hidden items.

While Dr. Pepperberg acknowledges that the brains of these birds are far different from the human brain, her experiments prove that African gray parrots can think and feel in ways that are similar to human thought processes and emotions.

10 Which word should go in blank (16)?

   F. presents

   G. presented

   H. present

11 Which word should go in blank (17)?

  A. within

  B. between

  C. beneath

12 Which word should go in blank (18)?

  F. recuests

  G. requests

  H. reqwcsts

13 Which word should go in blank (19)?

  A. aproksimatly

  B. aproximatly

  C. approximately

14 In which sentence is all **punctuation** correct?

  F. Tate bought his mother three things for her birthday; a bunch of flowers, a book of poetry, and a crystal necklace.

  G. Tate bought his mother three things for her birthday a bunch of flowers, a book of poetry, and a crystal necklace.

  H. Tate bought his mother three things for her birthday: a bunch of flowers, a book of poetry, and a crystal necklace.

15 In which sentence is all **capitalization** correct?

  A. Frank knew that Senator Redding had recently visited the Southwest.

  B. Frank knew that senator Redding had recently visited the Southwest.

  C. Frank knew that Senator Redding had recently visited the southwest.

16 In which sentence is all punctuation correct?

   F. Candice enjoys playing softball, tennis, and golf; she hates ballet.

   G. Candice enjoys playing softball, tennis and golf she hates ballet.

   H. Candice enjoys playing softball tennis, and golf, she hates ballet.

17 In which sentence is all capitalization correct?

   A. In my World history class, we learned about the european monarchs of the 1800s.

   B. In my World History class, we learned about the European monarchs of the 1800s.

   C. In my world History class, we learned about the European Monarchs of the 1800s.

18 Read the sentence in bold type.

   Nikki, before sending the sporting equipment to Hugh, asked him if she had remembered all the items in the correct order.

   Which sentence below most clearly expresses the meaning of the sentence in bold type?

   F. In the correct order, before sending the sporting equipment to Hugh, Nikki asked him if she had remembered all the items.

   G. Before sending the sporting equipment to Hugh, Nikki asked him if she had remembered all of the items in the correct order.

   H. Nikki asked him if she had remembered all of the items, in the correct order, before sending the sporting equipment to Hugh.

19 Combine the ideas below to create a logical sentence.

   Sasha stood in the lobby during the play's intermission.

   She looked at pictures.

   The pictures were of the actors.

   A. Sasha was standing in the lobby looking at pictures, during the play's intermission, of the actors.

   B. Looking at pictures of the actors, during the play's intermission, while Sasha was standing in the lobby.

   C. During the play's intermission, Sasha stood in the lobby and looked at pictures of the actors.

Exercise 4

Read the article "Amazing Ants." Choose the word or words that correctly complete questions 20 through 23. Then find the correct sentences in questions 24 through 29.

Amazing Ants

Ants are truly amazing creatures. Even though it is a very small insect, an ant has very strong legs. If we had legs as strong as ants' legs, we would be able to ___(16)___ as fast as a horse! An ant can lift twenty times its own body weight. Ants have some intellectual ___(17)___, too; they have many more brain cells than most creatures.

Ants also have very strong, scissor-like jaws. They have a great sense of smell and two stomachs. One stomach holds the food an ant will digest for itself, and the other stomach holds the food it will distribute to other ants ___(18)___ the colony.

But life for an ant isn't all rosy. Ants only live about fifty days—that is, if nothing eats them or ___(19)___ on them.

20 Which word should go in blank (16)?

    F. ran

    G. runs

    H. run

21 Which word should go in blank (17)?

    A. qualities

    B. qualities

    C. qualityes

22 Which word should go in blank (18)?

    F. alongside

    G. between

    H. throughout

23 Which word should go in blank (19)?

    A. step

    B. steps

    C. stepping

24 In which sentence is all **punctuation** correct?

    F. Afterward we watched a movie, and went to bed.

    G. Afterward we watched a movie and went to bed.

    H. Afterward, we watched a movie and went to bed.

25 In which sentence is all **capitalization** correct?

    A. My mom took me to East Greenberg Mall on Saturday.

    B. My Mom took me to east Greenberg mall on Saturday.

    C. My mom took me to East Greenberg Mall on saturday.

26 In which sentence is all **punctuation** correct?

    F. I saw monkeys lions, and bears, at the zoo.

    G. I saw monkeys, lions, and bears at the zoo.

    H. I saw monkeys, lions and, bears at the zoo.

27 In which sentence is all **capitalization** correct?

    A. We traveled on Intercoastal Air to reach the Grand Cayman islands.

    B. We traveled on Intercoastal air to reach the Grand Cayman Islands.

    C. We traveled on Intercoastal Air to reach the Grand Cayman Islands.

28 Read the sentence in bold type.

Greg and Wanda ran, to prove they were in peak condition, five miles on a warm, sunny day.

Which sentence below most clearly expresses the meaning of the sentence in bold type?

F. They ran five miles, Greg and Wanda, to prove they were in peak condition on a warm, sunny day.

G. On a warm, sunny day, Greg and Wanda, to prove they were in peak condition, ran five miles.

H. To prove they were in peak condition, Greg and Wanda ran five miles on a warm, sunny day.

29 Combine the ideas below to create a logical sentence.

Eve walked to the post office.

She saw a lost dog.

The dog was lying next to a tree.

A. While walking to the post office, Eve saw a lost dog lying next to a tree.

B. Seeing a lost dog lying next to a tree while Eve was walking to the post office.

C. Eve walked to the post office, yet a lost dog was lying next to a tree.

Answers

1 C

However provides an appropriate transition from sentence 4 to sentence 5 because the transition shows that though Derek's parents wish he would go to college, they will allow him to make his own choices.

Benchmark: LA.910.3.3.2 The student will revise by creating clarity and logic by maintaining central theme, idea, or unifying point and developing meaningful relationships among ideas.

2 H

The word *stuff* is vague and does not let the reader know what was being told. Of the answer choices, "funny stories" gives the reader the most detail about what Adrian was telling her family.

Benchmark: LA.910.3.3.3 The student will revise by creating precision and interest by elaborating ideas through supporting details (e.g., facts, statistics, expert opinions, anecdotes), a variety of sentence structures, creative language devices, and modifying word choices using resources and reference materials (e.g., dictionary, thesaurus) to select more effective and precise language.

3 A

Sentence 14 states that Derek was impressed with the campus. "There were so many things about Adrian's school that I found appealing" should be added because it links the idea that he was impressed to the things that Derek liked about the campus.

Benchmark: LA.910.3.3.1 The student will revise by evaluating the draft for development of ideas and content, logical organization, voice, point of view, word choice, and sentence variation.

4 F

The second paragraph is about Adrian's visit and what she said to her family. The fact that her behavior reminded Derek of their cousin Becky is off-topic. This sentence should be deleted from the paragraph.

Benchmark: LA.910.3.3.2 The student will revise by creating clarity and logic by maintaining central theme, idea, or unifying point and developing meaningful relationships among ideas.

5   C

The topic of the first paragraph is Derek's past plans for working after high school instead of attending college. This sentence should be added because it presents the details of Derek's past plan.

Benchmark: LA.910.3.3.3 The student will revise by creating precision and interest by elaborating ideas through supporting details (e.g., facts, statistics, expert opinions, anecdotes), a variety of sentence structures, creative language devices, and modifying word choices using resources and reference materials (e.g., dictionary, thesaurus) to select more effective and precise language.

6   G

Pamela presents many details about her trip; this is her only purpose. She is writing to inform her pen pal about her weekend in Miami.

Benchmark: LA.910.3.3.2 The student will revise by creating clarity and logic by maintaining central theme, idea, or unifying point and developing meaningful relationships among ideas.

7   B

The phrase "exciting and interesting attractions" are more specific than the words *places, stuff,* and *details* in the other answer choices.

Benchmark: LA.910.3.3.3 The student will revise by creating precision and interest by elaborating ideas through supporting details (e.g., facts, statistics, expert opinions, anecdotes), a variety of sentence structures, creative language devices, and modifying word choices using resources and reference materials (e.g., dictionary, thesaurus) to select more effective and precise language.

8   H

An example of the types of sculptures at Coral Castle would support the topic of the third paragraph.

Benchmark: LA. 910.3.3.1 The student will revise by evaluating the draft for development of ideas and content, logical organization, voice, point of view, word choice, and sentence variation.

9 B

The tone of this sentence is casual enough to fit the tone of the rest of the letter. The other choices are either too casual or too formal to fit with the tone of the rest of the letter.

Benchmark: LA. 910.3.3.1 The student will revise by evaluating the draft for development of ideas and content, logical organization, voice, point of view, word choice, and sentence variation.

10 G

Past tense is the proper verb form for this sentence.

Benchmark: LA. 910.3.4.4 The student will edit for correct use of possessives, subject/verb agreement, comparative and superlative adjectives and adverbs, and noun/pronoun agreement.

11 A

Within is the correct word to include in this sentence. *Between* signifies exchange involving only two people. *Beneath* does not make sense in the context of the sentence.

Benchmark: LA. 910.3.3.1 The student will revise by evaluating the draft for development of ideas and content, logical organization, voice, point of view, word choice, and sentence variation.

12 G

This answer choice is the correct spelling of the word *requests*.

Benchmark: LA. 910.3.4.1 The student will edit for correct use of spelling, using spelling rules, orthographic patterns, generalizations, knowledge of root words, prefixes, suffixes, knowledge of Greek, Latin, and Anglo-Saxon root words, and knowledge of foreign words commonly used in English *(laissez faire, croissant)*.

13 C

This answer choice is the correct spelling of the word *approximately*.

Benchmark: LA. 910.3.4.1 The student will edit for correct use of spelling, using spelling rules, orthographic patterns, generalizations, knowledge of root words, prefixes, suffixes, knowledge of Greek, Latin, and Anglo-Saxon root words, and knowledge of foreign words commonly used in English *(laissez faire, croissant)*.

14 H

This sentence is correctly punctuated. A colon is used to introduce a list of items.

Benchmark: LA. 910.3.4.3 The student will edit for correct use of punctuation, including commas, colons, semicolons, apostrophes, dashes, quotation marks, and underlining or italics.

15 A

Rules of capitalization are correctly applied in this sentence.

Benchmark: LA. 910.3.4.2 The student will edit for correct use of capitalization, including names of academic courses and proper adjectives.

16 F

This sentence is correctly punctuated.

Benchmark: LA. 910.3.4.3 The student will edit for correct use of punctuation, including commas, colons, semicolons, apostrophes, dashes, quotation marks, and underlining or italics.

17 B

Rules of capitalization are correctly applied in this sentence.

Benchmark: LA. 910.3.4.2 The student will edit for correct use of capitalization, including names of academic courses and proper adjectives.

18 G

This sentence clearly expresses the meaning of the sentence in bold type.

Benchmark: LA. 910.3.4.5 The student will edit for correct use of sentence formation, including absolutes and absolute phrases, infinitives and infinitive phrases, and use of fragments for effect.

19 C

This answer choice correctly combines the three ideas to create one complete, logical sentence.

Benchmark: LA. 910.3.4.5 The student will edit for correct use of sentence formation, including absolutes and absolute phrases, infinitives and infinitive phrases, and use of fragments for effect.

20 H

Run is the proper form of the verb to include in the sentence. It matches the subject of the sentence in number and tense.

Benchmark: LA. 910.3.4.4 The student will edit for correct use of possessives, subject/verb agreement, comparative and superlative adjectives and adverbs, and noun/pronoun agreement.

21 A

The word *quality* can only be made plural by deleting the *y* and adding the suffix *-ies*.

Benchmark: LA. 910.3.4.1 The student will edit for correct use of spelling, using spelling rules, orthographic patterns, generalizations, knowledge of root words, prefixes, suffixes, knowledge of Greek, Latin, and Anglo-Saxon root words, and knowledge of foreign words commonly used in English *(laissez faire, croissant)*.

22 H

Throughout is the proper word to convey the idea that the ants share food with all the other ants in the colony.

Benchmark: LA. 910.3.3.3 The student will revise by creating precision and interest by elaborating ideas through supporting details (e.g., facts, statistics, expert opinions, anecdotes), a variety of sentence structures, creative language devices, and modifying word choices using resources and reference materials (e.g., dictionary, thesaurus) to select more effective and precise language.

23 B

Steps is the proper form of the verb to include in this sentence.

Benchmark: LA. 910.3.4.4 The student will edit for correct use of possessives, subject/verb agreement, comparative and superlative adjectives and adverbs, and noun/pronoun agreement.

24 H

This sentence is correctly punctuated. It uses the comma properly.

Benchmark: LA. 910.3.4.3 The student will edit for correct use of punctuation, including commas, colons, semicolons, apostrophes, dashes, quotation marks, and underlining or italics.

25 A

The rules of capitalization are correctly applied in this sentence. All proper nouns are capitalized.

Benchmark: LA. 910.3.4.2 The student will edit for correct use of capitalization, including names of academic courses and proper adjectives.

26 G

This sentence is correctly punctuated. It uses commas properly.

Benchmark: LA. 910.3.4.3 The student will edit for correct use of punctuation, including commas, colons, semicolons, apostrophes, dashes, quotation marks, and underlining or italics.

27 C

The rules of capitalization are correctly applied in this sentence. All proper nouns are capitalized.

Benchmark: LA. 910.3.4.2 The student will edit for correct use of capitalization, including names of academic courses and proper adjectives.

28 H

This sentence clearly expresses the meaning of the sentence in bold type.

Benchmark: LA. 910. 3.4.5 The student will edit for correct use of sentence formation, including absolutes and absolute phrases, infinitives and infinitive phrases, and use of fragments for effect.

29 A

This answer choice correctly combines the three ideas to create one complete, logical sentence.

Benchmark: LA. 910. 3.4.5 The student will edit for correct use of sentence formation, including absolutes and absolute phrases, infinitives and infinitive phrases, and use of fragments for effect.

Chapter 8

Writing Applications

On the FCAT Writing test, you will respond to either an expository prompt or a persuasive prompt. For an expository prompt, you must describe, explain, or reflect upon something. For example, you might be asked to name the person in the world whom you admire most and explain why. For a persuasive prompt, you must express a point of view about a particular issue or controversy and try to convince your reader to agree with it. For example, you might be asked whether the study of a foreign language should be required in all high schools. Think about these applications as you read the remaining writing-skill benchmarks.

Writing Creatively

Benchmarks

- **LA.910.4.1.1** The student will write in a variety of expressive and reflective forms that use a range of appropriate strategies and specific narrative techniques, employ literary devices, and sensory descriptions.

- **LA.910.4.1.2** The student will incorporate figurative language, emotions, gestures, rhythm, dialogue, characterization, plot, and appropriate format.

As a creative writer, you have many tools at your disposal. You can use figurative language, such as similes, metaphors, and imagery, to bring vivid pictures or ideas to your reader's mind. You can use words to summon strong emotions. You can even use literary techniques, such as bits of dialogue or character descriptions, to make a point. Look at this example of vivid creative writing from Annie Dillard:

"A weasel is wild. Who knows what he thinks? He sleeps in his underground den, his tail draped over his nose. Sometimes he lives in his den for two days without leaving. Outside, he stalks rabbits, mice, muskrats, and birds, killing more bodies than he can eat warm, and often dragging the carcasses home. Obedient to instinct, he bites his prey at the neck, either splitting the jugular vein at the throat or crunching the brain at the base of the skull, and he does not let go. One naturalist refused to kill a weasel who was socketed into his hand deeply as a rattlesnake. The man could in no way pry the tiny weasel off, and he had to walk half a mile to water, the weasel dangling from his palm, and soak him off like a stubborn label."

Reread the last sentence of this passage. Notice the simile: *and soak him off like a stubborn label*. This image will stick in a reader's mind as persistently as the teeth of that weasel stuck in the naturalist's hand. Try to create phrases and images that your reader will remember.

Regardless of whether the prompt asks you for expository or persuasive writing, you should use some of the techniques of creative writing to make your essay more interesting. Strong images or metaphors are not just for use in expository writing. They can also help you persuade a reader effectively.

Writing to Inform

Benchmarks

- **LA.910.4.2.1** The student will write in a variety of informational/expository forms, including a variety of technical documents (e.g., how-to manuals, procedures, assembly directions).

- **LA.910.4.2.2** The student will record information and ideas from primary and/or secondary sources accurately and coherently, noting the validity and reliability of these sources and attributing sources of information.

- **LA.910.4.2.4** The student will write a business letter and/or memo that presents information purposefully and succinctly to meet the needs of the intended audience following a conventional format (e.g., block, modified block, memo, email).

- **LA.910.4.2.5** The student will write detailed travel directions and design an accompanying graphic using the cardinal and ordinal directions, landmarks, streets and highways, and distances.

- **LA.910.4.2.6** The student will write a work-related document (e.g., application, resume, meeting minutes, memo, cover letter, letter of application, speaker introduction, letter of recommendation).

On the FCAT Writing test, you may have to respond to a prompt with informative writing. For example, you might have to explain how to do something in step-by-step detail. You could describe how to raise a tent at a campsite or prepare a cheese omelet. In this kind of writing, it helps to be familiar with the format of how-to manuals or assembly instructions. Imagine that your reader knows nothing about the topic and has to be guided through the procedure step by step.

If the expository prompt leads you to mention a current event or event from history, you might rely on primary or secondary sources you have read or seen. Remember, you will not have access to research materials on the test, so whatever supporting facts and sources you mention have to come from your own memory. For example, you might explain that a fact comes from a TV news report or from a recent news magazine.

While you won't be tested on them, you should practice different forms of informative writing. You might write a business letter to get a refund from a company, or write a letter of application for a summer job. Go online to find the correct format for different kinds of letters and memos.

Speculating on Causes and Effects

Benchmark

- **LA.910.4.2.3** The student will write informational/expository essays that speculate on the causes and effects of a situation, establish the connection between the postulated causes or effects, offer evidence supporting the validity of the proposed causes or effects, and include introductory, body, and concluding paragraphs.

On the FCAT Writing test, you might write a special kind of informative essay that speculates on the possible causes or effects of some social change, program, or activity. For example, you could see the following prompt: "Write an essay about how social media have changed daily life in the United States. Discuss the positive and negative effects of these media."

In your response to a cause-and-effect prompt, state clearly the situation you are writing about, and try to make strong connections between the causes and effects in your essay. Be sure to offer valid reasons why something might cause something else to occur. In your last paragraph, sum up your line of reasoning.

Writing to Persuade

Benchmarks

- **LA.910.4.3.1** The student will write essays that state a position or claim, present detailed evidence, examples, and reasoning to support effective arguments and emotional appeals, and acknowledge and refute opposing arguments.
- **LA.910.4.3.2** The student will include persuasive techniques.

The other kind of prompt you are likely to see on the FCAT Writing test is a persuasive prompt. This asks you to state your position on an issue and support your position with facts, examples, and detailed evidence. For example, you might encounter a prompt like the following:

Writing Situation

The school board is contemplating making art a requirement for high school graduation.

Directions for Writing

What is your opinion about this issue? Some students insist that the study of art should be strictly an elective. Others think that learning about art and its techniques should be part of all students' basic education in culture. Write a letter to your school board representative in which you state your position on this question. Use facts and examples to support your point of view.

In writing a persuasive essay, make sure that you state your position about the issue clearly at the beginning. Then follow up by using whatever persuasive techniques seem most effective. The best method generally is to use facts and valid examples to support your opinion. You might provide a detailed example of a personal experience to make your point. You can also use arguments that appeal to the emotions of your reader; however, these need to be backed up with facts. You might try to imagine the strongest argument against your viewpoint and answer it with a reasonable response. At the end, sum up your position and supporting ideas. A successful persuasive essay should proceed logically, point by point, from the opening to a strong conclusion.

Sample Essays

Remember the writing prompts you read at the beginning of Chapter 5? The following are sample six-point responses to those prompts. Notice that the samples clearly respond to the prompt. They contain good opening and closing statements and progress logically from beginning to end. The essays are well developed and stay focused on the topic throughout. They contain few, if any, errors in usage, sentence construction, and mechanics.

Expository Prompt

Writing Situation

Most people have a favorite season or time of year.

Directions for Writing

Write an essay describing your favorite season. Discuss what makes this season special to you.

Sample Answer

My favorite season of the year is autumn. In autumn, the hot, humid summer air turns cool and crisp. The forest behind my house begins to change color. The lush greens of summer become an array of warm autumn hues like red, orange, brown, and gold. When the sun shines through the trees, it looks like the forest is a great fire trying to warm the gray sky. As I ride through the countryside, fields are dotted with bright orange pumpkins, and bright red apples hang from trees, ripe and ready for picking. At night, the temperature drops dramatically, and I can see my breath in the air. The smell of wood smoke from the chimneys of neighboring houses fills the air. On my porch, I listen to the sounds of the woods — twigs crackling in the dark blanket of the night forest and a light breeze scraping fallen leaves across the paved driveway. I snuggle deeper into a wool blanket to ward off the chill of a potential frost, and I sip warm apple cider with my family.

These tastes, sounds, smells, and sights of fall are special to me because I know that winter is on its way. I know that soon my family will be curled up on cozy chairs and couches next to a blazing fire. My house will take on a new warmth; not the hot, sticky air of summer but the warmth you feel when you first come in from the cold.

Persuasive Prompt

Writing Situation

To cut back on expenses, your principal has asked the school board for permission to cancel all field trips for the remainder of the year.

Directions for Writing

Think about how you feel about this issue. Some people think this is a good idea because they consider field trips "vacations" from learning and therefore an unnecessary expense. Write a letter to the school board explaining your position on the issue. Use facts and examples to develop your argument.

Sample Answer

Dear School Board:

School field trips should not be canceled for the rest of the school year. I understand how people might mistake a field trip for a mini-vacation from school. Students get to take a break from the monotony of a school day, get on a bus, and travel to a theater, an art museum, a science center, or a historical site. They get to watch plays, see magnificent works of art, try new inventions, or experience life as it was in the past.

What critics seem to forget, however, is that these field trips do not allow us to take a vacation from our education. On the contrary, field trips allow us to enhance what we've learned in the classroom and gain practical knowledge. While books, chalkboards, and lectures are certainly important, hands-on learning gives students the opportunity to take what they have learned and see how it is applied in real life. How much better you can appreciate a play by Shakespeare when you see it performed live! No art book of paintings and sculptures can replace the experience of seeing works of art in person. Why study a dry diagram of a flower when you can visit a greenhouse full of living examples of the most beautiful plants and flowers? Field trips provide students not only with a break from the monotony of an ordinary school day but also with a chance to supplement our classroom learning with valuable real-life experiences.

Yours truly,

FCAT 2.0 Reading
Practice Test

Directions: This Practice Test contains six reading passages and 56 multiple-choice questions. Mark your answers in the Answer Sheet section at the back of this book.

Read the article "Concerto for the Left Hand" before answering questions 1 through 7.

Concerto for the Left Hand

Inside a large concert hall in Paris in 1934, the audience applauds as the soloist seats himself at the piano bench and nods to the conductor. Following a brief opening passage by the orchestra, the pianist enters dramatically with a storm of chords struck up and down the keyboard. His playing is masterful, and his calm assurance on the stage holds the audience in thrall. However, there is one important difference in this pianist: his right sleeve hangs empty at his side. Those intricate trills and rapid glissandos are achieved with his left hand alone. The pianist's name is Paul Wittgenstein.

Wittgenstein was born in Vienna, Austria, in 1887. He was the seventh and next to last child of a fabulously wealthy and rather eccentric family. His father amassed a fortune in business, and passed on to his children his habit of independent thinking and his love of music. Some of Europe's greatest composers performed at the Wittgenstein Palais, a grand residence in the heart of Vienna. Paul's mother and father often played chamber music together for relaxation. All the Wittgenstein children could play multiple instruments and read music as naturally as prose.

Growing up, Paul set his heart on a career as a concert pianist. However, when World War I erupted in 1914, he enlisted and joined the fighting on the Eastern Front in what is now Poland. While on a scouting mission he was caught in an ambush by Russian troops, and a bullet shattered his right elbow. Subsequently his men managed to get him to a field hospital in a nearby town. There, doctors clumsily amputated his arm. When he awoke from the operation, Russian soldiers had stormed the town's walls and were holding the doctors and patients at gunpoint. Paul was taken prisoner and moved to a series of Russian camps, where he was held in squalid, freezing barracks with little food. To pass the time at one camp in Siberia, Paul drew a piano keyboard on a wooden crate and doggedly spent hours fingering his favorite pieces with his left hand while listening in his head to the imaginary result. A sympathetic diplomat with the Danish Red Cross noticed his dedicated routine. He succeeded in getting Paul transferred to a village hotel, where he could practice on an upright piano that was real, albeit rickety and out of tune. Finally, after months of negotiations, Paul and several other Austrians were freed in an exchange of prisoners. Paul returned to his family home and familiar keyboard.

Locking himself in his room for hours at a time, Paul set about devising new arrangements for the left hand of piano music by Bach, Chopin, and other composers. He developed tremendous strength and dexterity in his left hand, enabling him to produce a melodic line with his thumb and index finger while

Go On ▶

his other three fingers kept a rhythmic pulse. He also invented his own technique for making his one-handed playing sound like the work of two hands. He would depress the piano's pedal for added echo and flash his fingers over the keys at lightning speed from the upper register to the lower, enabling him to fool the ears of even the most expert musicians. Ironically, the most skeptical among his early listeners were probably his own family members. His older sister Hermine, for example, disliked his playing. "When I hear him practicing upstairs," she wrote to a friend, "not a single bar accords with my way of thinking and feeling." Ludwig Wittgenstein, the baby of the family and himself a celebrated philosopher, pointedly stayed away from his brother's concert appearances.

Nevertheless, in the years after the war, Paul pursued his dream with an astonishing vigor and single-mindedness. With money he inherited after his father's death, he commissioned some of the world's greatest composers to write piano concertos for the left hand. Ravel, Prokofiev, Strauss, and Schmidt were just some of the musicians who agreed to accept the technical challenge of writing such specialized music. To ensure that the concertos would be his property alone, Paul insisted that the composers grant him exclusive rights to perform the pieces in public. The generous fees that he paid certainly helped ease these negotiations.

Occasionally spats broke out between composers and Paul. With tastes that ran to the music of the eighteenth and nineteenth centuries, he sometimes failed to appreciate the virtues of modern music as purveyed by his commissioned writers. In addition, he was always opinionated and outspoken — in fact, he was unable to

Go On ▶

be less than candid when he did not understand a piece or disliked it entirely. For example, his experience with the French composer Maurice Ravel was anything but smooth. Then at the height of his fame, Ravel delivered to Paul a piano concerto that was melodic and full of drama, a virtuoso piece. Yet Paul was initially unimpressed and asked for several changes, which Ravel refused to make. When Paul premiered the concerto at a private gathering with Ravel in attendance, he changed several parts and cut out others. The composer was beside himself with rage. At first he swore that Paul would never play his concerto again in public, but at last the pair ironed out their differences. Paul agreed to perform the piece as written, and ended up playing it in concert halls the world over.

By the 1930s, Paul had become a sensation on the concert stage. Promoters throughout Europe and the United States clamored for his performances. Audiences offered thunderous applause to this strong-willed musician with his close-cropped hair, concentrated gaze, and nimble fingers. One critic described "the energy and skill of the artist who, if we close our eyes, deceives us into imagining a two-handed pianist: indeed sometimes in the power of his attack, into imagining two two-handed pianists." Paul Wittgenstein continued to play professionally for the next twenty years. The piano works that he commissioned are now considered classics. He proved that not even the loss of an arm could curtail the career of a dedicated musician and performer.

Answer questions 1 through 7. Base your answers on the article "Concerto for the Left Hand."

 1 Read this excerpt from the article.

> **His father amassed a fortune in business, and passed on to his children his habit of independent thinking and his love of music. Some of Europe's greatest composers performed at the Wittgenstein Palais, a grand residence in the heart of Vienna. Paul's mother and father often played chamber music together for relaxation. All the Wittgenstein children could play multiple instruments and read music as naturally as prose.**

In this excerpt, the author is discussing

A. the satisfactions of learning to play music at an early age.

B. the family background of Paul Wittgenstein.

C. the importance of music in the culture of Vienna.

D. the reasons why Europe produced so many great composers.

Go On ▶

2 Read this passage from the article.

> To pass the time at one camp in Siberia, Paul drew a piano keyboard on a wooden crate and doggedly spent hours fingering his favorite pieces with his left hand while listening in his head to the imaginary result. A sympathetic diplomat with the Danish Red Cross noticed his dedicated routine.

The author includes this passage mainly to show

    F. Paul's determination to develop his skill as a pianist.

    G. Paul's unrealistic ideas about playing the piano.

    H. the harsh conditions of prison camps in World War I.

    I. the value of the Red Cross in improving the conditions of prisoners.

3 Which of the following is NOT one of the tactics Paul used to start his career as a pianist?

    A. He developed arrangements for the left hand of music by great composers.

    B. He paid critics to attend his concerts and write favorable notices.

    C. He paid composers to write piano music for the left hand.

    D. He practiced a technique that enabled him to play rhythm and melody with one hand.

4 Read this sentence from the article.

> In addition, he was always opinionated and outspoken — in fact, he was unable to be less than candid when he did not understand a piece or disliked it entirely.

In this sentence, what does the word *candid* mean?

    F. difficult

    G. dishonest

    H. honest

    I. hateful

Go On ▶

5 The main reason that Paul paid composers to write music for him was that

   A. he needed very simple pieces that could be played with one hand.

   B. he loved modern music and wanted to play music in the modern style.

   C. he wanted to own the performing rights to the pieces that they wrote.

   D. he knew writing music to be played with one hand was technically very challenging.

6 Which of the following sentences is the BEST description of the attitude of Paul's family towards his playing?

   F. Paul's family made many sacrifices for him to help him be successful as a pianist.

   G. Paul's sister Hermine did not care for his playing, but his brother Ludwig strongly supported his career.

   H. Paul's family was mostly jealous of his success and popularity as a musician.

   I. Paul's family generally did not appreciate his talent as a musician and performer.

7 Why did the author write this article?

   A. to entertain readers with a story about feuding musicians.

   B. to inform readers about a remarkable musician who overcame a handicap to succeed.

   C. to convince readers that people with disabilities should be given a chance to succeed.

   D. to persuade readers that war should be abolished because of its disastrous effects on people like Paul Wittgenstein.

Go On ▶

Read the poem "The Tuft of Flowers" before answering questions 8 through 15.

The Tuft of Flowers

by Robert Frost

I went to turn the grass once after one
Who mowed it in the dew before the sun.

The dew was gone that made his blade so keen
Before I came to view the leveled scene.

I looked for him behind an isle of trees;
I listened for his whetstone[1] on the breeze.

But he had gone his way, the grass all mown,
And I must be, as he had been, — alone,

"As all must be," I said within my heart,
"Whether they work together or apart."

But as I said it, swift there passed me by
On noiseless wing a bewildered butterfly,

Seeking with memories grown dim o'er night
Some resting flower of yesterday's delight.

And once I marked his flight go round and round,
As where some flower lay withering on the ground.

And then he flew as far as eye could see,
And then on tremulous wing came back to me.

Go On ▶

I thought of questions that have no reply,
And would have turned to toss the grass to dry;

But he turned first, and led my eye to look
At a tall tuft of flowers beside a brook,

A leaping tongue of bloom the scythe[2] had spared
Beside a reedy brook the scythe had bared.

The mower in the dew had loved them thus,
By leaving them to flourish, not for us,

Nor yet to draw one thought of ours to him,
But from sheer morning gladness at the brim.

The butterfly and I had lit upon,
Nevertheless, a message from the dawn,

That made me hear the wakening birds around,
And hear his long scythe whispering to the ground,

And feel a spirit kindred[3] to my own;
So that henceforth I worked no more alone;

But glad with him, I worked as with his aid,
And weary, sought at noon with him the shade;

And dreaming, as it were, held brotherly speech
With one whose thought I had not hoped to reach.

Go On ▶

"Men work together," I told him from the heart,

"Whether they work together or apart."

1. whetstone: a stone for sharpening a blade

2. scythe: a curved bladed tool for cutting grass

3. kindred: related

Answer questions 8 through 15. Base your answers on the poem "The Tuft of Flowers."

8 What is the setting for this poem?

F. a small yard

G. a flower garden

H. a hardware store with lots of tools

I. a large field by a brook

9 Read the following line from the poem.

And hear his long scythe whispering to the ground,

This line contains an example of what kind of figurative language?

A. simile

B. symbolism

C. personification

D. hyperbole

10 Which word BEST describes the speaker of "The Tuft of Flowers"?

F. observant

G. carefree

H. melancholy

I. distrustful

Go On ▶

11 What causes the speaker to notice the tuft of flowers standing by the brook?

   A. the sudden gust of wind at his back

   B. the appearance of a shaft of sunlight

   C. the movement of a butterfly he is watching

   D. the words of the mower he is following

12 Read the following excerpt from the poem.

> **The mower in the dew had loved them thus,**
>
> **By leaving them to flourish,**

Another way to express the idea of *flourish* is

   F. grow and thrive.

   G. wither and die.

   H. droop.

   I. distract.

13 Which of the following does the author NOT use in organizing his material?

   A. rhyme

   B. stanzas

   C. repetition

   D. meter

14 The theme of this poem is the contrast between

   F. working in the country and working in the city.

   G. working alone and working together.

   H. working for pay and working for fun.

   I. working for oneself and working for someone else.

15 Why does the poet take the point of view of a field worker in this poem?

   A. to reinforce the worker's opinion that he needs help to do his job

   B. to demonstrate how hard the worker's life is

   C. to explore how the worker reacts when he sees the uncut flowers

   D. to show that a worker's mind can wander while at work

Go On ▶

Read the article "Daydreams Save the Day" before answering questions 16 through 28.

Daydreams Save the Day

by Ricardo Sanchez

Many students have gotten in trouble for daydreaming in class. It's not a good idea to be thinking about your new skateboard or our weekend plans when you should be learning algebra! It's rude to the instructor, and you might not learn what you need to know. However, many scientists agree that daydreaming itself isn't a bad thing at all. In fact, daydreams can make your life happier and healthier in numerous ways.

Some psychologists (scientists who study the mind) believe that the average person daydreams for many hours each day. Critics of daydreaming say that this is a dreadful waste of time. Daydreaming usually does not result in any obvious progress; it is usually seen as something that keeps people from making progress. This is not really the case, however. Sometimes daydreaming can help people sort out their minds and get their ideas in order so they can think and behave a lot more effectively. Their daydreams can make them more productive workers or students, and make future progress easier.

There are many negative stereotypes about daydreamers, such as they are lazy and they shirk responsibilities. While this description can be true, it is definitely not

Go On ▶

always the case. Sometimes daydreams actually give people a goal to work toward. For instance, writers might daydream about seeing their books in print, and this image builds determination to keep on writing. In this way, daydreams can be a method of visualizing success in the future. Some athletes use "positive thinking" visualizations while practicing. By thinking about their challenges and imagining success in the end, they tend to perform much better than athletes who have not prepared their minds.

Olympic diver Greg Louganis used this form of daydreaming to improve himself as a competitor and learn the most difficult dives. He would perform every step over and over in his mind until he visualized getting the dive exactly right. In his daydreaming mind, he had the routine so thoroughly memorized that he could almost feel it in his muscles and limbs. When it came time for the actual competition, he found that he was able to achieve a relaxed concentration and could block out distractions such as the screaming fans in the bleachers, the ever-present TV cameras, and all thoughts of doing the dive poorly. The result was an extraordinary series of gold-medal performances.

A third criticism of daydreams is that too much daydreaming can make people unhappy. Of course, people who daydream *all day* probably would lose track of the events of real life! They might start to "live in the past" or in some unrealistic dream world. But for people who do a regular amount of daydreaming, the practice can make them happier. This can happen in many ways.

For one, daydreaming allows the mind to relax. Especially in stressful times, giving your mind a break is a great idea. Taking a "mini-vacation" by daydreaming can make a person's brain feel energized and refreshed. These vacations are also great for overcoming boredom. Excessive boredom can have negative effects on people and cause them to feel gloomy and tired. A little daydreaming here and there can relieve the nasty effects of boredom.

Many psychologists think that daydreams can also help remove fear and conflict from our lives and prepare us for success in the real world. Just as athletes use daydreams to prepare for events, many people have found that daydreams help them learn to deal with themselves and others. If two people are not getting along, they might be able to daydream, or visualize, ways in which they could reconcile. They might even be able to use daydreams to imagine the other's point of view and find similarities or shared interests between themselves and the other person. Daydreaming can help us expand our minds, and that helps us find new ways to get along with others.

In much the same way, people can use daydreams to ease, and even conquer, their fears. For example, if a person has a powerful fear, or phobia, of heights, he or she might imagine safely climbing higher and higher on a hill. This can prepare the person to remain calm while climbing the hill. Positive-thinking daydreams can strengthen a person's courage considerably. Many people have used this simple technique to conquer their phobias.

There are many good kinds of daydreaming that help people improve their lives. However, bad types of daydreaming exist as well. Negative daydreaming occurs most frequently in the behavior we know as worrying. Some people get caught up in worries and spend their days nervously picturing all sorts of frightening and embarrassing

Go On ▶

events. Worries can have terrible effects on people's lives. Sometimes worries can keep people awake all night; other times, worries and stress can weaken the body, causing people to get sick more easily.

One of the best ways to combat negative daydreaming is to counter it with positive daydreaming. For instance, instead of worrying, you can take a more relaxed look at your problems. Reflect on the past and imagine some possibilities of the future, and then try to decide how to handle these thoughts. By using positive daydreams and visualizations, you may well be able to overcome many kinds of negative thoughts and feelings.

Daydreams play an important role in our daily lives, a role that not many people stop to consider. Good daydreams can make us healthy and happy, and bad daydreams can do just the opposite. But remember — no daydreams are good daydreams in algebra class!

Answer questions 16 through 28. Base your answers on the article "Daydreams Save the Day."

16 The author's main purpose for writing this article is most likely to

    F. entertain readers with stories of people who daydream too often.

    G. convince readers that daydreaming is more than a waste of time.

    H. teach readers how to analyze their own daydreams.

    I. explain the difference between positive and negative daydreaming.

17 Which is an example of negative daydreaming?

    A. visualizing the completion of a project before it is finished

    B. allowing your mind to wander for a few minutes

    C. concentrating on conquering a fear

    D. losing track of real life while thinking about the past

18 Which organizational pattern does the author use for the first half of the article?

    F. He poses questions about daydreaming to the reader and provides answers to them.

    G. He presents arguments against daydreaming and then offers opposing arguments.

    H. He lists different types of daydreaming and describes the positive effects of each one.

    I. He compares and contrasts positive and negative types of daydreaming.

Go On

19 Read this passage from the fourth paragraph of the article.

> **A third criticism of daydreams is that too much daydreaming can make people unhappy. Of course, people who daydream *all day* probably would lose track of the events of real life!**

In this passage, italics are used to

A. emphasize how absurd it would be to daydream all the time.

B. indicate that *all day* is an idiom with a special meaning.

C. show that the author is making a joke.

D. indicate that *all day* originally comes from a foreign language.

20 According to the article, why would athletes practice a form of daydreaming called "visualization"?

F. to ease their minds and help them sleep

G. to conquer a powerful fear

H. to achieve a relaxed concentration during competition

I. to reflect on the past and imagine some possibilities in the future

21 What does the author use to support the points he makes about daydreaming?

A. fictionalized anecdotes about daydreaming

B. personal conclusions based on research

C. common knowledge and folk wisdom about daydreaming

D. documented research from respected psychologists

22 According to the article, daydreams about conflicts with others are helpful because

F. they soothe us and keep us from feeling gloomy and tired.

G. they relax us as if we had taken a brief vacation.

H. they can assist us in understanding other people's feelings.

I. they have been shown to be effective in conquering phobias.

Go On ▶

23 Read this sentence from the article.

> **Especially in stressful times, giving your mind a break is a great idea.**

In which sentence does *break* have the same meaning as in the sentence above?

A. The golfer's tee shot hit a tree, but he got a lucky break when it bounced onto the green.

B. When the thunderstorm hit, everybody in the park made a break for their cars.

C. The team's new uniforms represent a surprising break with school tradition.

D. After three hours of hard work on her essay, Martha took a break and drank some iced tea on the patio.

24 The article indicates that, in contrast to negative stereotypes about daydreaming, many daydreamers

F. are lazy and shirk their responsibilities.

G. use their daydreams to work toward a goal of personal success.

H. use positive daydreams to build large, successful businesses.

I. are excessively bored and feel gloomy and tired.

25 Read this sentence from the article.

> **If two people are not getting along, they might be able to daydream, or visualize, ways in which they could reconcile.**

What does *reconcile* mean as it is used here?

A. restore to harmony

B. make consistent

C. submit to scrutiny

D. double-check for accuracy

Go On ▶

26 Which sentence BEST conveys the main idea of the passage?

F. Excessive daydreaming can make people unhappy.

G. Daydreaming in algebra class is always rude.

H. Though daydreaming seems bad, it has some good effects.

I. Daydreaming is most important as an aid to avoid boredom.

27 The organizational pattern that the author uses for the last part of the article could best be described as

A. comparison/contrast.

B. argument/support.

C. chronological order.

D. problem/solution

28 Which statement BEST summarizes the conclusion the author draws from his research in this article?

F. Daydreaming is the best way to sort out personal problems, achieve success, and relax your mind.

G. All forms of daydreaming allow your mind to take a break from the stresses of everyday life.

H. Daydreaming is acceptable as long as it does not interfere with important events in your life.

I. All forms of daydreaming are a waste of time and inhibit progress in your life.

Go On ▶

Read the article "Zora Neale Hurston" before answering questions 29 through 37.

Zora Neale Hurston
by Melanie Harris

Zora Neale Hurston was one of the most prolific black writers of 20th-century America, yet her work was largely unappreciated during her lifetime. Between the 1930s and 1960s, Hurston published seven books along with many short stories, plays and magazine articles. A combination of folklore and anthropology, her work differed from the politically slanted depictions of the struggles of blacks that were popular during her lifetime.

As a child Hurston was imaginative, colorful, and strong, traits she incorporated into many of her characters. Constantly reading and writing, she was introspective but passionate, so much so that her father once remarked that she would be hanged for sure. The fifth of eight children, Hurston was born around 1900 in Notasulga, Alabama. Her mother, Lucy, was a teacher, and her father was a carpenter and preacher who was elected mayor of their all-black community for three terms.

Hurston's mother died about a year after she was born, changing what would have been a typical childhood for Hurston into a tumultuous one. Her father remarried, and Hurston was rejected by her new stepmother and sent to live with various relatives, most of which lived in Eatonville, Florida. Eatonville, an all-black town where African Americans felt free to express themselves in a nondiscriminatory environment, made a favorable impression on Hurston that was reflected in her later writing. Hurston persevered in these years and worked her way through school as a maid and manicurist. After graduating from Morgan Academy in Baltimore in 1917, Hurston attended Howard University, where she met other writers and her future husband, Herbert Sheen. Hurston put her career above all else, however, and the couple's brief marriage ended in an amicable divorce. From 1928 to 1932, she studied anthropology and folklore at Columbia University and was later awarded a Guggenheim Fellowship for collecting folklore in Haiti and the British West Indies.

Go On ▶

Hurston arrived in New York City in 1925 during the Harlem Renaissance, an extraordinary movement of black literature and culture. With only $1.50 to her name, Hurston tried her hand at writing short stories. Her first stories to be published, such as "Spunk" and "John Redding Goes to Sea," appeared in black literary journals, and she began to make her name as a writer. Influenced by other artists in the Harlem Renaissance, who were starting to explore African American culture and express pride in their racial heritage, Hurston became interested in anthropology, particularly the study of black culture. For several years, she conducted research that was financed with grants and fellowships. One result of her work was her first novel, *Jonah's Gourd Vine*, which was a critical success. A year later she published *Mules and Men*, an investigation of voodoo practices in Florida and Louisiana, to positive reviews.

In 1937 Hurston produced her most famous novel, *Their Eyes Were Watching God*, about a black woman's quest for identity and fulfillment. Janie, the protagonist of the novel, learns about herself through a series of marriages and relationships with whites. Early critics dismissed the novel as a sentimental love story, but later it was praised as a complex study of a woman whose relationships were a metaphor for her identity. Hurston went on to write her autobiography, *Dust Tracks on a Road*, and in 1948 a last novel, *Seraph on the Suwanee*, about a poor white woman struggling to survive in Florida's citrus industry. *Seraph* was judged a failure, although much of the problem was that neither critics nor readers of the time were ready for a black female author to speak through white characters.

At the invitation of friends, Hurston returned to Florida, this time residing in Belle Glade. She lived in a one-room cabin and earned a meager living doing odd jobs, cleaning houses, and substitute teaching. Her last years were hard, as she suffered from the stomach ailments and money problems that had plagued her throughout her life. She died in a welfare home after suffering a severe stroke in 1960.

Despite the fact that her books were long out of print, interest in Hurston's writing surged in the 1970s. Old criticisms that she had failed to depict the evils of racism in her novels were replaced by more nuanced views that recognized the groundbreaking nature of her fictions. Ironically, her new admirers felt that her writing had been denied the recognition it deserved because of discrimination. Many black women writers, including Alice Walker, the author of *The Color Purple*, considered Hurston's original insights into black culture to be "genius." Walker published the article "In Search of Zora Neale Hurston" in *Ms.* magazine, and Hurston's books were republished to great acclaim. Hurston's concluding words in her autobiography reflect her outlook on the predicament of her life and the world: "Consider that with tolerance and patience, we goodly demons may breed a noble world in a few hundred generations or so."

Go On ▶

Answer questions 29 through 37. Base your answers on the article "Zora Neale Hurston."

29 Read this sentence from the article.

> Hurston's mother died about a year after she was born, changing what would have been a typical childhood for Hurston into a tumultuous one.

What does *tumultuous* mean as it is used here?

A. brilliant

B. turbulent

C. placid

D. tragic

30 According to the article, what is an important characteristic of Hurston's writing that she shared with other writers and artists of the Harlem Renaissance?

F. study of African American culture

G. focus on the effects of racism

H. interest in voodoo rites in Florida and Louisiana

I. emphasis on a woman's relationships

31 Which organizational pattern does the author use in this article?

A. She describes the similarities and differences between Hurston's work and her life.

B. She lists and explains reasons why the author's writing was so influential.

C. She relates the story of Hurston's career in chronological order.

D. She poses questions about the writer and then answers them.

Go On ▶

32 Read this sentence from the first paragraph of the article.

> **A combination of folklore and anthropology, her work differed from the politically slanted depictions of the struggles of blacks that were popular during her lifetime.**

Look at the word *slanted* in the sentence. Which of the following replacements for *slanted* has the most negative connotation?

F. engaged

G. biased

H. inclined

I. weighted

33 With which statement would the author of this article most likely agree?

A. Excellent writing is always recognized eventually by the reading public.

B. Hurston's fame as a writer, while late in coming, is richly deserved.

C. A typical, small-town childhood does not prepare a person for a life of fame.

D. Hurston's writing was not accepted easily because it was not realistic.

34 According to the evidence in the article, which of these reasons contributed most to the bad reviews for Hurston's last novel, *Seraph of Suwanee*?

F. People were not ready for a book with white characters written by a black woman.

G. The book was condescending toward the characters it portrayed.

H. Hurston did not know enough about the lives of the white characters she portrayed.

I. Hurston framed the novel as a sentimental love story, which disappointed critics.

Go On ▶

35   Read this sentence from the article.

> **Eatonville, an all-black town where African Americans felt free to express themselves in a nondiscriminatory environment, made a favorable impression on Hurston that was reflected in her later writing.**

Which of the following best restates the meaning of the sentence above?

A. Eatonville attracted African Americans who wanted to express their artistic ideas just as Hurston did later in her books.

B. Eatonville had special laws against discrimination, which Hurston approved of and described in her writings.

C. Hurston loved Eatonville because she learned to express her deepest feelings there.

D. Hurston enjoyed living in a town where race was not an issue, and her books contain this feeling.

36   Which subheading would be most appropriate for the last paragraph of the article on Zora Neale Hurston?

F. A Tragic Life

G. Alice Walker

H. Recognition at Last

I. Learning from the Past

37   Which pair of words best describes Zora Neale Hurston?

A. obedient and hard-working

B. independent and outspoken

C. insightful and sympathetic

D. intelligent and misunderstood

Go On ▶

Read the excerpt from the story "A Wagner Matinee" before answering questions 38 through 45.

Excerpt from
"A Wagner Matinee"
by Willa Cather

I received one morning a letter, written in pale ink on glassy, blue-lined notepaper, and bearing the postmark of a little Nebraska village. This communication . . . was from my Uncle Howard and informed me that his wife had been left a small legacy by a bachelor relative who had recently died, and that it would be necessary for her to go to Boston to attend to the settling of the estate. He requested me to meet her at the station and render her whatever services might be necessary. . . .

When the train arrived I had some difficulty in finding my aunt. She was the last of the passengers to alight, and it was not until I got her into the carriage that she seemed really to recognize me. She had come all the way in a day coach; her linen duster had become black with soot, and her black bonnet gray with dust, during the journey. . . .

My Aunt Georgiana had been a music teacher at the Boston Conservatory, somewhere back in the latter sixties. One summer, while visiting in the little village among the Green Mountains where her ancestors had dwelt for generations, she had kindled the callow fancy of the most idle and shiftless of all the village lads, and had conceived for this Howard Carpenter one of those extravagant passions. . . . When she returned to her duties in Boston, Howard followed her, and the upshot of this inexplicable infatuation was that she eloped with him, eluding the reproaches of her family and the criticisms of her friends by going with him to the Nebraska frontier. Carpenter, who, of course, had no money, had taken a homestead in Red Willow County, fifty miles from the railroad. . . . For thirty years my aunt had not been further than fifty miles from the homestead. . . .

I owed to this woman most of the good that ever came my way in my boyhood, and had a reverential affection for her. During the years when I was riding herd for my uncle, my aunt, after cooking the three meals—the first of which was ready at six o'clock in the morning—and putting the six children to bed, would often stand until midnight at her ironing board, with me at the kitchen table beside her, hearing me recite Latin declensions and conjugations, gently shaking me when my drowsy head sank down over a page of irregular verbs. It was to her, at her ironing or mending, that I read my first Shakespeare, and her old textbook on mythology was the first that ever came into my empty hands. She taught me my scales and exercises, too--on the little parlor organ, which her husband had bought her after fifteen years. . . .

Go On ▶

When my aunt appeared on the morning after her arrival she was still in a semi-somnambulant state. . . . I had planned a little pleasure for her that afternoon, to repay her for some of the glorious moments she had given me when we used to milk together in the straw-thatched cowshed and she, because I was more than usually tired, or because her husband had spoken sharply to me, would tell me of the splendid performance of the *Huguenots* she had seen in Paris, in her youth. At two o'clock the Symphony Orchestra was to give a Wagner program, and I intended to take my aunt; though, as I conversed with her I grew doubtful about her enjoyment of it. Indeed, for her own sake, I could only wish her taste for such things quite dead, and the long struggle mercifully ended at last. . . . She questioned me absently about various changes in the city, but she was chiefly concerned that she had forgotten to leave instructions about feeding half-skimmed milk to a certain weakling calf, "old Maggie's calf, you know, Clark," she explained, evidently having forgotten how long I had been away. . . .

I asked her whether she had ever heard any of the Wagnerian operas and found that she had not. . . . I began to think it would have been best to get her back to Red Willow County without waking her, and regretted having suggested the concert. From the time we entered the concert hall, however, she was a trifle less passive and inert, and for the first time seemed to perceive her surroundings. I had felt some trepidation lest she might become aware of the absurdities of her attire, or might experience some painful embarrassment at stepping suddenly into the world to which she had been dead for a quarter of a century. . . .

When the musicians came out and took their places, she gave a little stir of anticipation and looked with quickening interest down over the rail at that invariable grouping, perhaps the first wholly familiar thing that had greeted her eye since she had left old Maggie and her weakling calf. I could feel how all those details sank into her soul, for I had not forgotten how they had sunk into mine when I came fresh from plowing forever and forever between green aisles of corn, where, as in a treadmill, one might walk from daybreak to dusk without perceiving a shadow of change. . . . I recalled how, in the first orchestra I had ever heard, those long bow strokes seemed to draw the heart out of me, as a conjurer's stick reels out yards of paper ribbon from a hat.

The first number was the *Tannhauser* overture. When the horns drew out the first strain of the Pilgrim's chorus my Aunt Georgiana clutched my coat sleeve. Then it was I first realized that for her this broke a silence of thirty years; the inconceivable silence of the plains. . . .

The overture closed; my aunt released my coat sleeve, but she said nothing. . . . What, I wondered, did she get from it? She had been a good pianist in her day I knew, and her musical education had been broader than that of most music teachers of a quarter of a century ago. She had often told me of Mozart's operas and Meyerbeer's, and I could remember hearing her sing, years ago, certain melodies of Verdi's. When I had fallen ill with a fever in her house she used to sit by my cot in the evening—when the cool, night wind blew in through the faded mosquito netting tacked over the window, and I lay watching a certain bright star that burned red above the cornfield--

Go On ▶

and sing "Home to our mountains, O, let us return!" in a way fit to break the heart of a Vermont boy near dead of homesickness already.

I watched her closely through the prelude to *Tristan and Isolde,* trying vainly to conjecture what that seething turmoil of strings and winds might mean to her, but she sat mutely staring at the violin bows that drove obliquely downward, like the pelting streaks of rain in a summer shower. Had this music any message for her? . . .

Soon after the tenor began the "Prize Song," I heard a quick drawn breath and turned to my aunt. Her eyes were closed, but the tears were glistening on her cheeks, and I think, in a moment more, they were in my eyes as well. It never really died, then-- the soul that can suffer so excruciatingly and so interminably; it withers to the outward eye only; like that strange moss which can lie on a dusty shelf half a century and yet, if placed in water, grows green again. . . .

Her lip quivered and she hastily put her handkerchief up to her mouth. From behind it she murmured, "And you have been hearing this ever since you left me, Clark?" Her question was the gentlest and saddest of reproaches. . . .

My aunt wept quietly, but almost continuously, as a shallow vessel overflows in a rainstorm. From time to time her dim eyes looked up at the lights which studded the ceiling, burning softly under their dull glass globes; doubtless they were stars in truth to her. I was still perplexed as to what measure of musical comprehension was left to her, she who had heard nothing but the singing of gospel hymns at Methodist services in the square frame schoolhouse on Section Thirteen for so many years. I was wholly unable to gauge how much of it had been dissolved in soapsuds, or worked into bread, or milked into the bottom of a pail. . . .

The concert was over; the people filed out of the hall chattering and laughing, glad to relax and find the living level again, but my kinswoman made no effort to rise. The harpist slipped its green felt cover over his instrument; the flute players shook the water from their mouthpieces; the men of the orchestra went out one by one, leaving the stage to the chairs and music stands, empty as a winter cornfield.

I spoke to my aunt. She burst into tears and sobbed pleadingly. "I don't want to go, Clark, I don't want to go!"

I understood. For her, just outside the door of the concert hall, lay the black pond with the cattle-tracked bluffs; the tall, unpainted house, with weather-curled boards; naked as a tower, the crook-backed ash seedlings where the dishcloths hung to dry; the gaunt, molting turkeys picking up refuse about the kitchen door.

Go On ▶

Now answer questions 38 through 45. Base your answers on the story "A Wagner Matinee."

38   What is another way of saying "she had kindled the callow fancy"?

F.   She had attracted someone's attention.

G.   She had lit something on fire.

H.   She was dressed very beautifully.

I.   She had inspired a young artist.

39   Before the concert, the nephew is concerned about all the following EXCEPT

A.   his aunt is too tired to enjoy the show.

B.   his aunt is too preoccupied with the farm to listen with attention.

C.   his aunt will not like the orchestral music.

D.   his aunt will feel out of place in the clothes she is wearing.

40   What is the central conflict of the story?

F.   the rivalry between nephew and aunt

G.   the question of whether the aunt should attend the concert

H.   the need to balance farm life and city life

I.   the revival of a forgotten passion

41   Read this sentence from the story.

> I could feel how all those details sank into her soul, for I had not forgotten how they had sunk into mine when I came fresh from plowing forever and forever between green aisles of corn, where, as in a treadmill, one might walk from daybreak to dusk without perceiving a shadow of change.

In this sentence, the author emphasizes the theme of

A.   the satisfaction of doing a job well.

B.   the hardship and monotony of country life.

C.   the difficulty of choosing between art and real life.

D.   the comfort and security of life on a farm.

Go On ▶

42 When the narrator in the story says "like that strange moss which can lie on a dusty shelf half a century," to what is he comparing the love of music?

F. a plant that cannot seem to flower

G. a plant that can come back to life

H. a plant that never loses its bloom

I. a plant that has dried up and died

43 Which word best describes the narrator's overall tone in the story?

A. reflective

B. objective

C. humorous

D. resentful

44 "A Wagner Matinee" was first published in 1905. What has changed today that would affect the main idea of the story?

F. Communication is mostly done by email and text instead of by letter.

G. Travel is done mostly by airplane and automobile instead of by train.

H. Music is available on the radio or on recordings.

I. Farming is done with large machines and scientific methods.

45 At the end of the story, Aunt Georgiana realizes that she

A. should not have attended the concert.

B. should have devoted her life to teaching music.

C. has missed out on certain things she loved in life.

D. misses the farm and her comfortable life there.

Go On ▶

Read the article "The Hawks in Your Backyard" before answering questions 46 through 56.

The Hawks in Your Backyard

by Eric Wagner

Bob Rosenfield stares up into the high canopy of a Douglas fir in Joanie Wenman's backyard, in the suburbs of Victoria, British Columbia. "Where's the nest again?" he asks.

"It's the dark spot near the top, about 100 feet or so up," says Andy Stewart. "The first good branch is around 70 feet," he adds helpfully.

"All right!" Rosenfield says. "Let's go get the kids." He straps on a pair of steel spurs and hefts a coil of thick rope. Hugging the tree — his arms barely reach a third of the way around it — he starts to climb, and soon falls into a labored rhythm: *chunk-chunk* as the spurs bite into the furrowed bark; gaze up; scout a route; feel for a grip with his fingertips; hug the trunk, *chunk-chunk*. Those of us pacing beneath listen to him grunt and huff. As he nears the nest, the female Cooper's hawk dives at him with an increasing, screeching fervor: *kak-kak-kak-kak-kak!*

"Woah!" Rosenfield yells. "Boy, she's mad!"

"Man, I hate watching him do this," Stewart mutters. Most people, he says (his tone implies he means most "sane" people), would use a climbing lanyard or some other safety device should they, say, get thumped on the head by an irate Cooper's hawk and lose their grip and fall. "But not Bob."

At last, Rosenfield reaches the nest. "We got four chicks!" he calls down. "Two males, two females!" He rounds them up ("C'mere, you!") and puts them in an old backpack. He uses the rope to lower the chicks to the ground. Stewart gathers up the backpack and takes the chicks to a large stump. They are about 19 days old, judging by the hint of mature feathers emerging from their down. He weighs them, measures the lengths of their various appendages and draws a little blood for DNA typing.

Meanwhile, Rosenfield stays in the canopy, gazing off into the middle distance. After the chicks have been hoisted back to the nest, I ask Stewart what Rosenfield does while he waits. "I don't know for sure," Stewart says. He chuckles. "I think he likes to watch the hawks fly underneath him."

Go On ▶

Rosenfield, a biologist at the University of Wisconsin, Stevens Point, has been free-climbing absurdly tall trees in pursuit of Cooper's hawks for more than 30 years. Cooper's hawks are about the size of a crow, although females are a third again as large as males, a size disparity apparent even in chicks. The sexes otherwise look alike, with a slate back, piercing red eyes and russet-streaked breast, the exact color of which varies with geography. Rosenfield has worked with other, perhaps more superficially impressive species in more superficially impressive places — gyrfalcons in Alaska, peregrine falcons in Greenland. But even though he's most likely to study Cooper's hawks in a city, he has a special fondness for them. "They're addicting," he says. "DNA really outdid itself when it figured out how to make a Cooper's hawk."

Not everyone thinks so. With their short, rounded wings and long tail, Cooper's hawks are well adapted to zip and dodge through tangled branches and thick underbrush in pursuit of prey. They occasionally eat small mammals, like chipmunks or rats, but their preferred quarry is birds. Cooper's hawks were the original chicken hawks, so called by American colonists because of their taste for unattended poultry. Now they are more likely to offend by snatching a songbird from a backyard birdfeeder, and feelings can be raw. After a local newspaper ran a story about the Victoria project, Stewart received a letter detailing the Cooper's hawk's many sins. "Two pages," he says. "Front and back."

Due in part to such antipathy, Cooper's hawks were heavily persecuted in the past. Before 1940, some researchers estimate, as many as half of all first-year birds were shot. In the eastern United States, leg bands from hawks that had been shot were returned to wildlife managers at rates higher than those of ducks, "and it's legal to hunt those," Rosenfield says. Heavy pesticide use in the 1940s and '50s likely led to eggshell thinning, which further depleted populations. On top of that, much of the birds' forest habitat was lost to logging and development. The species' predicament was thought so dire that, in 1974, *National Geographic* published an article asking, "Can the Cooper's Hawk Survive?"

It was this worry that brought Rosenfield to Cooper's hawks in 1980, in Wisconsin, when the state listed the species as threatened. "They had a bit of a conundrum on their hands," Rosenfield says. Once a species is listed, the state has to put in place a plan for its recovery. "How do you call a bird recovered if you don't know how many there are in the first place?" he says. So he went in search of them. First, he looked in places they were supposed to be: in mixed forests, or next to rivers. But he started to hear about hawks in odd places. There were reports of them nesting in towns and cities, in places like Milwaukee. If so, their habits were not in keeping with conventional raptor natural history.

As he heard from more colleagues around North America, Rosenfield expanded his study and confirmed that Cooper's hawks are thriving in

Go On ▶

urban areas. He now works with populations in Stevens Point, as well as Albuquerque, New Mexico and Victoria, where the hawks were first detected in 1995. He goes to each place for a week or so each summer to catch adults and band chicks with local biologists. (Stewart, who himself has studied Cooper's hawks yards for 17 years, is a retired biologist formerly with the British Columbia Ministry of the Environment.) More often than not, the people he and his colleagues visit not only invite them to conduct research on their property, but they also take an active interest in the birds' welfare. "It's good PR for the hawks," Rosenfield says. "People get to see them up close, and then maybe they hate them a little less."

In cities, Rosenfield has found, Cooper's hawks can take advantage of a near bottomless supply of pigeons, sparrows and starlings. Unlike other species that stray into cities, Cooper's hawks are as likely to survive there as in more natural habitats, and pairs produce similar numbers of chicks. "We're seeing some of the highest nesting densities in cities," Rosenfield says. Not only that, cities may be one of the best options for the long-term viability of the species. In Victoria, Cooper's hawk populations are stable. In Milwaukee, their numbers are increasing rapidly.

In the end, Rosenfield suspects that Cooper's hawks may not have been so rare after all. It may just be that people weren't going to the right places. They sought them in forests and mountains, when really all they needed to do was go to their own backyards and look up.

The next day, we go back to the Douglas fir behind Joanie Wenman's house. This time Rosenfield is going for the chick's parents. He sets up a 12-foot-high fine-mesh "mist net," concealing it among firs and big leaf maples. He and Stewart tether a long-suffering captive barred owl to a stand a few feet from the net — Cooper's hawks hate barred owls — and place a speaker beneath it. In the early years, Rosenfield tells me, trapping the adult hawks was hard. "We had to do so much to hide the nets," he says. "Because Coops have eyes like — well, you know."

We retreat as the speaker blasts out different renditions of Cooper's hawk distress calls. After a few minutes, we hear a series of *kaks*. "There she is," Stewart whispers. We look and see the female glowering at the owl from a branch 50 feet above it. She *kaks* again, and then dives, steep and swift. The owl flails off its perch as the hawk sweeps over its head and slams into the net. "Got her!" Rosenfield yells. He sprints over to the hawk as she thrashes, thoroughly trussing herself, and carefully extracts her. He hands her off to Stewart, who takes her vitals as Wenman watches, asking the occasional question about the hawk's biology.

When Stewart is finished, he gives the female to Rosenfield. "Aren't you something," Rosenfield says. He holds her out, appraises her, strokes her back. The female glares at him. "Hey, want to hear something cool?" he asks Wenman. He moves the female toward her head. Wenman jerks back. "Don't worry," Rosenfield laughs. "It'll be fine!" Wenman does not

Go On ▶

look entirely convinced, but she makes herself stand still. Rosenfield gently brings the female toward her again; Wenman flinches — she can't help it — but Rosenfield nods encouragingly as he presses the bird's chest to Wenman's ear. Wenman cocks her head, hears the hawk's wild thudding heart. Her eyes widen at the strength of the sound, and she smiles.

Answer questions 46 through 56. Base your answers on the article "The Hawks in Your Backyard."

46   Read this excerpt from the article.

> **Now they are more likely to offend by snatching a songbird from a back-yard birdfeeder, and feelings can be raw. After a local newspaper ran a story about the Victoria project, Stewart received a letter detailing the Cooper's hawk's many sins. "Two pages," he says. "Front and back."**

In the excerpt, the author is pointing out that

   F.   the Cooper's hawk behaves unpredictably and so is misunderstood.

   G.   the Cooper's hawk often feeds on other birds, which angers people.

   H.   the Cooper's hawk is the victim of bad publicity, as in the local newspaper story.

   I.   the Cooper's hawk's instincts lead it to hunt other birds that are nuisances to homeowners.

47   Bob Rosenfield began his study of Cooper's hawks because

   A.   he was concerned that the species was in great danger.

   B.   he suspected that the dire state of the species was overstated.

   C.   he had been attacked by a Cooper's hawk in the past.

   D.   he knew the real reason why their numbers were growing.

Go On ▶

48 Which of the following is NOT a factor that led experts to think Cooper's hawks were endangered?

    F. Pesticide use years ago had probably thinned their eggshells and harmed their young.

    G. Logging and development had destroyed much of their habitat.

    H. Hunters had shot them at rates higher than that for ducks.

    I. Predators had thinned their population since they were not adapted to fly through tangled underbrush.

49 Read this sentence from the article.

> **Rosenfield, a biologist at the University of Wisconsin, Stevens Point, has been free-climbing absurdly tall trees in pursuit of Cooper's hawks for more than 30 years.**

In the sentence, the word *absurdly* is used to suggest that

    A. the trees are not really so tall.

    B. Rosenfield is daring in his ability to climb such tall trees.

    C. Rosenfield should look for Cooper's hawks in other locations.

    D. the trees are far from beautiful.

50 According to the article, a key difference between Cooper's hawks and similar species is that

    F. Cooper's hawks can survive in urban areas.

    G. Cooper's hawks require a dense forest environment to survive.

    H. Cooper's hawks occasionally eat small mammals, such as rats.

    I. Cooper's hawks have colors that can vary with geography.

51 According to the article, Cooper's hawks are difficult to trap because

    A. the females are a third larger than males.

    B. they can zip and dodge through tangled branches.

    C. they have exceptionally keen eyesight.

    D. they are exceptionally intelligent.

Go On ▶

52 Read the following passage from the article.

> **"They had a bit of a conundrum on their hands," Rosenfield says. Once a species is listed, the state has to put in place a plan for its recovery. "How do you call a bird recovered if you don't know how many there are in the first place?" he says.**

What is the meaning of the word *conundrum*?

F. a unique opportunity

G. a complicated problem

H. a hopeless situation

I. a lucky development

53 The reader can conclude from evidence in the article that the author most likely views Rosenfield's work with Cooper's hawks as

A. dangerous and foolhardy.

B. difficult but pointless.

C. challenging and rewarding.

D. dull and repetitive.

54 The biologists employ speakers that blare Cooper's hawk distress calls in order to

F. determine how many hawks are in the area.

G. capture a barred owl.

H. keep the adult hawks from approaching.

I. attract the adult hawks.

55 Which sentence from the article is most closely related to the idea behind the title, "The Hawks in Your Backyard"?

A. "Bob Rosenfield stares up into the high canopy of a Douglas fir in Joanie Wenman's backyard, in the suburbs of Victoria, British Columbia."

B. "They sought them in forests and mountains, when really all they needed to do was go to their own backyards and look up."

C. "Now they are more likely to offend by snatching a songbird from a backyard birdfeeder, and feelings can be raw."

D. "He goes to each place for a week or so each summer to catch adults and band chicks with local biologists."

Go On ▶

56   With which statement would the author of this article most likely agree?

F.   Biologists' fieldwork on Cooper's hawks should be focused on more popular species.

G.   Despite evidence of stable numbers of Cooper's hawks, they probably should be a protected species.

H.   Due to the work of biologists like Bob Rosenfield, people who might ordinarily dislike Cooper's hawks take an interest in them.

I.   Cooper's hawks are a growing nuisance to homeowners and need to be relocated to forested areas.

STOP

FCAT Writing Practice Test

$$1$$

For the FCAT Writing, you will be given an answer book with a prompt inside. You will have 45 minutes to read the prompt, plan what you want to write, and write your response. A separate planning sheet will be provided. You will respond to a prompt that asks you to explain or a prompt that asks you to persuade.

You should write your response neatly and show that you can organize and express your thoughts clearly and completely. You may not use a dictionary or other reference materials.

Directions for Responding to the Prompt

On the actual test, the prompt will appear in a box on the prompt page. It is important to use the planning sheet to jot down ideas and organize your writing. Although the planning sheet is not scored, you must turn it in with your test.

Planning Sheet

Remember, use this sheet for planning what you will write. The writing on this sheet will *not* be scored. On the FCAT only the writing in the writing folder will be scored. An Answer Sheet for the writing prompt is provided on page 285.

Persuasive Prompt

Writing Situation

Your parents are not sure that after-school jobs are valuable for high school students.

Directions for Writing

Think about the effect that an after-school job has had on you or other students you know. Now write to convince your parents that after-school jobs are valuable for high school students.

Go On ▶

Planning Sheet

Answers
for
Practice Test

Practice Reading Test 1 Answers

1 **The correct answer is B, the family background of Paul Wittgenstein.**

In the passage, the author describes the financial success of Wittgenstein's father, the concerts staged in the family home, and the musical endeavors of his parents and siblings. The focus of the passage is on Paul's family background. The passage does not focus on why it might be satisfying to learn about music at an early age, why music was an important part of Viennese culture, or why so many great composers came from Europe.

Type of text: Informational

Benchmark: LA.910.2.2.3 The student will organize information to show understanding or relationships among facts, ideas, and events (e.g., representing key points within text through charting, mapping, paraphrasing, summarizing, comparing, contrasting, or outlining).

2 **The correct answer is F, Paul's determination to develop his skill as a pianist.**

The author includes phrases such as *doggedly spent hours* and *his dedicated routine* to show that Paul had tremendous determination to succeed as a pianist. The author does not indicate that Paul's ideas are unrealistic. Information about the harsh prison conditions and the valuable efforts of the Red Cross are incidental to the author's purpose here.

Type of text: Informational

Benchmark: LA.910.1.6.8 The student will identify advanced word/phrase relationships and their meanings.

3 **The correct answer is B, He paid critics to attend his concerts and write favorable notices.**

According to the article, Paul *set about devising new arrangements for the left hand of keyboard music by Bach, Chopin, and other composers;* he also *commissioned some of the world's greatest composers to write piano concertos for the left hand;* and he *developed tremendous strength and dexterity in his left hand, enabling him to produce a melodic line with his thumb and index while his other three fingers kept a rhythmic pulse.* However, the article makes no mention of paying critics to attend concerts or write favorable reviews.

Type of text: Informational

Benchmark: LA.910.1.7.3 The student will determine the main idea or essential message in grade-level or higher texts through inferring, paraphrasing, summarizing, and identifying relevant details.

4 **The correct answer is H, honest.**

The word *candid* means "honest" or "forthright." Paul could not lie about his true opinion when it came to judging a composition. Someone who is opinionated and outspoken could be said to be *candid*.

Type of text: Informational

Benchmark: LA.910.1.6.3 The student will use context clues to determine the meaning of unfamiliar words.

5 **The correct answer is C, he wanted to own the performing rights to the pieces that they wrote.**

The article points out that *to ensure that the concertos would be his property alone, Paul insisted that the composers grant him exclusive rights to perform the pieces in public,* and that the large fees he paid helped him get those rights more easily. The article does not indicate that Paul could play only simple pieces, and it specifically says that he did not particularly like modern music. Also, while writing music for the left hand was certainly challenging, it was not the main reason for his commissioning of new works.

Type of text: Informational

Benchmark: LA.910.1.7.4 The student will identify cause-and-effect relationships in text.

6 **The correct answer is I, Paul's family generally did not appreciate his talent as a musician and performer.**

According to the article, Paul's family did not support his career as a pianist and apparently did not believe in his talent. His sister disliked his approach to playing, and his brother declined to attend his concerts. The best summary of their attitude is answer choice I.

Type of text: Informational

Benchmark: LA.910.1.7.3 The student will determine the main idea or essential message in grade-level or higher texts through inferring, paraphrasing, summarizing, and identifying relevant details.

7 **The correct answer is B, to inform readers about a remarkable musician who overcame a handicap to succeed.**

The article is mostly about Paul Wittgenstein's struggle to become a successful musician despite the loss of his right arm. The author's main purpose was to inform readers about his life and career. The incident about his feud with a composer was only part of the article. The author's main purpose was not to convince the reader about anything, even though the article might affect a reader's opinions about war and about people with certain disabilities.

Type of text: Informational

Benchmark: LA.910.1.7.2 The student will analyze the author's purpose and/or perspective in a variety of texts and understand how they affect meaning.

8 **The correct answer is I, a large field by a brook.**

Mowing takes place in a yard or field; the narrator has to search for the person who is mowing, so he must be in a large field; and there is "a tall tuft of flowers beside a brook."

Type of text: Poetry

Benchmark: LA.910.2.1.2 The student will analyze and compare a variety of traditional, classical, and contemporary literary works, and identify the literary elements of each (e.g., setting plot, characterization, conflict).

9 **The correct answer is C, personification.**

The swishing scythe's blade is compared to a person whispering, so the type of figurative language employed is personification.

Type of text: Poetry

Benchmark: LA.910.2.1.5 The student will analyze and develop an interpretation of a literary work by describing an author's use of literary elements (e.g., theme, point of view, characterization, setting, plot), and explain and analyze different elements of figurative language (e.g., simile, metaphor, personification, hyperbole, symbolism, allusion, imagery).

10 **The correct answer is F, observant.**

The speaker of the poem notices the movements of the butterfly and the tuft of flowers that has been left standing. He is very *observant,* or apt to notice things.

Type of text: Poetry

Benchmark: LA.910.1.7.3 The student will determine the main idea or essential message in grade-level or higher texts through inferring, paraphrasing, summarizing, and identifying relevant details.

11 **The correct answer is C, the movement of a butterfly he is watching.**

The speaker sees the tuft of flowers because "he [the butterfly] turned first, and led my eye to look/At a tall tuft of flowers beside a brook." The speaker doesn't notice them because of the wind, a shaft of sunlight, or the mower's words.

Type of text: Poetry

Benchmark: LA.910.1.7.4 The student will identify cause-and-effect relationships in text.

12 **The correct answer is F, grow and thrive.**

The mower loves the flowers so he or she leaves them to thrive and remain beautiful.

Type of text: Poetry

Benchmark: LA.910.1.6.5 The student will relate new vocabulary to familiar words.

13 **The correct answer is C, repetition.**

The poet employs rhyme, stanzas, and meter to give his poem a strong framework. However, he doesn't repeat any lines word for word.

Type of text: Poetry

Benchmark: LA.910.2.1.3 The student will explain how meaning is enhanced through various features of poetry, including sound (e.g., rhythm, repetition, alliteration, consonance, assonance), structure (e.g., meter, rhyme scheme), and graphic elements (e.g., line length, punctuation, word position).

14 **The correct answer is G, working alone and working together.**

At the beginning of the poem, the speaker feels that he is working alone, but at the end of the poem he realizes he is actually working alongside the mower who came before him. The other suggestions do not fit the details of the poem.

Type of text: Poetry

Benchmark: LA.910.1.7.5 The student will analyze a variety of text structures (e.g., comparison/contrast, cause/effect, chronological order, argument/support, lists) and text features (main headings with subheadings) and explain their impact on meaning in text.

15 **The correct answer is C, to explore how the worker reacts when he sees the uncut flowers.**

Assuming the point of view of a field worker enables the author to explore the worker's feelings of brotherhood and togetherness with the unseen mower after the worker sees the tuft of flowers left uncut. There is no evidence that the author wants to show that the worker needs help or is working too hard. Although the worker ponders many things as he works, the author does not seem concerned that his mind is wandering. Instead, the worker's thoughts are very focused and philosophical.

Type of text: Poetry

Benchmark: LA.910.2.1.5 The student will analyze and develop an interpretation of a literary work by describing an author's use of literary elements (e.g., theme, point of view, characterization, setting, plot), and explain and analyze different elements of figurative language (e.g., simile, metaphor, personification, hyperbole, symbolism, allusion, imagery).

16 **The correct answer is G, convince readers that daydreaming is more than a waste of time.**

While the author does discuss positive and negative daydreaming, his main purpose is to show the many ways that daydreaming can benefit people's lives.

Type of text: Informational

Benchmark: LA.910.1.7.2 The student will analyze the author's purpose and/or perspective in a variety of texts and understand how they affect meaning.

17   **The correct answer is D, losing track of real life while thinking about the past.**

In the fourth paragraph, the author points out that daydreaming all day and losing track of real life and real events can lead to people "living in the past," which can be harmful. This is a form of negative daydreaming.

Type of text: Informational

Benchmark: LA.910.2.2.2 The student will use information from the text to answer questions or to state the main idea or provide relevant details.

18   **The correct answer is G, He presents arguments against daydreaming and then offers opposing arguments.**

For the first half of the article, the author discusses several criticisms of daydreaming and then presents opposing arguments explaining the positive aspects of daydreaming.

Type of text: Informational

Benchmark: LA.910.1.7.5 The student will analyze a variety of text structures (e.g., comparison/contrast, cause/effect, chronological order, argument/support, lists) and text features (main headings with subheadings) and explain their impact on meaning in text.

19   **The correct answer is A, emphasize how absurd it would be to daydream all the time.**

The author italicizes the words *all day* to emphasize how outlandish it would be to daydream constantly. The phrase is not an idiom, and while the author is using exaggeration he is not really making a joke. Of course, *all day* does not come from a foreign language.

Type of text: Informational

Benchmark: LA.910.2.2.1 The student will analyze and evaluate information form text features (e.g., transitional devices, table of contents, glossary, index, bold or italicized text, headings, charts and graphs, illustrations, subheadings).

20 **The correct answer is H, to achieve a relaxed concentration during competition.**

In his example about diver Greg Louganis, the author points out that Louganis used visualization so that he would be more relaxed and focused during an actual competition. Daydreaming can be used to conquer a strong fear or to reflect on the past and imagine possibilities in the future, but these effects are not connected to visualization in the article. Nowhere in the article is daydreaming and visualization recommended as a sleep aid, although that might be one result of feeling more relaxed.

Type of text: Informational

Benchmark: LA.910.1.7.4 The student will identify cause-and-effect relationships in text.

21 **The correct answer is B, personal conclusions based on research.**

Because there is so much information about different types of daydreaming in this article, the reader can assume that the author did some research on daydreaming. There are no fictionalized anecdotes about daydreaming, and while the author mentions psychologists in the article, no documented research is referred to. Rather than using common knowledge and folk wisdom to support his points, the author tends to show how they are usually wrong in some way.

Type of text: Informational

Benchmark: LA.910.6.2.2 The student will organize, synthesize, analyze, and evaluate the validity and reliability of information from multiple sources (including primary and secondary sources) to draw conclusions using a variety of techniques, and correctly use standardized citations.

22 **The correct answer is H, they can assist us in understanding other people's feelings.**

The author states that *some people might even be able to use daydreams to imagine the other's point of view and find similarities or shared interests between themselves and the other person.*

Type of text: Informational

Benchmark: LA.910.2.2.2 The student will use information from the text to answer questions or to state the main idea or provide relevant details.

23 **The correct answer is D, After three hours of hard work on her essay, Martha drank some iced tea for a break.**

Both the excerpted sentence and the sentence in option D use the word *break* in a context that means "a respite from something difficult, such as work, stress, or responsibility."

Type of text: Informational

Benchmark: LA.910.1.6.9 The student will determine the correct meaning of words with multiple meanings in context.

24 **The correct answer is G, use their daydreams to work toward a goal of personal success.**

The correct answer is G. Answer choices F and I do not contrast with negative stereotypes about daydreaming because they are themselves negative results of daydreaming. Nowhere does the author say that daydreamers use their daydreams specifically to build businesses. He does say that *sometimes daydreams actually give people a goal to work toward.*

Type of text: Informational

Benchmark: LA.910.1.7.7 The student will compare and contrast elements in multiple texts.

25 **The correct answer is A, restore to harmony.**

As it is used here, *reconcile* means to make up, or to restore harmony between people. The words *not getting along* provide a context clue to the meaning.

Type of text: Informational

Benchmark: LA.910.1.6.3 The student will use context clues to determine meanings of unfamiliar words.

26 **The correct answer is H, Though daydreaming seems bad, it has some good effects.**

All these ideas are discussed in the article, but the main idea of the entire passage is that while daydreaming has negative connotations, it can actually be beneficial for you.

Type of text: Informational

Benchmark: LA.910.1.7.3 The student will determine the main idea or essential message in grade-level or higher texts through inferring, paraphrasing, summarizing, and identifying relevant details.

27 **The correct answer is D, problem/solution.**

At the end of the article, the author uses a problem/solution organizational pattern. The author explains that there are negative types of daydreaming and discusses the problems associated with negative daydreaming. For example, the author explains that people who fear heights may worry if they have to climb something high. The author then provides a solution to this problem: People who fear heights can imagine completing the task safely and successfully, and use this as motivation. The problem of negative daydreaming is solved by positive daydreaming.

Type of text: Informational

Benchmark: LA.910.1.7.5 The student will analyze a variety of text structures (e.g., comparison/contrast, cause/effect, chronological order, argument/support, lists) and text features (main headings with subheadings) and explain their impact on meaning in text.

28 **The correct answer is H, Daydreaming is acceptable as long as it does not interfere with important events in your life.**

The correct answer is H. The author never claims that daydreaming is the "best" way to deal with problems or clear your mind, as indicated by answer choice F. Choices G and I lump all forms of daydreaming together, which makes part of each statement incorrect.

Type of text: Informational

Benchmark: LA.910.2.2.3 The student will organize information to show understanding or relationships among facts, ideas, and events (e.g., representing key points within text through charting, mapping, paraphrasing, summarizing, comparing, contrasting, or outlining).

29 **The correct answer is B, turbulent.**

The death of Hurston's mother ensured that her childhood was no longer *placid,* but *turbulent,* or filled with change and upheaval. A *tumultuous* childhood may have tragic elements, but the word does not mean "tragic."

Type of text: Informational

Benchmark: LA.910.1.6.5 The student will relate new vocabulary to familiar words.

30 **The correct answer is F, study of African American culture.**

The answer is found directly in the article: *Influenced by other artists in the Harlem Renaissance, who were starting to explore African American culture and express pride in their racial heritage, Hurston became interested in anthropology, particularly the study of black culture.*

Type of text: Informational

Benchmark: LA.910.1.7.7 The student will compare and contrast elements in multiple texts.

31 **The correct answer is C, She relates the story of Hurston's career in chronological order.**

The author relates the story of Zora Neale Hurston's life and career in chronological order, starting with her childhood and progressing through her death.

Type of text: Informational

Benchmark: LA.910.1.7.5 The student will analyze a variety of text structures (e.g., comparison/contrast, cause/effect, chronological order, argument/support, lists) and text features (main headings with subheadings) and explain their impact on meaning in text.

32 **The correct answer is G, biased.**

The word *biased* is the most negative of the four choices because it contains the idea of a rigid preference without a strong supporting reason. The other words have more positive connotations of presenting ideas in a persuasive way.

Type of text: Informational

Benchmark: LA.910.1.6.6 The student will distinguish denotative and connotative meanings of words.

33 **The correct answer is B, Hurston's fame as a writer, while late in coming, is richly deserved.**

In several places, the author points out how the early critics of Hurston's work were slow to recognize the greatness and innovation of her work. This indicates that the author believes Hurston's fame, while delayed, was well deserved. The author does not seem to expect excellent writing to always be appreciated, nor does she focus on whether or not Hurston's writing was realistic. The opinion about a small-town childhood does not come from the article.

Type of text: Informational

Benchmark: LA.910.1.7.2 The student will analyze the author's purpose and/or perspective in a variety of texts and understand how they affect meaning.

34 **The correct answer is F, People were not ready for a book with white characters written by a black woman.**

According to the article, Hurston's novel *Seraph of Suwanee* got bad reviews mainly because *neither critics nor readers of the time were ready for a black female author to speak through white characters*. No one claimed the book was condescending toward the characters or that Hurston didn't know enough about the kinds of characters in her book. The criticism about a sentimental love story was leveled against one of Hurston's earlier novels.

Type of text: Informational

Benchmark: LA.910.2.2.2 The student will use information from the text to answer questions or to state the main idea or provide relevant details.

35 **The correct answer is D, Hurston enjoyed living in a town where race was not an issue, and her books contain this feeling.**

The key idea is that the residents of Eatonville felt comfortable in an atmosphere without racism and that Hurston enjoyed this atmosphere and expressed its influence in her writing. Answer choice D restates this idea best.

Type of text: Informational

Benchmark: LA.910.1.6.8 The student will identify advanced word/phrase relationships and their meanings.

36 **The correct answer is H, Recognition at Last.**

Most of the article describes how Hurston's work was not appreciated and how her life ended tragically, but the last paragraph focuses on her work finally receiving the respect it deserved. While Alice Walker is mentioned in the last paragraph, she is not the main focus.

Type of text: Informational

Benchmark: LA.910.2.1.3 The student will organize information to show understanding or relationships among facts, ideas, and events (e.g., representing key points within text through charting, mapping, paraphrasing, summarizing, comparing, contrasting, or outlining).

37 **The correct answer is D, intelligent and misunderstood.**

The article mentions more than one instance in Hurston's life when her intelligent work was misunderstood by readers and critics, so the words in Answer Choice D are the best description.

Type of text: Informational

Benchmark: LA.910.1.7.3 The student will determine the main idea or essential message in grade-level or higher texts through inferring, paraphrasing, summarizing, and identifying relevant details).

38 **The correct answer is F, She had caught someone's attention.**

Willa Cather writes in the more ornate style of her era. *To kindle the callow fancy* meant to attract the romantic attention of a young person. Students should note, as a context clue, that the narrator's aunt soon eloped with the young man whose "callow fancy" she had kindled.

Type of text: Literary

Benchmark: LA.910.2.1.9 The student will identify, analyze, and compare the differences in English language patterns and vocabulary choices of contemporary and historical texts.

39 **The correct answer is C, his aunt will not like the orchestral music.**

The nephew recalls that his aunt was a music teacher and always loved orchestral music, so he doesn't worry that she will not like the music. He does reflect that *when my aunt appeared on the morning after her arrival she was still in a semi-somnambulant state,* or sleepy state. He notices that *she was chiefly concerned that she had forgotten to leave instructions about feeding half-skimmed milk to a certain weakling calf.* He also worries that *she might become aware of the absurdities of her attire.*

Type of text: Literary

Benchmark: LA.910.2.1.5 The student will analyze and develop an interpretation of a literary work by describing an author's use of literary elements (e.g., theme, point of view, characterization, setting, plot), and explain and analyze different elements of figurative language (e.g., simile, metaphor, personification, hyperbole, symbolism, allusion, imagery).

40 **The correct answer is I, the revival of a forgotten passion.**

The key conflict in the story is the revival of the aunt's old passion for music. For a person with an abiding love of music, the Wagner concert was overwhelmingly beautiful to her since she had *heard nothing but the singing of gospel hymns at Methodist services . . . for so many years.* There is no rivalry between the nephew and aunt; they have an affectionate relationship. The question of the aunt attending the concert is quickly decided by the nephew. The contrast between farm life and city life is implicit in the story, but does not form the main conflict.

Type of text: Literary

Benchmark: LA.910.2.1.5 The student will analyze and develop an interpretation of a literary work by describing an author's use of literary elements (e.g., theme, point of view, characterization, setting, plot), and explain and analyze different elements of figurative language (e.g., simile, metaphor, personification, hyperbole, symbolism, allusion, imagery).

41 **The correct answer is B, the hardship and monotony of country life.**

The correct answer is B. Cather is emphasizing how dull and difficult the farm work is in the narrator's memory. She describes the monotony as *plowing forever and forever between green aisles of corn,* and mentions that *one might walk from daybreak to dusk without perceiving a shadow of change.* The work is described as being like a treadmill.

Type of text: Literary

Benchmark: LA.910.2.1.4 The student will identify and analyze universal themes and symbols across genres and historical periods, and explain their significance.

42 **The correct answer is G, a plant that can come back to life.**

The narrator is comparing the love of music to a plant that appears to be dead but revives when put in water *(can lie on a dusty shelf half a century and yet, if placed in water, grows green again)*. This image represents the revival of his aunt's love of music.

Type of text: Literary

Benchmark: LA.910.2.1.5 The student will analyze and develop an interpretation of a literary work by describing an author's use of literary elements (e.g., theme, point of view, characterization, setting, plot), and explain and analyze different elements of figurative language (e.g., simile, metaphor, personification, hyperbole, symbolism, allusion, imagery).

43 **The correct answer is A, reflective.**

Willa Cather's narrator in this story reflects on his own past and that of his aunt in some detail. He is not really objective, as he imaginatively enters into his aunt's predicament. His tone is certainly not resentful or humorous.

Type of text: Literary

Benchmark: LA.910.2.1.7 The student will analyze, interpret, and evaluate an author's use of descriptive language (e.g., tone, irony, mood, imagery, pun, alliteration, onomatopoeia, allusion), figurative language (e.g., symbolism, metaphor, personification, hyperbole), common idioms, and mythological and literary allusions, and explain how they impact meaning in a variety of texts.

44 **The correct answer is H, Music is available on the radio or on recordings.**

The change that would affect the main idea of the story is that music is available today on the radio or on recordings. The narrator's aunt had no means to hear orchestral music on her farm in Nebraska so her experience at the concert was very emotional for her. The other changes mentioned would not have as great an effect on the story's main idea.

Type of text: Literary

Benchmark: LA.910.2.1.8 The student will explain how ideas, values, and themes of a literary work often reflect the historical period in which it was written.

45 The correct answer is C, has missed out on certain things she loved in life.

The narrator's aunt becomes increasingly emotional as she listens to the music, and then cries out at the end, "I don't want to go, Clark, I don't want to go!" This indicates that she has been struck by the beauty of the music and regrets missing out on attending concerts and hearing such music regularly. She doesn't regret attending the concert, and the text doesn't mention any regret about not teaching music. Instead of missing her farm at the end, Aunt Georgiana probably feels depressed at the thought of its homely aspects — which the narrator thinks about in the last paragraph.

Type of text: Literary

Benchmark: LA.910.2.1.1 The student will analyze and compare historically and culturally significant works of literature, identifying the relationships among the major genres (e.g., poetry, fiction, nonfiction, short story, dramatic literature, essay) and the literary devices unique to each, and analyze how they support and enhance the theme and main ideas of the text.

46 The correct answer is G, the Cooper's hawk often feeds on other birds, which angers many people.

The author says the Cooper's hawk is *more likely to offend by snatching a songbird* and that *feelings can be raw.* And Stewart received a letter *detailing the Cooper's hawk's many sins.* These phrases indicate that people become angry at the behavior of the Cooper's hawk.

Type of text: Informational

Benchmark: LA.910.1.6.8 The student will identify advanced word/phrase relationships and their meanings.

47 The correct answer is A, he was concerned that the species was in great danger.

The article says: *The species' predicament was thought so dire that, in 1974,* National Geographic *published an article asking, "Can the Cooper's Hawk Survive?". . . It was this worry that brought Rosenfield to Cooper's hawks in 1980, in Wisconsin, when the state listed the species as threatened.* Early on, Rosenfield did not have any reason to suspect that the data on Cooper's hawks was faulty. He hadn't been attacked in the past, and he didn't realize the truth about their growing numbers until later in his research.

Type of text: Informational

Benchmark: LA.910.6.2.2 The student will organize, synthesize, analyze, and evaluate the validity and reliability of information from multiple sources (including primary and secondary sources) to draw conclusions using a variety of techniques, and correctly use standardized citations.

48 **The correct answer is I, Predators had thinned their population since they were not adapted to fly through tangled underbrush.**

Choice I is the correct answer. The article states that the Cooper's hawk is actually well adapted to fly through tangled underbrush, and no mention is made of danger from predators other than humans. The other factors are all listed in the text.

Type of text: Informational

Benchmark: LA.910.2.2.2 The student will use information from the text to answer questions or to state the main idea or provide relevant details.

49 **The correct answer is B, Rosenfield is daring in his ability to climb such tall trees.**

The author is suggesting that the trees are *absurdly* or *ridiculously* tall for Rosenfield to free-climb. He is inferring that Rosenfield is undaunted by the height of the trees. The tone of the passage reveals the meaning to the reader.

Type of text: Informational

Benchmark: LA.910.2.1.7 The student will analyze, interpret, and evaluate an author's use of descriptive language (e.g., tone irony, mood, imagery, pun, alliteration, onomatopoeia, allusion), figurative language (e.g., symbolism, metaphor, personification, hyperbole), common idioms, and mythological and literary allusions, and explain how they impact meaning in a variety of texts.

50 **The correct answer is F, Cooper's hawks can survive in urban areas.**

According to the article, *unlike other species that stray into cities, Cooper's hawks are as likely to survive there as in more natural habitats, and pairs produce similar numbers of chicks.*

Type of text: Informational

Benchmark: LA.910.1.7.7 The student will compare and contrast elements in multiple texts.

51 **The correct answer is C, they have exceptionally keen eyesight.**

The author of the article writes: *In the early years, Rosenfield tells me, trapping the adult hawks was hard. "We had to do so much to hide the nets," he says. "Because Coops have eyes like — well, you know."* Of course Rosenfield is saying that "Coops" have "eyes like hawks," a proverbial expression that means they have keen eyesight. The article does say that female Cooper's hawks are a third larger than males and that Cooper's hawks can zigzag through underbrush, but neither is the reason given for the difficulty in trapping them. The article doesn't say verbatim that Cooper's hawks are exceptionally intelligent.

Type of text: Informational

Benchmark: LA.910.2.2.3 The student will organize information to show understanding or relationships among facts, ideas, and events (e.g., representing key points within text through charting, mapping, paraphrasing, summarizing, comparing, contrasting, or outlining).

52 **The correct answer is G, a complicated problem.**

The state has "a complicated problem" in trying to plan for the recovery of a species of bird whose numbers are unknown. Answer choice G is correct.

Type of text: Informational

Benchmark: LA.910.1.6.5 The student will relate new vocabulary to familiar words.

53 **The correct answer is C, challenging and rewarding.**

The author focuses on the challenging aspects of Rosenfield's work, such as retrieving chicks from tall trees and searching for Cooper's hawks from isolated forests to towns and cities. He also depicts Rosenfield's affection for the species ("Aren't you something," Rosenfield says), which would make his work with them more rewarding.

Type of text: Informational

Benchmark: LA.910.1.7.2 The student will analyze the author's purpose and/or perspective in a variety of texts and understand how they affect meaning.

54 **The correct answer is I, attract the adult hawks.**

At the beginning of the section about trapping the Cooper's hawks, the author writes: *This time Rosenfield is going for the chick's parents.* In the event, only the mother bird appears.

Type of text: Informational

Benchmark: LA.910.1.7.5 The student will analyze a variety of text structures (e.g., comparison/contrast, cause/effect, chronological order, argument/support, lists) and text features (main headings with subheadings) and explain their impact on meaning in text.

55 **The correct answer is B, "They sought them in forests and mountains, when really all they needed to do was go to their own backyards and look up."**

The main idea behind the title of the article is that the Cooper's hawk needn't be sought only in forest areas but often can be found in urban areas such as someone's backyard. Answer choice B is correct because it contains this idea.

Type of text: Informational

Benchmark: LA.910.1.7.3 The student will determine the main idea or essential message in grade-level or higher texts through inferring, paraphrasing, summarizing, and identifying relevant details.

Benchmark: LA.910.1.7.6 The student will analyze and evaluate similar themes or topics by different authors across a variety of fiction and nonfiction selections.

56 **The correct answer is H, Due to the work of biologists like Bob Rosenfield, people who might ordinarily dislike Cooper's hawks take an interest in them.**

At one point in the article, the author writes: *More often than not, the people he and his colleagues visit not only invite them to conduct research on their property, but they also take an active interest in the birds' welfare. "It's good PR for the hawks," Rosenfield says. "People get to see them up close, and then maybe they hate them a little less."* The author never indicates that biologists' work should focus on other species. He points to evidence of stable numbers of Cooper's hawks to show that they are not so rare as was feared. Finally, while the author would probably agree that Cooper's hawks can be a nuisance to some homeowners, he does not seem to want them relocated from their urban habitat.

Type of text: Informational

Benchmark: LA.910.1.7.2 The student will analyze the author's purpose and/or perspective in a variety of texts and understand how they affect meaning.

Practice Writing Test 1 Sample Answer

I think that after-school jobs are valuable for high school students for a number of reasons. First, merely seeking an after-school job gives a student a taste of what it is like to look for full-time employment. A student must first hunt down a job opportunity through the use of a newspaper, the Internet, or by word of mouth. Then the student must request, fill out, and submit an application for the desired position. If the student is called for an interview, he or she will then experience the interview process. This is a valuable set of skills to develop, because most adults must take these same steps when seeking full-time employment. A student who has had even limited experience in this process is far more prepared to pursue a job after graduation than one who has not.

Second, obtaining a part-time job is valuable for a high school student because it gives the student experience in completing necessary tasks and taking orders from authority figures outside the home environment. Many high school-age young people become accustomed to rebelling against parental requests and orders, even when completing the simplest tasks around the home. Often this rebellion at home is met with only mild repercussions; most punishments for bad behavior at home involve the removal of certain privileges for a short amount of time. Young adults need to learn that their actions have consequences in the real world. Holding a part-time job can teach a person the importance of respecting and submitting to authority figures. Certainly many adults with full-time jobs must do the same on a daily basis.

Finally, holding a part-time job introduces a young adult to the discipline of financial independence and responsibility. A high school student can achieve a great sense of satisfaction by earning his or her own paychecks for the first time. This also weans young people away from their financial dependence on their parents, and teaches them how to live on a budget and decide which expenses are most important at the time. A student who is particularly conscious of finances may choose to save his or her income — another valuable skill that often translates into real-world success. For these reasons, I believe that seeking and working at part-time jobs can be very beneficial to high school students.

FCAT 2.0 Reading
Practice Test

2

Directions: This Practice Test contains six reading passages and 56 multiple-choice questions. Mark your answers in the Answer Sheet section at the back of this book.

Read the article "Shipwreck in a Cornfield" before answering questions 1 through 7.

Shipwreck in a Cornfield

When most people think of a shipwreck, they imagine the remains of a huge wooden or metal boat crashed along the bottom of the ocean. Fish swim in and out of the mangled boat's hull, and coral and seaweed cling to its sides. Meanwhile, divers with scuba gear and cameras paddle their way into the depths to explore inside the long-forgotten vessel. They might find anything from old pottery to rusty cannons to pirate gold, but one thing is certain: the deep, cold water has swallowed up the ship and kept it secret for a very long time.

Surprisingly, though, water is not always a necessary element in shipwreck explorations. Few people realize that many important shipwrecks can be found on land. Trading skiffs, warships, and pirate galleons alike have been found buried deep in riverbeds, hilltops, and cornfields throughout the world.

The seemingly unlikely event of a boat being buried is actually fairly common. There are millions of boats in the world, and thousands of bodies of water that can be accessed by boats. That means there are numerous opportunities for ships to sink, and, indeed, ships do sink on a regular basis. Let's say a ship is traveling down a river and it springs a leak, founders, strikes the bottom of the river, and sinks into the mud. Over subsequent years, more mud and sediment build up on top of the shipwreck, partially or wholly concealing it.

The next step in this process is more unlikely but still not uncommon. The river may change its course by covering a new section of land, or beginning to flow in a different direction. Many things can cause a river to change its course, including damming, erosion, and floods. After the river has moved, its old riverbed (where the shipwreck still lies) is uncovered. Former riverbeds have rich, moist soil and make excellent farmlands. If a farmer finds such soil and plants there, the crops will likely grow well. Within a short time, the land will permanently lose any similarity to a riverbed; a casual observer would not realize that a river ever used to traverse it. An observer would certainly never dream that there might be a shipwreck buried beneath it.

Go On ▶

In 1988, brothers David and Greg Hawley found the wreck of a steamboat that sank on September 5, 1856 — and they found it buried forty-five feet underground in the middle of a farmer's cornfield.

The Hawleys had first learned about the steamboat, named the *Arabia*, while reading an old newspaper. According to the article, the ship had sunk in the Missouri River a mile below the town of Parkville, Missouri. The brothers were puzzled; they could find Parkville on a modern map, but there was no river anywhere near it. How could there conceivably be a ship there?

David Hawley found an old map of the town, and it was immediately evident to him that the Missouri River had once flowed near Parkville. The river, also known as the Big Muddy, had changed course over the years. To get wood to power steamboats like the Arabia, workers had cut down trees that grew on the shoreline. With the tree roots gone, there was nothing left to prevent the banks from eroding. Dirt fell into the river, dragging trees and stumps along with it. Over time the riverbank had eroded so much that the river changed its course.

To find the old course of the river, the Hawleys decided to compare the old and new maps and figure out what land used to be part of the riverbed. After drawing up a new map, they marked off all the land within a mile of Parkville and then visited some local farmers and obtained permission to enter their cornfields with metal detectors. The Hawleys were not hoping to uncover old coins or jewelry — they were searching for a shipwreck.

It didn't take long before the brothers' metal detectors located the huge metal boilers and engines of the old steamship. Caught up in the thrill of discovery, the Hawleys and some friends gathered some money and launched into a massive effort to excavate the deeply sunken artifact. The project was costly and time consuming, but the diggers were determined to bring this piece of history back to the surface.

It wasn't as easy as scooping up sand with a shovel. To the Hawleys' dismay, they found that the field was solid, but there was plenty of water underneath. As they dug into the sandy soil, they discovered a miniature river of muddy water coursing below. Undeterred, they built twenty irrigation wells and constructed water pumps nearby to drain water from the excavation site. They had to work fast, too; if they didn't find the ship by spring, heavy rains might arrive and wash away all their efforts.

After almost five months of strenuous labor, the brothers and their helpers finally sighted the superstructure of the *Arabia*. Although it was filled with mud, they were eventually able to clean it out and explore inside. They were the first people to set foot in the boat in more than a hundred years, and the items they found had not seen sunlight in just as long.

The *Arabia* was an invaluable time capsule, containing everything from unopened suitcases to jars of blueberry pie filling, all well preserved by the mud. The searchers also found crates of Asian silk, British dishes, South American tobacco, and French perfume. There was no doubt that the *Arabia* was a well-stocked trading ship.

Examining the long-lost ship also revealed clues to its demise. The Hawleys learned that the *Arabia* was carrying hundreds of tons of freight and passengers when it struck a submerged walnut tree — doubtless one of the "snags" that came from the eroding

Go On ▶

riverbank. Like a spear, the tree ripped open the ship and sent it foundering toward the riverbed. Although the passengers escaped unharmed, the freight, and the ship itself, fell quickly into the mud. (The *Arabia* was not the only ship to sink in the area, either; the researchers believe that hundreds of ships went down, and many are still buried in farmers' fields.)

Although the Hawleys had at first hoped to find golden treasures on board the *Arabia*, they quickly realized that all the history they were rescuing was indeed the real treasure. Their hard work had barely begun; the next steps were to save the artifacts from deteriorating. The delicate items, such as fabrics and foods, had been preserved in cold, watery mud for decades; brought out of the water, they would quickly rot. Every item from the ship had to be carefully stabilized using many different techniques, including soaking, freezing, and coating with wax.

Next, the Hawleys had to find a place to store the thousands of relics. The team eventually established a museum dedicated to the history of the *Arabia* and its passengers. More than 100,000 people visit the museum each year to catch a unique glimpse of the past — a piece of seafaring history rescued from deep in the dirt.

Answer questions 1 through 7. Base your answers on the article "Shipwreck in a Cornfield."

1 The author's main purpose in writing this article is to

   A. explain how readers can dig up their own buried shipwrecks.

   B. present the history of the *Arabia* and tell the story of how it sank.

   C. describe the Hawleys' project and offer information on buried shipwrecks.

   D. persuade readers to investigate local history to see if any buried shipwrecks are in the area.

2 According to the article, what caused the Missouri River to change course?

   F. A dam was built upriver.

   G. A huge flood made the river overflow its banks.

   H. Farmers diverted the water to irrigate their land.

   I. Erosion due to lumbering broke down the riverbanks.

Go On ▶

3 Judging from information in the article, what would be the BEST way to find out if a river has changed its course?

   A. Use a metal detector to see if any shipwrecks lie underground in the area.

   B. Find an old map of the area to see the course of the river years ago.

   C. Consult records to see if there have been any major floods in the area in the last century.

   D. Ask a farmer or property owner to describe any changes in the river's course over the years.

4 Read this sentence from the article.

   Let's say a ship is traveling down a river and it springs a leak, founders, strikes the bottom of the river, and sinks into the mud.

   In this sentence, what does the word *founders* mean?

   F. drops below the surface

   G. builds momentum

   H. explodes suddenly

   I. floats aimlessly

5 Read this sentence from the article.

   Although the Hawleys had at first hoped to find golden treasures on board the *Arabia*, they quickly realized that all the history they were rescuing was indeed the real treasure.

   The reader can conclude from evidence in the article that the author most likely views the Hawleys' work in finding the *Arabia* as being

   A. unrewarding and tiresome.

   B. interesting and valuable to history.

   C. interesting but environmentally questionable.

   D. physically challenging but well-paid.

Go On ▶

6   When the author says that the *Arabia* "was an invaluable time capsule," this means that

    F.   it was worth more than a modern ocean liner.

    G.   it was airtight like a space capsule.

    H.   it preserved items from the past.

    I.   it should be exhibited at fairs and carnivals.

7   Which of the following is the BEST summary of the information in the last two paragraphs?

    A.   The Hawleys and their team worked hard to preserve the relics from the *Arabia*, placed them in a new museum, and then began to search for other wrecked steamboats in the area.

    B.   After rescuing the *Arabia* from the cornfield, the Hawleys sold thousands of its relics to pay for a new museum where the old steamboat could be seen by the public.

    C.   The Hawleys finally got 100,000 people to contribute to building a museum to store the *Arabia* and its artifacts.

    D.   Once the Hawleys had dug out the *Arabia*, they worked to preserve its artifacts and started a museum to put them on public display.

Go On ▶

Read the excerpt from *A Doll's House* before answering questions 8 through 15.

Excerpt from A Doll's House

by Henrik Ibsen

In this scene, Nora Helmer is confronted by a man named Nils Krogstad from whom she illegally and secretly borrowed money to pay for a trip to help her ill husband, Torvald. Over the years, Nora has worked hard and saved to pay back the money to Krogstad, and the loan is almost fully repaid. However, Torvald is Krogstad's boss at the bank and has been considering firing Krogstad from his post.

KROGSTAD (*controlling himself*): Listen to me, Mrs. Helmer. If necessary, I am prepared to fight for my small post in the Bank as if I were fighting for my life.

NORA: So it seems.

KROGSTAD: It is not only for the sake of the money; indeed, that weighs least with me in the matter. There is another reason—well, I may as well tell you. My position is this. I daresay you know, like everybody else, that once, many years ago, I was guilty of an indiscretion.

NORA: I think I have heard something of the kind.

KROGSTAD: The matter never came into court; but every way seemed to be closed to me after that. So I took to the business that you know of. I had to do something; and, honestly, don't think I've been one of the worst. But now I must cut myself free from all that. My sons are growing up; for their sake I must try and win back as much respect as I can in the town. This post in the Bank was like the first step up for me—and now your husband is going to kick me downstairs again into the mud.

NORA: But you must believe me, Mr. Krogstad; it is not in my power to help you at all.

KROGSTAD: Then it is because you haven't the will; but I have means to compel you.

NORA: You don't mean that you will tell my husband that I owe you money?

KROGSTAD: Hm!—suppose I were to tell him?

Go On ▶

NORA: It would be perfectly infamous of you. (*Sobbing*.) To think of his learning my secret, which has been my joy and pride, in such an ugly, clumsy way—that he should learn it from you! And it would put me in a horribly disagreeable position—

KROGSTAD: Only disagreeable?

NORA (*impetuously*): Well, do it, then!—and it will be the worse for you. My husband will see for himself what a blackguard you are, and you certainly won't keep your post then.

KROGSTAD: I asked you if it was only a disagreeable scene at home that you were afraid of?

NORA: If my husband does get to know of it, of course he will at once pay you what is still owing, and we shall have nothing more to do with you.

KROGSTAD (*coming a step nearer*): Listen to me, Mrs. Helmer. Either you have a very bad memory or you know very little of business. I shall be obliged to remind you of a few details.

NORA: What do you mean?

KROGSTAD: When your husband was ill, you came to me to borrow two hundred and fifty pounds.

NORA: I didn't know any one else to go to.

KROGSTAD: I promised to get you that amount—

NORA: Yes, and you did so.

KROGSTAD: I promised to get you that amount, on certain conditions. Your mind was so taken up with your husband's illness, and you were so anxious to get the money for your journey, that you seem to have paid no attention to the conditions of our bargain. Therefore it will not be amiss if I remind you of them. Now, I promised to get the money on the security of a bond which I drew up.

NORA: Yes, and which I signed.

KROGSTAD: Good. But below your signature there were a few lines constituting your father a surety for the money; those lines your father should have signed.

NORA: Should? He did sign them.

KROGSTAD: I had left the date blank; that is to say your father should himself have inserted the date on which he signed the paper. Do you re-member that?

NORA: Yes, I think I remember—

KROGSTAD: Then I gave you the bond to send by post to your father. Is that not so?

Go On ▶

NORA: Yes.

KROGSTAD: And you naturally did so at once, because five or six days afterwards you brought me the bond with your father's signature. And then I gave you the money.

NORA: Well, haven't I been paying it off regularly?

KROGSTAD: Fairly so, yes. But—to come back to the matter in hand—that must have been a very trying time for you, Mrs. Helmer?

NORA: It was, indeed.

KROGSTAD: Your father was very ill, wasn't he?

NORA: He was very near his end.

KROGSTAD: And died soon afterwards?

NORA: Yes.

KROGSTAD: Tell me, Mrs. Helmer, can you by any chance remember what day your father died?—on what day of the month, I mean.

NORA: Papa died on the 29th of September.

KROGSTAD: That is correct; I have ascertained it for myself. And, as that is so, there is a discrepancy (*taking a paper from his pocket*) which I cannot account for.

NORA: What discrepancy? I don't know—

KROGSTAD: The discrepancy consists, Mrs. Helmer, in the fact that your father signed this bond three days after his death.

NORA: What do you mean? I don't understand—

KROGSTAD: Your father died on the 29th of September. But, look here; your father dated his signature the 2nd of October. It is a discrepancy, isn't it? (*Nora is silent.*) Can you explain it to me? (*Nora is still silent.*) It is a remarkable thing, too, that the words "2nd of October," as well as the year, are not written in your father's handwriting but in one that I think I know. Well, of course it can be explained; your father may have forgotten to date his signature, and someone else may have dated it haphazard before they knew of his death. There is no harm in that. It all depends on the signature of the name; and that is genuine, I suppose, Mrs. Helmer? It was your father himself who signed his name here?

NORA (*after a short pause, throws her head up and looks defiantly at him*): No, it was not. It was I that wrote papa's name.

KROGSTAD: Are you aware that is a dangerous confession?

NORA: In what way? You shall have your money soon.

KROGSTAD: Let me ask you a question; why did you not send the paper to your father?

Go On ▶

NORA: It was impossible; papa was so ill. If I had asked him for his signature, I should have had to tell him what the money was to be used for; and when he was so ill himself I couldn't tell him that my husband's life was in danger—it was impossible.

KROGSTAD: It would have been better for you if you had given up your trip abroad.

NORA: No, that was impossible. That trip was to save my husband's life; I couldn't give that up.

KROGSTAD: But did it never occur to you that you were committing a fraud on me?

NORA: I couldn't take that into account; I didn't trouble myself about you at all. I couldn't bear you, because you put so many heartless difficulties in my way, although you knew what a dangerous condition my husband was in.

KROGSTAD: Mrs. Helmer, you evidently do not realise clearly what it is that you have been guilty of. But I can assure you that my one false step, which lost me all my reputation, was nothing more or nothing worse than what you have done.

NORA: You? Do you ask me to believe that you were brave enough to run a risk to save your wife's life.

KROGSTAD: The law cares nothing about motives.

NORA: Then it must be a very foolish law.

KROGSTAD: Foolish or not, it is the law by which you will be judged, if I produce this paper in court.

NORA: I don't believe it. Is a daughter not to be allowed to spare her dying father anxiety and care? Is a wife not to be allowed to save her husband's life? I don't know much about law; but I am certain that there must be laws permitting such things as that. Have you no knowledge of such laws—you who are a lawyer? You must be a very poor lawyer, Mr. Krogstad.

KROGSTAD: Maybe. But matters of business—such business as you and I have had together—do you think I don't understand that? Very well. Do as you please. But let me tell you this—if I lose my position a second time, you shall lose yours with me. (*He bows, and goes out through the hall.*)

NORA (*appears buried in thought for a short time, then tosses her head*). Nonsense! Trying to frighten me like that!—I am not so silly as he thinks. (*Begins to busy herself putting the children's things in order.*) And yet—? No, it's impossible! I did it for love's sake.

Go On ▶

Answer questions 8 through 15. Base your answers on the excerpt from *A Doll's House.*

8 In this scene, Krogstad has come to see Nora because he wants her to

    F. help him keep his job.

    G. finish paying her debt to him.

    H. help him get a better job at the bank.

    I. tell her husband the truth.

9 Nora and Krogstad are alike in all the following ways EXCEPT

    A. they both are guilty of breaking the law.

    B. they both want to hide certain facts from Torvald.

    C. they both made sacrifices to help Torvald when he was ill.

    D. they both are in danger of losing something precious.

10 Read the following line from the play.

> **"The discrepancy consists, Mrs. Helmer, in the fact that your father signed this bond three days after his death."**

Which of the following words is closest in meaning to *discrepancy*?

    F. penalty

    G. oddity

    H. inconsistency

    I. formality

11 Which pair of words BEST describes Krogstad?

    A. sarcastic and disrespectful

    B. intelligent and cunning

    C. nervous and unfriendly

    D. arrogant and boastful

Go On ▶

12 The reader can infer from Krogstad's words that he lost his reputation in the city because

    F. he was harassing women like Nora to pay back their loans.

    G. he was stealing money from the bank.

    H. he was a poor lawyer.

    I. he did something dishonest years ago.

13 Torvald is important to this drama mainly because he

    A. wields power over Nora and Krogstad.

    B. stole money to get Nora out of debt.

    C. forged a signature to get a loan from Krogstad.

    D. has suspicions about Nora's relationship with Krogstad.

14 Which of the following titles gives the main idea of this scene from *A Doll's House*?

    F. A Lost Reputation

    G. The Dying Father

    H. The Forged Signature

    I. The Desperate Journey

15 Which is the BEST description of the theme of this scene?

    A. The evil people do lives on after them.

    B. A person will do desperate things for love.

    C. No one is above the law.

    D. Money is the root of all evil.

Go On ▶

Read the article "East Meets West" before answering questions 16 through 28.

East Meets West

Before the United States was even a hundred years old, it faced problems that threatened to tear it to pieces. In the 1860s, the country endured the Civil War, which nearly ripped the northern and southern states apart. During that time, there was also a great divide between the eastern and western territories. America's East and West were separated — not by war but by distance and lack of transportation. As the Civil War raged, a great innovation was chosen that would pull the country back together: a transcontinental railroad line reaching from one end of the nation to the other.

In the 1800s, trains were a powerful and important means of transportation. People viewed these "iron horses" as awesome technology, much as we might view spaceships or supersonic jet planes today. Trains could move large amounts of people and cargo over land much more easily and effectively than horses or oxen could. Just as important, trains became a symbol to war-weary Americans. If railroad tracks could be built across the nation, they would unite the states and make America powerful again.

Today, in the age of space travel and jets, this might seem an easy task. However, at the time, building a rail system was an extremely challenging feat. In the East, railroad tracks only reached as far as Nebraska. Meanwhile, in the West, railroads only ran north and south, making no attempt to connect with the East. There was a gap of about seventeen hundred miles between the eastern and western rail lines that kept the two halves of the nation apart.

Most people relied on wagon trains or long sea voyages to travel between the East and West. However, more and more people wanted to find another, more convenient way. A railroad would offer them a perfect opportunity. Investors and shopkeepers supported this idea because a railroad would help to encourage new towns full of potential buyers and sellers. Many investors and fortune hunters in the East were also excited to travel westward in search of gold.

Other Americans simply loved the idea of a new way to explore the country and learn about different places and ideas. In the 1800s, people did not have a complete picture of America because much of it had barely

Go On ▶

been explored. In the cities of the East, people could only look at artists' paintings of the beauty of the West and guess at what it might look like in person. They wanted to see for themselves the buffalo roaming the prairies and the mountain goats climbing the Sierra Nevadas.

Much of the early debate about the line concerned what route it should take: a central route across the Sierra Nevada mountains through Clipper Gap and Donner Pass, or a southern path through Texas to California that would avoid the mountains. Reports from Pony Express riders, who routinely rode from the east to California, convinced planners that winter snows in the mountains were passable and that the central route was more feasible for the proposed railroad. In 1862, Congress passed a bill authorizing the line and President Abraham Lincoln signed it into law. Two companies were hired for the job: the Union Pacific would build westward from Council Bluffs, a town near Omaha, Nebraska, while the Central Pacific would lay tracks eastward from Sacramento, California. These companies became two of the most famous competitors in American history.

Of course, building the new railroad line required an enormous amount of labor. The Union Pacific sent teams of scouts and engineers westward to sketch out the line the tracks would follow. Next, vast construction gangs were sent out to begin grading, or leveling, the land — often in stretches of a hundred miles or more. Then came an army of track-laying crews, more than ten thousand workers and as many animals. These crews also included blacksmiths, carpenters, engineers, masons, surveyors, and cooks. Their task was to actually install the railroad tracks, which required hundreds of tons of steel bars and timber ties. The huge Union Pacific teams included many Irish immigrant laborers, Mormon workers from across the Utah area, and later, when the Civil War ended, veterans from both the Union and Confederate armies. The Union Pacific gangs were able to work quickly and cover a lot of territory, mainly because most of the land in the East was flat and because it was easier to get supplies from nearby cities.

Working from the West, the Central Pacific had neither of these advantages. The western terrain was much harsher, largely made up of dense forests and mountains. Every mile presented new challenges, and the company spent years tunneling and bridging its way across the hilly terrain. Over the course of the project, the Central Pacific built 15 tunnels, the longest measuring 1,659 feet. There were also problems getting supplies to the workers. Timber was available along the route, but all the steel rails and other materials (including the trains themselves) had to be shipped in by sea. The Central Pacific workforce was substantially made up of Chinese immigrants. The Chinese workers were paid less than their counterparts on the Union Pacific gangs, who received one to three dollars a day. Eventually the Chinese workers grew disenchanted about their working situation and wages, and they struck — successfully — for

Go On ▶

higher pay. Workers for both companies endured monumental hardships during construction of the railroad, often fainting from the heat of prairie summers or freezing in the cold of the western mountains.

Company officials drove their workers hard for the sake of profit. Each company made $16,000 per mile on a level grade, $32,000 in the high plains, and $48,000 in the mountains. Miles of extra track were laid to pad revenues and profits; when the construction teams had almost met, they were instructed to lay tracks parallel to one another to increase the precious miles. In addition, each company received grants of land along the right-of-way of the route. The moneymaking potential of the project was almost endless.

Finally, on May 10, 1869, the workers of the Union Pacific and Central Pacific met in Utah at a place called Promontory Point. The Central Pacific had laid almost 700 miles of track, and the Union Pacific more than a thousand miles of track. Company officials and politicians from many states raced to Promontory Point for the big ceremony. Parades with bands from across the United States ushered in a new age of rail travel for America, and five states donated gold or silver spikes to be hammered into the rails to finish the project. California's governor Leland Stanford pounded in the final golden spike — gold-plated actually, since pure gold would have been too soft for the purpose. A simple message, "DONE", was telegraphed across the nation to announce that the East and West had been united at last. As the dignitaries left for their gala dinners and balls, workers replaced the golden spikes with simple steel ones. The greatest engineering feat of the nineteenth century was complete.

Answer questions 16 through 28. Base your answers on the article "East Meets West."

 Which sentence from the article provides the best evidence that constructing the Transcontinental Railroad would be challenging?

    F.   "There was a gap of about seventeen hundred miles between the eastern and western rail lines that kept the two halves of the nation apart."

    G.   "The Union Pacific gangs were able to work quickly and cover a lot of territory, mainly because most of the land in the East was flat and because it was easier to get supplies from nearby cities."

    H.   "Two companies were hired for the job: the Union Pacific would build westward from Council Bluffs, a town near Omaha, Nebraska, while the Central Pacific would lay tracks eastward from Sacramento, California."

    I.   "However, more and more people wanted to find another, more convenient way."

17　Which organizational pattern does the author use in this article?

   A.　He raises arguments about why the new railroad line was needed and supports his arguments with contemporary facts.

   B.　He lists the important benefits of the Transcontinental Railroad and its major drawbacks.

   C.　He explains why a great East-West railroad line was needed and how it was built.

   D.　He describes the similarities and differences between railroads in the West and East.

18　With which statement would the author of this article most likely agree?

   F.　It is unrealistic to think that ordinary people would want to visit many places in a sprawling nation such as the United States.

   G.　In the 1800s railroads may have seemed like a marvelous technology, but they were not a very reliable means of transportation.

   H.　The vast amounts of money spent on the Transcontinental Railroad could have been used for many better purposes.

   I.　It is not surprising that the projects that most benefited Americans were long and difficult.

19　Read this sentence from the article.

   Reports from Pony Express riders, who routinely rode from the east to California, convinced planners that winter snows in the mountains were passable and that the central route was more feasible for the proposed railroad.

In this sentence, the word *feasible* means

   A.　practical.

   B.　expensive.

   C.　risky.

   D.　urgent.

20　The workforces of the Central Pacific and Union Pacific were similar in that

   F.　both had to deal with steep mountains.

   G.　both included large numbers of immigrant workers.

   H.　both received their supplies from nearby cities.

   I.　both were paid the same amount for their labor.

Go On ▶

21 According to the evidence in the article, which of these reasons contributed most to the slower pace of the Central Pacific's progress?

  A. The federal government did not support the Central Pacific's work.

  B. The Central Pacific lacked sufficient timber to make rail ties.

  C. Central Pacific owners lacked the financial incentives that the Union Pacific owners had.

  D. Much of the Central Pacific's route included dense forests and mountains.

22 Which subhead would be most appropriate for the last paragraph of this article?

  F. The Grand Finale

  G. California's Railways

  H. Steel Versus Gold

  I. A Nation Divided

23 Read this sentence from the article.

> Miles of extra track were laid to pad revenues and profits; when the construction teams had almost met, they were instructed to lay tracks parallel to one another to increase the precious miles.

Which phrase has the same meaning as the phrase *to pad revenues and profits* in the sentence above?

  A. to protect the company's finances from disclosure

  B. to increase the amount of money made

  C. to cushion the investors from losing money

  D. to change the way bookkeeping on the project was done

24 The author wrote this article mainly to

  F. describe what life was like for an immigrant worker in the 1860s.

  G. convince readers that the Civil War damaged America's sense of unity.

  H. inform readers about the history of one of America's greatest construction projects.

  I. explain why such a large-scale project was only possible in the simpler economy of the 1800s.

Go On ▶

25 Read this passage from the article.

> **The Chinese workers were paid less than their counterparts on the Union Pacific gangs, who received one to three dollars a day. Eventually the Chinese workers grew disenchanted about their working situation and wages, and they struck — successfully — for higher pay.**

What does *disenchanted* mean as it is used here?

A. bitterly divided

B. completely unreasonable

C. accustomed to hardship

D. free from illusion

26 The fact that the Transcontinental Railroad would create new towns full of potential buyers and sellers appealed mostly to

F. Americans who were weary of the Civil War.

G. investors and shopkeepers with an eye on business.

H. engineers in search of new technical challenges.

I. travelers seeking new and exciting places to visit.

27 Based on information in the article, which sentence BEST describes the attitude of railroad company officials toward their task?

A. It was their duty to the nation.

B. It was a very profitable venture.

C. It was impractical and dangerous.

D. It was the best way to unite the nation.

28 If you were filing this article for a research project, in which of the following categories would you place it?

F. Immigration in the Nineteenth Century

G. Geography of the American Nation

H. Transportation and Its Effects on America

I. Settlers in the American West

Go On ▶

Read the article "MP3: Decompressed" before answering questions 29 through 37.

MP3: Decompressed

Aside from the fact that MP3 players store and play music, how much do you really know about the multifarious gadgets?

What Does MP3 Stand For?

Though most people can explain what an MP3 file is, they usually have a difficult time with the specifics—for instance, explaining what the *M*, the *P*, and the *3* represent. The MP3 format, or the technology of shrinking a music file, developed from a technology known as MPEG. That acronym stands for Moving Pictures Expert Group, a group of innovators who have taken on the responsibility of developing ways to store, send, and view moving pictures and audio. The technology they created for sharing compressed digital video files is also called MPEG. That takes care of *M* and *P*, but what about *3*?

The primary goal of the Moving Pictures Expert Group is to create and then enhance files. The group meets about three times a year to discuss their research and their developments in the field of video compression. First they created audio layer I and audio layer II, both of which worked but stripped a lot of quality from music. Then the group created audio layer III, which allowed people to shrink music into files in which the quality remains intact.

So there you have it. An MP3 is really a Moving Picture Expert Group Audio Layer III file. No wonder they shortened the name.

A Timeline of MP3 Development

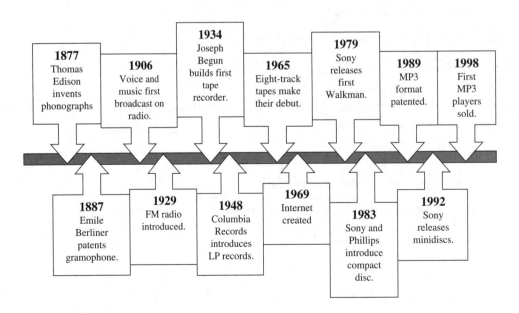

Go On ▶

How Much Quality Is Lost?

MP3 technology continues to improve, and innovators of the technology use the human ear as their inspiration. These innovators are masters of the art of psychoacoustic compression, or shrinking files to include only what is perceivable to the human ear.

The human ear can only pick up fragments of sound for two reasons. First, some tones are just imperceptible to the human ear. Second, if one instrument produces a loud sound, the human ear cannot perceive the fainter tones underlying it.

Scientists use a process called perceptual noise shaping to remove sounds from music that the human ear cannot perceive. You might notice minor differences between an analog (or traditional) recording and an MP3 file of the same song because compression removes subtleties that are beyond detection by the human ear. You can notice only slight differences when you listen to an MP3, but if you compared the playback of an MP3 file to that of an analog recording on a high-fidelity system, the difference in quality would be quite noticeable.

How Compressed Is an MP3?

Audio Layer III provides a 12:1 ratio from analog to digital, which means a file is compressed to one-twelfth its original size. If you were to download one song from a CD onto your computer, it would take up about 40 million bytes (or 40 megabytes) of computer space. If you compress that music file into an MP3 file, it will only take up about 3.5 megabytes of computer space.

What Is Inside an MP3 Player?

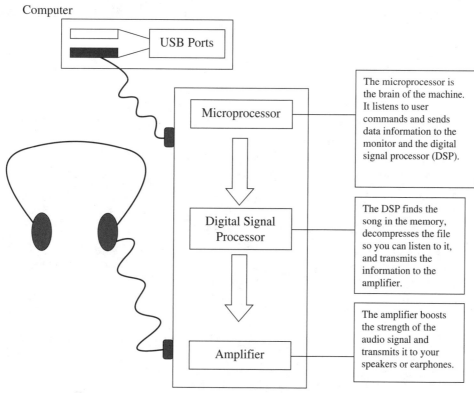

Computer

USB Ports

Microprocessor

The microprocessor is the brain of the machine. It listens to user commands and sends data information to the monitor and the digital signal processor (DSP).

Digital Signal Processor

The DSP finds the song in the memory, decompresses the file so you can listen to it, and transmits the information to the amplifier.

Amplifier

The amplifier boosts the strength of the audio signal and transmits it to your speakers or earphones.

Go On ▶

If you could open up your tiny music storage device, you would be amazed at what goes on inside! That slim, shiny machine contains tiny parts that make music come alive. Check out the illustration of how MPEG audio layer III coding comes out of an MP3 player as music.

So What Should I Get?

There are two basic types of MP3 player to choose from, each with its own advantages and disadvantages:

- A **flash MP3** player has no moving parts inside and therefore cannot store very much information—only about 200 songs. However, you do not have to worry about your music skipping. These devices are very inexpensive compared with their more complex counterparts, the hard-drive MP3 players. If you want to use your device primarily for exercise, the flash MP3 player is the machine for you.

- A **hard-drive MP3** player can have as much memory as some computers and, also like your computer, can store any type of file, not just MP3s. This type of player can also hold photos, video, or text files and can be used to transport files from one computer to another. The primary benefit of a hard-drive device is that it can store so much information. The drawbacks are that more space means more breakable parts, a bigger price tag, and a bulkier, heavier player. Finally, the music can skip if you jostle the device too much.

As with any purchase, you should educate yourself and then make a decision to purchase based on your personal preferences. Whichever type of player you choose, you will have a greater appreciation for the device now that you know all that is going on inside!

Go On ▶

Answer questions 29 through 37. Base your answers on the article "MP3: Decompressed."

29 According to the evidence in the article, which of the following features contributed most to the popularity of hard-drive MP3 players?

A. the ability to store a large amount of information

B. a smaller price tag

C. the ability to play during exercise

D. unbreakable parts

30 Read this passage from the article.

> The MP3 format, or the technology of shrinking a music file, developed from a technology known as MPEG. That acronym stands for Moving Pictures Expert Group, a group of innovators who have taken on the responsibility of developing ways to store, send, and view moving pictures and audio.

What is the meaning of *acronym* in this passage?

F. a word that means the opposite of a particular term

G. a word that stands for a complex scientific term

H. a word formed from the first letters of the words in a compound term

I. a word used by scientists and inventors to refer to one of their innovations

31 What is the main purpose of the subheadings in this article?

A. to introduce the topic of each section of text

B. to introduce the topic of each section of text and each illustration

C. to emphasize the cause-effect structure of the article

D. to answer important questions about the subject matter

Go On ▶

32 Which statement from the article provides the BEST evidence of the versatility of MP3 players?

F. "As with any purchase, you should educate yourself and then make a decision to purchase based on your personal preferences."

G. "That slim, shiny machine contains tiny parts that make music come alive."

H. "These innovators are masters of the art of psychoacoustic compression, or shrinking files to include only what is perceivable to the human ear."

I. "This type of player can also hold photos, video, or text files and can be used to transport files from one computer to another."

33 According to the author, the best thing to do before buying an MP3 player is to

A. ask to see the inside of the MP3 player and examine the circuitry in detail.

B. read articles about the benefits and drawbacks of various MP3 players.

C. query several people who already own MP3 players about their sound quality and mechanical performance.

D. focus only on flash MP3 players because they have no moving parts and you do not have to worry about music skipping.

34 The main purpose of the diagram under the heading "What Is Inside an MP3 Player?" is to

F. explain the history of MP3 players.

G. show what an MP3 player looks like.

H. explain how an MP3 player works.

I. teach how to repair an MP3 player.

35 The article states that *Some tones are just imperceptible to the human ear.* Which of the following best restates the idea in this sentence?

A. Some sounds are simply too low or too high for a person to hear.

B. Some musical notes sound harsh when heard together.

C. Humans can hear some tones more clearly than others.

D. The differences between most musical sounds are not apparent to the ordinary human ear.

Go On ▶

36   The ability to compress audio files is important to computer users because

     F.   compressed digital files are much less expensive than analog files.

     G.   compressed files require the use of a digital signal processor.

     H.   compression removes unwanted sounds from a music file.

     I.   compressed files take up much less space on a computer.

37   Which of the following would be a better subheading for the first graphic than "A Timeline of MP3 Development"?

     A.   A List of Innovators in MP3 Technology

     B.   A Timeline of Innovations in Recorded Music Up to MP3

     C.   A Timeline of Important Events in Music History

     D.   A Comparison of Analog and Digital Music Technologies

Go On ▶

Read the story "The Interlopers" before answering questions 38 through 45.

The Interlopers

by H. H. Munro (Saki)

In a forest of mixed growth somewhere on the eastern spurs of the Carpathians, a man stood one winter night watching and listening, as though he waited for some beast of the woods to come within the range of his vision, and, later, of his rifle. But the game for whose presence he kept so keen an outlook was none that figured in the sportsman's calendar as lawful and proper for the chase; Ulrich von Gradwitz patrolled the dark forest in quest of a human enemy.

The forest lands of Gradwitz were of wide extent and well stocked with game; the narrow strip of precipitous woodland that lay on its outskirt was not remarkable for the game it harbored or the shooting it afforded, but it was the most jealously guarded of all its owner's territorial possessions. A famous lawsuit, in the days of his grandfather, had wrested it from the illegal possession of a neighboring family of petty landowners; the dispossessed party had never acquiesced in the judgment of the Courts, and a long series of poaching episodes and similar scandals had embittered the relationships between the families for three generations. The neighbor feud had grown into a personal one since Ulrich had come to be head of his family; if there was a man in the world whom he detested and wished ill to it was Georg Znaeym, the inheritor of the quarrel and the tireless game-snatcher and raider of the disputed border-forest.

Ulrich strayed away by himself from the watchers whom he had placed in ambush on the crest of the hill, and wandered far down the steep slopes amid the wild tangle of undergrowth, peering through the tree trunks and listening through the whistling and skirling of the wind and the restless beating of the branches for sight and sound of the marauders. If only on this wild night, in this dark, lone spot, he might come across Georg Znaeym, man to man, with none to witness — that was the wish that was uppermost in his thoughts. And as he stepped round the trunk of a huge beech he came face to face with the man he sought.

The two enemies stood glaring at one another for a long silent moment. Each had a rifle in his hand, each had hate in his heart and murder uppermost in his mind. The chance had come to give full play to the passions of a lifetime. But a man who has been brought up under the code of a restraining civilization cannot easily nerve himself to shoot down his neighbor in cold blood and without word spoken, except for an offense against his hearth and honor. And before the moment of hesitation had given way to action a deed of Nature's own violence overwhelmed them both. A fierce shriek of the storm had been answered by a splitting crash over their heads, and before they could leap aside a mass of falling beech tree had thundered down on them. Ulrich von Gradwitz found himself stretched on the ground, one arm numb beneath him and the other held almost as helplessly in a tight tangle of forked branches, while both legs were pinned beneath the fallen mass. His heavy shooting-

Go On ▶

boots had saved his feet from being crushed to pieces, but if his fractures were not as serious as they might have been, at least it was evident that he could not move from his present position till some one came to release him. The descending twig had slashed the skin of his face, and he had to wink away some drops of blood from his eyelashes before he could take in a general view of the disaster. At his side, so near that under ordinary circumstances he could almost have touched him, lay Georg Znaeym, alive and struggling, but obviously as helplessly pinned down as himself. All round them lay a thick-strewn wreckage of splintered branches and broken twigs.

"So you're not killed, as you ought to be, but you're caught, anyway," Georg cried. "Caught fast. Ho, what a jest, Ulrich von Gradwitz snared in his stolen forest. There's real justice for you!"

And he laughed again, mockingly and savagely.

"I'm caught in my own forest-land," retorted Ulrich. "When my men come to release us you will wish, perhaps, that you were in a better plight than caught poaching on a neighbor's land, shame on you."

Georg was silent for a moment; then he answered quietly:

"Are you sure that your men will find much to release? I have men, too, in the forest tonight, close behind me, and THEY will be here first and do the releasing. When they drag me out from under these cursed branches it won't need much clumsiness on their part to roll this mass of trunk right over on the top of you. Your men will find you dead under a fallen beech tree. For form's sake I shall send my condolences to your family."

"It is a useful hint," said Ulrich fiercely. "My men had orders to follow in ten minutes time, seven of which must have gone by already, and when they get me out — I will remember the hint. Only as you will have met your death poaching on my lands I don't think I can decently send any message of condolence to your family."

"Good," snarled Georg, "good. We fight this quarrel out to the death, you and I and our foresters, with no cursed interlopers to come between us. Death and good riddance to you, Ulrich von Gradwitz."

"The same to you, Georg Znaeym, forest-thief, game-snatcher."

Both had now given up the useless struggle to free themselves from the mass of wood that held them down; Ulrich limited his endeavors to an effort to bring his one partially free arm near enough to his outer coat-pocket to draw out his wine-flask. Even when he had accomplished that operation it was long before he could manage the unscrewing of the stopper or get any of the liquid down his throat. Nevertheless, the wine was warming and reviving to the wounded man, and he looked across with something like a throb of pity to where his enemy lay, just keeping the groans of pain and weariness from crossing his lips.

"Could you reach this flask if I threw it over to you?" asked Ulrich suddenly. "Let us drink, even if tonight one of us dies."

"No, I can scarcely see anything; there is so much blood caked round my eyes," said Georg, "and in any case I don't drink wine with an enemy."

Ulrich was silent for a few minutes, and lay listening to the weary screeching of the wind. An idea was slowly forming and growing in his brain, an idea that gained strength every time that he looked across at the man who was fighting so grimly

Go On ▶

against pain and exhaustion. In the pain and languor that Ulrich himself was feeling the old fierce hatred seemed to be dying down.

"Neighbor," he said presently, "do as you please if your men come first. It was a fair compact. But as for me, I've changed my mind. If my men are the first to come you shall be the first to be helped, as though you were my guest. We have quarreled like devils all our lives over this stupid strip of forest, where the trees can't even stand upright in a breath of wind. Neighbor, if you will help me to bury the old quarrel I – I will ask you to be my friend."

Georg Znaeym was silent for so long that Ulrich thought, perhaps, he had fainted with the pain of his injuries. Then he spoke slowly and in jerks.

"How the whole region would stare and gabble if we rode into the market square together. And if we choose to make peace among our people there is none other to interfere, no interlopers from outside. . . . I would never fire a shot on your land, save when you invited me as a guest; and you should come and shoot with me down in the marshes where the wildfowl are. In all the countryside there are none that could hinder if we willed to make peace. I never thought to have wanted to do other than hate you all my life, but I think I have changed my mind about things too, this last half-hour. Ulrich von Gradwitz, I will be your friend."

For a space both men were silent, turning over in their minds the wonderful changes that this dramatic reconciliation would bring about. And each prayed a private prayer that his men might be the first to arrive, so that he might be the first to show honorable attention to the enemy that had become a friend.

Presently, as the wind dropped for a moment, Ulrich broke silence.

"Let's shout for help," he said. "In this lull our voices may carry a little way."

"They won't carry far through the trees and undergrowth," said Georg, "but we can try. Together, then."

The two raised their voices in a prolonged hunting call.

There was silence again for some minutes, and then Ulrich gave a joyful cry.

"I can see figures coming through the wood. They are following in the way I came down the hillside."

Both men raised their voices in as loud a shout as they could muster.

"They hear us! They've stopped. Now they see us. They're running down the hill towards us," cried Ulrich.

"How many of them are there?" asked Georg.

"I can't see distinctly," said Ulrich. "Nine or ten."

"Then they are yours," said Georg. "I had only seven out with me."

"They are making all the speed they can, brave lads," said Ulrich gladly.

"Are they your men?" asked Georg. "Are they your men?" he repeated impatiently as Ulrich did not answer.

"No," said Ulrich with a laugh, the idiotic chattering laugh of a man unstrung with hideous fear.

"Who are they?" asked Georg quickly, straining his eyes to see what the other would gladly not have seen.

"Wolves."

Go On ▶

Now answer questions 38 through 45. Base your answers on the story "The Interlopers."

38   The forest setting is important to this story for all the following reasons EXCEPT

    F.   Ulrich and Georg become trapped under a fallen tree in the forest.

    G.   ownership of part of the forest is the source of the conflict between Ulrich and Georg.

    H.   it is difficult for Ulrich to see clearly in the dense underbrush of the forest.

    I.   Ulrich depends on income from timber in the forest, and Georg is intent on stealing the wood.

39   Read this passage from the story.

> **"Neighbor," he said presently, "do as you please if your men come first. It was a fair compact. But as for me, I've changed my mind. If my men are the first to come you shall be the first to be helped, as though you were my guest."**

In which sentence is *compact* used in the same sense as in the passage above?

    A.   A compact car generally sells for less than a larger sedan.

    B.   The cook pressed down on the sandwich with a spatula to make it thinner and more compact.

    C.   Before she went onstage, the actress checked her makeup in the mirror of her compact.

    D.   All the farmers in the county made an informal compact to share the grain elevator.

40   At one point in the story, Georg says,

> **"In all the countryside there are none that could hinder if we willed to make peace."**

Which of the following BEST restates this idea in a modern idiom?

    F.   "Even if we want peace, we can't bring it about by ourselves."

    G.   "Peace and friendship are just what the people in this area need."

    H.   "There's no one around here to stop us if we wanted to be friends."

    I.   "The people in our area are not likely to approve of our friendship."

Go On ▶

41   The main reason that Ulrich and Georg are enemies is that

    A.   their families have had a longtime dispute over a strip of forest land.

    B.   Ulrich's grandfather stole a strip of forest land from Georg's grandfather.

    C.   Georg is jealous of the wealth of Ulrich's family.

    D.   Ulrich swore he would kill Georg if he ever found him on his property.

42   Read the following sentence from the story.

> **And before the moment of hesitation had given way to action a deed of Nature's own violence overwhelmed them both.**

This sentence contains an example of what kind of literary device?

    F.   symbolism

    G.   flashback

    H.   personification

    I.   simile

43   Until the end of the story, the main theme of "The Interlopers" seems to be

    A.   the importance of justice.

    B.   how enemies can become friends.

    C.   the dangers of the natural world.

    D.   people are often not what they seem.

44   The most likely reason the author wrote this story was to

    F.   inspire readers with a tale about an unlikely friendship.

    G.   entertain readers with a tale about unpredictable fate.

    H.   describe the unique relationship between two wealthy landowners.

    I.   convince readers that everyone is capable of changing for the better.

45   The word *interlopers* in the title of the story refers to

    A.   Ulrich's and Georg's men.

    B.   the wolves.

    C.   the game in the forest.

    D.   Ulrich and Georg.

Go On ▶

Read the article "The All-American Girls' Baseball League" before answering questions 46 through 56.

The All-American Girls' Baseball League

In the 1940s, many young men enlisted in the armed forces and were sent overseas to fight in World War II. The absence of so many men greatly affected the economy of the United States, leaving a large number of businesses with dozens of positions to fill. In some situations, women left the domestic sphere to join the workforce. This became an exciting time for countless women who had never been employed outside the home. Many had jobs manufacturing war materials, some became substitute teachers in local schools, and others worked in health care. Of course, factories, hospitals, and schools were not the only enterprises that needed a solution to the lack of men.

The world of professional sports, a field composed almost entirely of men, was particularly hard hit by the war. Baseball, America's national pastime, saw many of its star players trade in bats and balls for helmets and rifles.

Go On ▶

Many teams in the minor leagues were disbanded, and even some major league clubs faced empty stadiums and financial hardship. However, one man figured out a way to bring fans back to the game.

In 1943, Philip K. Wrigley started the All-American Girls' Professional Baseball League. Wrigley, who inherited a major chewing gum company and the Chicago Cubs after his father's death in 1932, recognized America's need for entertainment during this stressful wartime period. Because of a shortage of men, Wrigley decided to create a baseball league made up entirely of women athletes. Scouts scoured the country to find talented young women to take the field. Some of the women played on local softball teams, while others had only played baseball in backyard games with male relatives and friends.

Recognizing that the idea of women playing baseball would be shocking to many people at the time, Wrigley and his associates carefully composed a strict code of conduct that held the players accountable for their actions on and off the field. The women of the new league were amazing athletes, but they were also expected to be shining examples of femininity. Along with a manager and a coach, each team was assigned a female chaperone to ensure that the players behaved in an appropriate manner. After practicing their hitting and fielding skills during the day, the girls were required to take night classes in hygiene and etiquette. They were expected to look their best at all times. The uniforms included a short skirt, and the players wore makeup at all times, even during games. The required skirts made it particularly difficult to slide when stealing bases, but the women's protests about this problem were ignored.

The rules of play were similar to those for regular baseball, with a few modifications made to the field and the types of equipment that the women used. The league's first four teams — the Racine Belles, the Kenosha Comets, The Rockford Peaches, and the South Bend Blue Sox — started the inaugural season in May 1943. The teams were hosted by small cities outside Chicago, where the league was headquartered. Resourceful owners had to find ad hoc solutions to early challenges, such as the use of small community ballparks and grandstands, to get the league up and running. While it was curiosity that initially lured many people to the games, the women's performance on the field kept fans coming back every week. More than 175,000 fans attended games in the first season. Wrigley took the opportunity to expand the league to neighboring cities in the following years.

The women ballplayers in Wrigley's league were overjoyed to be able to play a game they loved and earn a living doing it. Even though people enjoyed the girls' league, there was never a doubt that the men fighting overseas were still on the minds of players and spectators both. At the start of most games, the two teams would form a "V" for victory around home plate as "The Star Spangled Banner" was played. Many of the women players also visited wounded soldiers at local hospitals to show their support for the war effort.

Go On ▶

The league continued to grow as the war went on. Teams were added in Milwaukee and Minneapolis, and total attendance reached 450,000 in 1945, the year World War II ended. Some league cities even formed junior teams where girls under the age of fourteen could learn the basics of the game and play against each other. After the war, women's games continued to attract thousands of fans to every game. But Major League Baseball, with many of its former stars returning healthy and ready to play, returned to prominence. After a peak attendance figure of 910,000 fans in 1948, interest in the All-American Girls' Professional Baseball League started to wane. In 1954, the league disbanded after 12 years of operation.

Although the league existed for only a short period, it left a lasting impression not only on baseball but on sports in general, proving that women could succeed as professional athletes. In 1992 the league's story was made into a popular motion picture. *A League of Their Own* was a fictionalized account of the 1943 season, but it introduced a new generation to the extraordinary women who not only played a sharp brand of baseball but also broke down barriers and raised morale in America during the difficult days of World War II. In October 1988 the Baseball Hall of Fame added an exhibit honoring the women of the AAGBL. Decades after their groundbreaking efforts, these pioneering women ballplayers continue to inspire young girls everywhere to break down barriers and do their very best.

Answer questions 46 through 56. Base your answers on the article "The All-American Girls' Baseball League."

46 The main idea the author wants to convey in this article is that

    F. World War II forced women to take over jobs once held by men.

    G. the women of the All-American Girls' Baseball League were portrayed in a 1992 motion picture.

    H. the All-American Girls' Baseball League left a lasting impression on the sport of baseball and on American society.

    I. since World War II, American women have been more active in the workforce and have found increased opportunities to compete in professional sports.

Go On ▶

47 Compared to men's major league baseball, the game in the women's league was

    A. exactly the same regarding rules, equipment, and playing field.

    B. slightly different regarding equipment and playing field.

    C. slightly different regarding rules of the game and number of players on the field.

    D. radically different regarding rules of the game, such as having four strikes instead of three.

48 Read the following passage from the article.

> **The uniforms included a short skirt, and the players wore makeup at all times, even during games. The required skirts made it particularly difficult to slide when stealing bases, but the women's protests about this problem were ignored.**

The author included this passage to demonstrate that

    F. the women ballplayers had little influence on how the league was run.

    G. the owner of the women's baseball league treated the players very badly.

    H. the style of baseball was not important to the owner of the women's league.

    I. the owner of the women's league did not want the players stealing bases.

49 What is the meaning of the word *scoured* as used in this sentence from the third paragraph of the article?

> **Scouts scoured the country to find talented young women to take the field.**

    A. emptied

    B. rubbed

    C. harassed

    D. searched

Go On ▶

50 Which phrase BEST describes the public's initial feelings about the All-American Girls' Baseball League?

    F. very curious

    G. completely uninterested

    H. extremely shocked

    I. wildly enthusiastic

51 According to the article, players in the AAGBL wore short skirts and makeup because

    A. Wrigley sold more tickets if the players looked pretty.

    B. the owners expected them to be examples of femininity.

    C. the players themselves demanded it.

    D. the rules of polite society pressured them to do it.

52 Read the following sentence from the article.

> Resourceful owners had to find ad hoc solutions to early challenges, such as the use of small community ballparks and grandstands, to get the league up and running.

Which best expresses the meaning of the Latin phrase *ad hoc* as it is used here?

    F. impractical

    G. unscrupulous

    H. makeshift

    I. ideal

53 According to the article, which statement is correct?

    A. Before the formation of Wrigley's league, women had never played baseball anywhere.

    B. Attendance at women's league baseball games was poor, and the league disbanded as soon as World War II ended.

    C. The women's baseball league lacked enough quality athletes to be a success.

    D. Wrigley's women's baseball league was an example of how the absence of men during World War II gave women their first opportunity to work outside their homes.

Go On ▶

54   Read the following sentence from the last paragraph of the article.

> **Decades after their groundbreaking efforts, these pioneering women ballplayers continue to inspire young girls everywhere to break down barriers and do their very best.**

The phrase *groundbreaking efforts* refers to which of the following?

F.   the girls' skill as baseball players

G.   the girls' success in becoming the first female professional ballplayers

H.   the girls' introduction to a new generation of fans via a motion picture

I.   the girls' loyalty to the men who were away fighting in the war

55   According to the article, which of the following was the main reason for the decline of the All-American Girls' Baseball League?

A.   The female ballplayers gradually left the league to get married and start families.

B.   Major League Baseball demanded that the women's baseball league stop competing with it.

C.   Major League Baseball's attendance revived when its star players returned from fighting the war.

D.   The level of play in the All-American Girls' Baseball League became much worse in the 1950s.

56   With which of the following statements would the author of this article most likely agree?

F.   There is an urgent need in the U.S. for a new girls' professional baseball league.

G.   World War II had nothing but damaging effects on the sport of baseball.

H.   The All-American Girls' Professional Baseball League was an important step for women in sports.

I.   The All-American Girls' Professional Baseball League was an amusing stunt that never had a chance to succeed.

FCAT Writing
Practice Test

2

For the FCAT Writing, you will be given an answer book with a prompt inside. You will have 45 minutes to read the prompt, plan what you want to write, and write your response. A separate planning sheet will be provided. You will respond to a prompt that asks you to explain or a prompt that asks you to persuade.

You should write your response neatly and show that you can organize and express your thoughts clearly and completely. You may not use a dictionary or other reference materials.

Directions for Responding to the Prompt

On the actual test, the prompt will appear in a box on the prompt page. It is important to use the planning sheet to jot down ideas and organize your writing. Although the planning sheet is not scored, you must turn it in with your test.

Planning Sheet

Remember, use this sheet for planning what you will write. The writing on this sheet will *not* be scored. On the FCAT only the writing in the writing folder will be scored. An Answer Sheet for the writing prompt is provided on page 291.

Expository Prompt

Writing Situation

It is often said that a true friend is someone you can rely on. What other qualities does a true friend have?

Directions for Writing

Think about the most important qualities in a true friend. Now write to explain what qualities a true friend should have and why they are important.

Planning Sheet

Planning Sheet

Answers
for
Practice Test

2

Practice Reading Test 2 Answers

1 **The correct answer is C, describe the Hawleys' experience and offer information on buried shipwrecks.**

In the article, the author provides background information on how shipwrecks become buried away from a river channel and then describes the Hawleys' experience in raising the shipwreck out of the ground. The author is not mainly interested in encouraging readers to dig up a buried boat or in telling the history of the *Arabia,* although some details of its wreck are given. The author does not seek to persuade readers to investigate possible buried shipwrecks in their own areas.

Type of text: Informational

Benchmark: LA.910.1.7.2 The student will analyze the author's purpose and/or perspective in a variety of texts and understand how they affect meaning.

2 **The correct answer is I, Erosion due to lumbering broke down the riverbanks.**

In the article, the author explains what caused the river's course to change: *To get wood to power steamboats like the* Arabia, *workers had cut down trees that grew on the shoreline. With the tree roots gone, there was nothing left to prevent the banks from eroding. Dirt fell into the river, dragging trees and stumps along with it. Over time the riverbank had eroded so much that the river changed its course.*

Type of text: Informational

Benchmark: LA.910.1.7.4 The student will identify cause-and-effect relationships in text.

3 **The correct answer is B, Find an old map of the area to see the course of the river years ago.**

The author describes how the Hawleys looked at an old map to discover that the Missouri River in their area had changed course. The other methods of detection would not have helped or would not have been as effective.

Type of text: Informational

Benchmark: LA.910.2.2.2 The student will use information from the text to answer questions or to state the main idea or provide relevant details.

4 **The correct answer is F, drops below the surface.**

It is clear from the context that the meaning of *founders* is "sinks or drops below the surface of the water." Answer choice F is correct.

Type of text: Informational

Benchmark: LA.910.1.6.3 The student will use context clues to determine the meaning of unfamiliar words.

5 **The correct answer is B, interesting and historically valuable.**

The author says that the Hawleys were *caught up in the thrill of discovery and determined to bring this piece of history back to the surface.* The sample sentence for this question points out that the history of the steamship was the real treasure. All these details indicate that the author thinks their work is interesting and historically valuable.

Type of text: Informational

Benchmark: LA.910.1.7.3 The student will determine the main idea or essential message in grade-level or higher texts through inferring, paraphrasing, summarizing, and identifying relevant details.

6 **The correct answer is H, it preserved items from the past.**

According to the article, the *Arabia* contained *everything from unopened suitcases to jars of blueberry pie filling, all well preserved by the mud.* This indicates that it is a time capsule in the sense of preserving items from the past.

Type of text: Informational

Benchmark: LA.910.1.6.8 The student will identify advanced word/phrase relationships and their meanings.

7 **The correct answer is D, Once the Hawleys had dug out the *Arabia,* they worked to preserve its artifacts and started a museum to put them on public display.**

Answer choice D is the best summary of the information in the final two paragraphs. Choice A incorrectly states that the Hawleys and their team began to search for other wrecked steamboats in the area. Choice B incorrectly says that they sold thousands of the Arabia's relics to pay for a new museum. Choice C incorrectly says that 100,000 people contributed to building a new museum.

Type of text: Informational

Benchmark: LA.910.2.1.3 The student will organize information to show understanding or relationships among facts, ideas, and events (e.g., representing key points within text through charting, mapping, paraphrasing, summarizing, comparing, contrasting, or outlining).

8 **The correct answer is F, help him keep his job.**

Nora is married to Torvald, Krogstad's boss. Torvald wants to fire Krogstad from his post at the bank, and Krogstad admits, "I am prepared to fight for my small post in the Bank as if I were fighting for my life." Because Nora borrowed money from Krogstad illegally, he believes he has leverage to make her help him keep his job. If she does not, he threatens to tell Torvald about the illegality of the loan.

Type of text: Drama

Benchmark: LA.910.2.1.2 The student will analyze and compare a variety of traditional, classical, and contemporary literary works, and identify the literary elements of each (e.g., setting plot, characterization, conflict).

9 **The correct answer is C, they both made sacrifices to help Torvald when he was ill.**

Nora made a sacrifice by signing illegally for an urgent loan so that she could go to Torvald when he was ill. Krogstad made no such sacrifice himself.

Type of text: Drama

Benchmark: LA.910.2.1.5 The student will analyze and develop an interpretation of a literary work by describing an author's use of literary elements (e.g., theme, point of view, characterization, setting, plot), and explain and analyze different elements of figurative language (e.g., simile, metaphor, personification, hyperbole, symbolism, allusion, imagery).

10 **The correct answer is H, inconsistency.**

In this sentence, Krogstad refers to a *discrepancy,* or an *inconsistency* between facts: Mrs. Helmer's father could not have signed the bond three days after his death.

Type of text: Drama

Benchmark: LA.910.1.6.3 The student will use context clues to determine meanings of unfamiliar words.

11 **The correct answer is B, intelligent and cunning.**

In this scene, Krogstad uses his knowledge of business and the law against Nora and threatens to expose her illegal loan if she fails to help him. This demonstrates that he is both smart and sneaky. He is not sarcastic and disrespectful; he maintains a civil tone throughout. He may be nervous, but his words seem calm and well chosen. He is not arrogant and boastful, only confident that Nora will have to do as he insists.

Type of text: Drama

Benchmark: LA.910.2.1.2 The student will analyze and compare a variety of traditional, classical, and contemporary literary works, and identify the literary elements of each (e.g., setting plot, characterization, conflict).

12 **The correct answer is I, he did something dishonest years ago.**

Krogstad says at the beginning of the scene: *My position is this. I daresay you know, like everybody else, that once, many years ago, I was guilty of an indiscretion. . . . The matter never came into court; but every way seemed to be closed to me after that.* This "indiscretion that never came into court" is probably a crime of some sort that "everybody" knows about and holds against him.

Type of text: Drama

Benchmark: LA.910.2.1.6 The student will create a complex, multi-genre response to the reading of two or more literary works, describing and analyzing an author's use of literary elements (e.g., theme, point of view, characterization, setting, plot), and explain and analyze different elements of figurative language (e.g., simile, metaphor, personification, hyperbole, symbolism, allusion, imagery), and analyzing an author's development of time and sequence through the use of complex literary devices such as foreshadowing and flashback.

13 **The correct answer is A, wields power over Nora and Krogstad.**

Since Nora fears what will happen if Torvald finds out about her loan, and Krogstad fears that Torvald will fire him from the bank, Torvald has power over both Nora and Krogstad. Torvald did not steal money to get Nora out of debt. It was Nora who forged the signature on the bond. Nowhere is there an indication that Torvald has suspicions about Nora and Krogstad.

Type of text: Drama

Benchmark: LA.910.2.1.2 The student will analyze and compare a variety of traditional, classical, and contemporary literary works, and identify the literary elements of each (e.g., setting plot, characterization, conflict).

14 **The correct answer is H, The Forged Signature.**

In the scene, the most important idea is the revelation that Nora forged her father's signature on the bond and so Krogstad has a way to compel her to help him. Krogstad's lost reputation, Nora's dying father, and her desperate journey to help her husband are mentioned in the scene, but none of them are the main focus of the scene.

Type of text: Drama

Benchmark: LA.910.2.1.1 The student will analyze and compare historically and culturally significant works of literature, identifying the relationships among the major genres (e.g., poetry, fiction, nonfiction, short story, dramatic literature, essay) and the literary devices unique to each, and analyze how they support and enhance the theme and main ideas of the text.

15 **The correct answer is B, A person will do desperate things for love.**

At the end of the scene, Nora says, "No, it's impossible! I did it for love's sake." In other words, she was heedless of the law when it was a question of saving her husband's life. Answer choice A is not correct because Nora's father is the only character that has died, and he did not commit an evil act. Answer choice C is closer to the theme, but Nora doesn't claim to be above the law; instead she argues that the law should take into account people's motives. Answer choice D is incorrect because Nora did not want the money for any greedy purpose but rather to help her get to her husband.

Type of text: Drama

Benchmark: LA.910.1.7.6 The student will analyze and evaluate similar themes or topics by different authors across a variety of fiction and nonfiction selections.

Benchmark: LA.910.2.1.4 The student will identify and analyze universal themes and symbols across genres and historical periods, and explain their significance.

16 **The correct answer is F, "There was a gap of about seventeen hundred miles between the eastern and western rail lines that kept the two halves of the nation apart."**

The statement that the labor of two companies was required for the project (choice H) indicates that it would be challenging, but the best evidence is in the statement that a gap of seventeen hundred miles had to be crossed with new tracks, an enormous task.

Type of text: Informational

Benchmark: LA.910.2.2.2 The student will use information from the text to answer questions or to state the main idea or provide relevant details.

17 **The correct answer is C, He explains why a great east-west railroad line was needed and how it was built.**

The author begins by giving reasons why Americans wanted a nationwide railroad line and then explains in detail how the project was completed.

Type of text: Informational

Benchmark: LA.910.1.7.5 The student will analyze a variety of text structures (e.g., comparison/contrast, cause/effect, chronological order, argument/support, lists) and text features (main headings with subheadings) and explain their impact on meaning in text.

18 **The correct answer is I, It is not surprising that the projects that most benefited Americans were long and difficult.**

The author clearly shows an understanding that important, beneficial projects often require a long time and plenty of difficult work. For example, the author says that *building the new railroad line required an enormous amount of labor* and describes the completed railroad as *the greatest engineering feat of the nineteenth century*. The author actually says that many people wanted the railroad built so that they could explore the vast nation, so choice F is incorrect. Also, the author points out that travel by rail was much easier and more effective than using horses or oxen. Although the author acknowledges that huge amounts of money were spent on the project, nowhere does the author say that the money should have been used for something else.

Type of text: Informational

Benchmark: LA.910.1.7.2 The student will analyze the author's purpose and/or perspective in a variety of texts and understand how they affect meaning.

19 **The correct answer is A, practical.**

Since the winter snows in the mountains did not make the central route impassable, it was considered a more practical alternative than the southern route.

Type of text: Informational

Benchmark: LA.910.1.6.5 The student will relate new vocabulary to familiar words.

20 **The correct answer is G, both included large numbers of immigrant workers.**

The item that the workforces had in common is choice G. The Central Pacific company hired large numbers of Chinese immigrant workers, while the Union Pacific employed many Irish immigrant workers. Only the Central Pacific workforce had to deal with the harsh terrain of steep mountains. Only the Union Pacific workforce received their supplies from nearby cities. And the Union Pacific workers were paid more for their labor than the Chinese who made up most of the Central Pacific workforce.

Type of text: Informational

Benchmark: LA.910.2.2.3 The student will organize information to show understanding or relationships among facts, ideas, and events (e.g., representing key points within text through charting, mapping, paraphrasing, summarizing, comparing, contrasting, or outlining).

21 **The correct answer is D, Much of the Central Pacific's route included dense forests and mountains.**

According to the article, *the western terrain was much harsher, largely made up of dense forests and mountains. Every mile presented new challenges, and the [Central Pacific] company spent years tunneling and bridging its way across the hilly terrain.* This contributed to the slower pace of progress for the Central Pacific.

Type of text: Informational

Benchmark: LA.910.1.7.4 The student will identify cause-and-effect relationships in text.

22 **The correct answer is F, The Grand Finale.**

Since the last paragraph deals with the ceremony celebrating the completion of the Transcontinental Railroad, the most appropriate subhead would be "The Grand Finale." The paragraph is not about California's railways. The properties of steel spikes and gold-plated ones are mentioned only in passing. With the driving of the last spikes at Promontory Point, the east and west sides of the nation were no longer divided but united by a single railroad line.

Type of text: Informational

Benchmark: LA.910.1.7.3 The student will determine the main idea or essential message in grade-level or higher texts through inferring, paraphrasing, summarizing, and identifying relevant details.

23 **The correct answer is B, to increase the amount of money made.**

To *pad* something is to "increase the amount in a needless or fraudulent manner." *Revenues and profits* refer to the amounts of money the railroad companies were making. The companies were laying unnecessary miles of track in order to get more money for the project. Answer choice B has the meaning closest to the phrase in the article.

Type of text: Informational

Benchmark: LA.910.1.6.8 The student will identify advanced word/phrase relationships and their meanings.

24 **The correct answer is H, inform readers about the history of one of America's greatest construction projects.**

The author does not focus on the life of an immigrant worker, although the harsh working conditions are mentioned. The author also mentions how the Civil War damaged the country's sense of unity, but this is not a main purpose of the article. The author briefly explains why many Americans favored the new railroad line, but again this is not a main focus. The author's chief purpose is to provide information about the history of the construction project.

Type of text: Informational

Benchmark: LA.910.1.7.2 The student will analyze the author's purpose and/or perspective in a variety of texts and understand how they affect meaning.

25 **The correct answer is D, free from illusion.**

The root word of *disenchanted* is *enchant,* which means "to be under a spell or fooled by an illusion." To be disenchanted then is to be freed from such a spell (the prefix *dis-* means "not"). The passage is saying that the Chinese workers were no longer under the illusion that their working situation was fair.

Type of text: Informational

Benchmark: LA.910.1.6.7 The student will identify and understand the meaning of conceptually advanced prefixes, suffixes, and root words.

26 **The correct answer is G, investors and shopkeepers with an eye on business.**

This answer comes directly from the text of the article: *Investors and shopkeepers supported this idea because a railroad would help to encourage new towns full of potential buyers and sellers.*

Type of text: Informational

Benchmark: LA.910.2.2.2 The student will use information from the text to answer questions or to state the main idea or provide relevant details.

27 **The correct answer is B, It was a very profitable venture.**

The article indicates that railroad company officials were chiefly interested in the project as a profitable venture. For example, the article says: *Company officials drove their workers hard for the sake of profit. Each company made $16,000 per mile on a level grade, $32,000 in the high plains, and $48,000 in the mountains. . . . The moneymaking potential of the project was almost endless.* They did not mainly see the project as their duty to the nation or the best way to unite the country. The officials seemed to have little concern about the practicality and danger of the project.

Type of text: Informational

Benchmark: LA.910.6.2.2 The student will organize, synthesize, analyze, and evaluate the validity and reliability of information from multiple sources (including primary and secondary sources) to draw conclusions using a variety of techniques, and correctly use standardized citations.

28 **The correct answer is H, Transportation and Its Effects on America.**

The information in this article would be most helpful in writing about transportation and its effects on America. The article focuses on how the Transcontinental Railroad helped to unite the country, speed up coast-to-coast travel, and spur business development in cities and towns along the route. Immigrant workers and the geography and topography of the West and Midwest are mentioned in the article, but are not the main focus. The topic of settlers in the West is addressed only indirectly in the possibility of new settlements appearing in response to the new railroad.

Type of text: Informational

Benchmark: LA.910.1.7.3 The student will determine the main idea or essential message in grade-level or higher texts through inferring, paraphrasing, summarizing, and identifying relevant details.

29 **The correct answer is A, the ability to store a large amount of information.**

The second bulleted point in the last section says, *The primary benefit of a hard-drive device is that it can store so much information.*

Type of text: Informational

Benchmark: LA.910.2.2.2 The student will use information from the text to answer questions or to state the main idea or provide relevant details.

30 **The correct answer is H, a word formed from the first letters of the words in a compound term.**

The passage indicates that MPEG is an *acronym* that stands for **M**oving **P**ictures **E**xpert **G**roup. Therefore, an acronym must be a word made up of the first letters of the words in a compound term.

Type of text: Informational

Benchmark: LA.910.1.6.3 The student will use context clues to determine meanings of unfamiliar words.

31 **The correct answer is B, to introduce the topic of each section of text and each illustration.**

The subheadings in this article introduce the topic of each text section and each illustration. The article doesn't have a cause-effect structure and the subheadings mainly ask questions instead of answering them.

Type of text: Informational

Benchmark: LA.910.6.1.1 The student will explain how text features (e.g., charts, maps, diagrams, subheadings, captions, illustrations, graphs) aid the reader's understanding.

32 **The correct answer is I, "This type of player can also hold photos, video, or text files and can be used to transport files from one computer to another."**

Versatility means the ability to do many different things. Answer choice I is the best example of an MP3 player's versatility since it explains the many different ways in which it can be used.

Type of text: Informational

Benchmark: LA.910.1.7.3 The student will determine the main idea or essential message in grade-level or higher texts through inferring, paraphrasing, summarizing, and identifying relevant details.

33 **The correct answer is B, read articles about the benefits and drawbacks of various MP3 players.**

In discussing what MP3 device is best to purchase, the author says: *As with any purchase, you should educate yourself and then make a decision to purchase based on your personal preferences.* A good way to educate oneself is to read articles that discuss the advantages and disadvantages of the different devices. The author suggests looking inside an MP3 player only to see the tiny working parts, not to check for quality. Talking to other owners of an MP3 might be a good way to research a purchase, but the author doesn't mention this. The author does mention that flash MP3 players do not skip, but this is not raised as a decisive reason for purchasing one.

Type of text: Informational

Benchmark: LA.910.1.7.2 The student will analyze the author's purpose and/or perspective in a variety of texts and understand how they affect meaning.

34 **The correct answer is F, explain how an MP3 player works.**

Although the subheading is about what is inside an MP3 player, the text in the diagram explains how the parts of the player operate to produce the music. The other graphic deals with the history of MP3s. The graphic does not show a picture of an actual MP3 player or explain how to repair one.

Type of text: Informational

Benchmark: LA.910.6.1.1 The student will explain how text features (e.g., charts, maps, diagrams, subheadings, captions, illustrations, graphs) aid the reader's understanding.

35 **The correct answer is A, Some sounds are simply too low or too high for a person to hear.**

The word *imperceptible* means "unable to be perceived." The idea of the sentence is that some tones, or sounds, simply cannot be heard by the human ear — probably because they are too low or too high in frequency to be picked up. Of the four answer choices, A restates this idea best.

Type of text: Informational

Benchmark: LA.910.1.6.8 The student will identify advanced word/phrase relationships and their meanings.

36 **The correct answer is I, compressed files take up much less space on a computer.**

According to the article, *If you were to download one song from a CD onto your computer, it would take up about 40 million bytes (or 40 megabytes) of computer space. If you compress than music file into an MP3 file, it will only take up about 3.5 megabytes of computer space.* The article does not indicate that compressed files are less expensive. It is not relevant to the question that compressed files require a digital signal processor. Compression does remove some sounds from an audio file, but that is not the main reason the technology is important to computer users.

Type of text: Informational

Benchmark: LA.910.1.7.4 The student will identify cause-and-effect relationships in text.

37 **The correct answer is B, A Timeline of Innovations in Recorded Music Up to MP3.**

The graphic is a timeline and not a list, so choice A is incorrect. The graphic covers events in the history of recorded music, not just music in general, so choice C is incorrect. The graphic identifies important events regarding analog recorded music, but it does not compare analog to digital. Answer choice B is the best replacement for the subheading since the graphic is a timeline of innovations in the technology of recorded music and not just in the development of the MP3.

Type of text: Informational

Benchmark: LA.910.2.2.1 The student will analyze and evaluate information from text features (e.g., transitional devices, table of contents, glossary, index, bold or italicized text, headings, charts and graphs, illustrations, subheadings).

38 **The correct answer is I, Ulrich depends on income from timber in the forest, and Georg is intent on stealing the wood.**

Answer choice I is correct. There is no mention in the story of Ulrich depending on the forest timber for income. Georg is accused of poaching game, not timber. The other items are all ways in which the forest setting is important to the story.

Type of text: Literary

Benchmark: LA.910.2.1.2 The student will analyze and compare a variety of traditional, classical, and contemporary literary works, and identify the literary elements of each (e.g., setting, plot, characterization, conflict).

39 **The correct answer is D, All the farmers in the county made an informal compact to share the grain elevator.**

In the quoted passage, the word *compact* means "an agreement." Answer choice D uses the word in this sense.

Type of text: Literary

Benchmark: LA.910.1.6.9 The student will determine the correct meaning of words with multiple meanings in context.

40 **The correct answer is H, "There's no one around here to stop us if we wanted to be friends."**

Answer choice H is the best restatement of the idea in the quotation. To *hinder* is "to block or stop," and *willed to make peace* is almost the same idea as "wanted to be friends."

Type of text: Literary

Benchmark: LA.910.2.1.9 The student will identify, analyze, and compare the differences in English language patterns and vocabulary choices of contemporary and historical texts.

41 **The correct answer is A, their families have had a longtime dispute over a strip of forest land.**

According to the text of the story, *a famous lawsuit, in the days of [Ulrich's] grandfather, had wrested [the land] from the illegal possession of a neighboring family of petty landowners; the dispossessed party had never acquiesced in the judgment of the Courts, and a long series of poaching episodes and similar scandals had embittered the relationships between the families for three generations.* Choice B is incorrect because it was Georg's family who was accused of illegally possessing the land, not Ulrich's. Nowhere does the text say that Georg is jealous of Ulrich's wealth. Ulrich wants to kill Georg at the beginning of the story, but that is a result of the feud, not its cause.

Type of text: Literary

Benchmark: LA.910.2.1.5 The student will analyze and develop an interpretation of a literary work by describing an author's use of literary elements (e.g., theme, point of view, characterization, setting, plot), and explain and analyze different elements of figurative language (e.g., simile, metaphor, personification, hyperbole, symbolism, allusion, imagery).

42 **The correct answer is H, personification.**

In the quoted sentence, Nature is personified as someone committing a deed of violence, much as the protagonists were about to do.

Type of text: Literary

Benchmark: LA.910.2.1.5 The student will analyze and develop an interpretation of a literary work by describing an author's use of literary elements (e.g., theme, point of view, characterization, setting, plot), and explain and analyze different elements of figurative language (e.g., simile, metaphor, personification, hyperbole, symbolism, allusion, imagery).

43 **The correct answer is B, how enemies can become friends.**

Until the surprise ending, the main theme of the story seems to be the almost incredible reconciliation of the old enemies, Ulrich and Georg. So answer choice B is the best answer. Answer choice C is one theme of the story up to the end (as in the danger of the tree falling in the storm), but it is revealed as the main theme only with the surprise ending and the arrival of the wolves.

Type of text: Literary

Benchmark: LA.910.1.7.6 The student will analyze and evaluate similar themes or topics by different authors across a variety of fiction and nonfiction selections.

Benchmark: LA.910.2.1.4 The student will identify and analyze universal themes and symbols across genres and historical periods, and explain their significance.

44 **The correct answer is G, entertain readers with a story about unpredictable fate.**

The author's most likely purpose in writing this story was to employ a surprise ending to entertain readers and make them think about the unpredictability of fate. He undercuts any inspiring effect with the story's ending. The story is not mainly concerned with describing the relationship between Ulrich and Georg.

Type of text: Literary

Benchmark: LA.910.1.7.2 The student will analyze the author's purpose and/or perspective in a variety of texts and understand how they affect meaning.

45 **The correct answer is B, the wolves.**

The word *interloper* means "someone who intrudes or interferes." Earlier in the story Georg says, "We fight this quarrel out to the death, you and I and our foresters, with no cursed interlopers to come between us." However, the wolves are the real interlopers, who will "interfere" with Georg and Ulrich by killing them.

Type of text: Literary

Benchmark: LA.910.1.6.3 The student will use context clues to determine meanings of unfamiliar words.

Benchmark: LA.910.1.7.3 The student will determine the main idea or essential message in grade-level or higher texts through inferring, paraphrasing, summarizing, and identifying relevant details.

46 The correct answer is H, the All-American Girls' Baseball League left a lasting impression on the sport of baseball and on American society.

In the last paragraph, the author writes: *Although the league existed for only a short period, it left a lasting impression not only on baseball but on sports in general, proving that women could succeed as professional athletes. . . . extraordinary women who not only played a sharp brand of baseball but also broke down barriers and raised morale in America during the difficult days of World War II.* The article mentions that women took over men's jobs during the war and that the women of the All-American Girls' Professional Baseball League were portrayed in a film, but neither of these ideas is the main focus. The fact that since World War II American women have been more active in the workforce and have had increased opportunities in pro sports is hinted at in the last paragraph but is not the main idea of the article.

Type of text: Informational

Benchmark: LA.910.2.2.2 The student will use information from the text to answer questions or to state the main idea or provide relevant details.

47 The correct answer is B, slightly modified regarding equipment and playing field.

The fifth paragraph of the article states: *The rules of play were similar to those for regular baseball, with a few modifications made to the field and the types of equipment that the women used.* "A few modifications" as to the field and equipment indicates that the women's game was only slightly different from Major League Baseball.

Type of text: Informational

Benchmark: LA.910.2.2.3 The student will organize information to show understanding or relationships among facts, ideas, and events (e.g., representing key points within text through charting, mapping, paraphrasing, summarizing, comparing, contrasting, or outlining).

48 The correct answer is F, the women ballplayers had little influence on how the league was run.

The author includes the passage to show how little input the professional women ballplayers had about something as basic as their uniforms even when they affected their ability to play the game properly. This allows the reader to infer that the ballplayers were completely controlled by the league owners.

Type of text: Informational

Benchmark: LA.910.1.7.2 The student will analyze the author's purpose and/or perspective in a variety of texts and understand how they affect meaning.

49 **The correct answer is D, searched.**

In this sentence, *scoured* means "to search thoroughly" — in this case, to find young women who could play baseball.

Type of text: Informational

Benchmark: LA.910.1.6.9 The student will determine the correct meaning of words with multiple meanings in context.

50 **The correct answer is F, very curious.**

The article states that *while it was curiosity that initially lured many people to the games, the women's performance on the field kept fans coming back every week.* So fans were very curious at the beginning of the league.

Type of text: Informational

Benchmark: LA.910.2.2.2 The student will use information from the text to answer questions or to state the main idea or provide relevant details.

51 **The correct answer is B, the owners expected them to be examples of femininity.**

While it is probably true that Wrigley expected to sell more tickets if the players looked pretty, in the fourth paragraph the author points out that the girls were expected to be feminine at all times. That is the main reason they were required to wear skirts and makeup during games.

Type of text: Informational

Benchmark: LA.910.1.7.4 The student will identify cause-and-effect relationships in text.

52 **The correct answer is H, makeshift.**

The term *ad hoc* typically means "suited to the situation" or "used from what is immediately available." In other words, the owners had to find *improvised* or *makeshift* solutions to their problems in starting the new league quickly.

Type of text: Informational

Benchmark: LA.910.1.6.11 The student will identify the meaning of words and phrases form other languages commonly used by writers of English (e.g., *ad hoc, ex post facto, RSVP*).

53 **The correct answer is D, Wrigley's women's baseball league was an example of how the absence of men during World War II gave women their first opportunity to work outside their homes.**

In the first paragraph, the author explains that the lack of men allowed many women to join the workforce for the first time. The second paragraph indicates that this situation led Wrigley to start his women's baseball league. It is not correct that women had never baseball anywhere before the league began. Attendance at women's league games was strong, and the league endured into the 1950s. Also, the league apparently had plenty of quality athletes to be successful.

Type of text: Informational

Benchmark: LA.910.2.2.3 The student will organize information to show understanding or relationships among facts, ideas, and events (e.g., representing key points within text through charting, mapping, paraphrasing, summarizing, comparing, contrasting, or outlining).

54 **The correct answer is G, the girls' success in becoming the first female professional ballplayers.**

In the sentence, the girls' *groundbreaking efforts* refers to their success in breaking down barriers that kept women from making a living as professional athletes. This is one of the main ideas of the article.

Type of text: Informational

Benchmark: LA.910.1.7.3 The student will determine the main idea or essential message in grade-level or higher texts through inferring, paraphrasing, summarizing, and identifying relevant details.

55 **The correct answer is C, Major League Baseball's attendance revived when its star players returned from fighting the war.**

The next to last paragraph in the article states that *Major League Baseball, with many of its former stars returning healthy and ready to play, returned to prominence. After a peak attendance figure of 910,000 fans in 1948, interest in the All-American Girls' Professional Baseball League started to wane. In 1954, the league disbanded after 12 years of operation.* This indicates that when Major League Baseball became very popular again, the women's game began to lose its audience.

Type of text: Informational

Benchmark: LA.910.2.2.2 The student will use information from the text to answer questions or to state the main idea or provide relevant details.

56   **The correct answer is H, The All-American Girls' Professional Baseball League showed that women could succeed as professional athletes.**

In the last paragraph, the author writes: *Although the league existed for only a short period, it left a lasting impression not only on baseball but on sports in general, proving that women could succeed as professional athletes.* This indicates that the author would agree that the women's pro baseball league was an important step for women who wanted to succeed in sports.

Type of text: Informational

Benchmark: LA.910.1.7.2 The student will analyze the author's purpose and/or perspective in a variety of texts and understand how they affect meaning.

Practice Writing Test 2 Sample Answer

In my opinion, a true or genuine friend should be honest, loyal, and trustworthy. These are the traits I look for in a friend. While I consider myself to have many friends, like most people I have only a few true friends on whom I can rely. Each of them has these qualities in abundance.

Honesty is a very important trait in a friend. Suppose you are dressed to go out and you are wearing something you think looks good on you — but it really doesn't. A true friend will take you aside and tell you to change. My friend Lisa is such a friend. Lisa is honest with me, but if she criticizes it is always in a gentle manner. When I liked a boy and he didn't really like me, Lisa told me the truth, not just what I wanted to hear. Honesty like that is invaluable.

Loyalty is another very important quality. A true friend will stick with you even when you make a fool of yourself. Last semester, when I was walking down the steps to the school cafeteria, I slipped and fell in front of what seemed like the whole student body. Well, I was much more embarrassed than hurt. Lots of people guffawed. But my friends Lisa and Tina did not laugh. They simply helped me up and were more concerned with whether or not I was hurt than what others thought. They are my true friends.

True friends can also be trusted. They will not say bad things about you behind your back. If they have a problem with something you have done, they will tell you about it personally instead of grousing about you to other people. You always know that your true friends would never intentionally do anything to hurt you. That is the beauty of having an honest, loyal, and trustworthy friend.

FCAT 2.0
Reading and Writing Answer Sheets for Practice Test

Answer all the questions that appear in Practice Test 1 on these Answer Sheets. Answer multiple-choice questions by filling in the bubble for the answer you select. Write your response to the writing prompt on the lines provided.

1. Ⓐ Ⓑ Ⓒ Ⓓ 2. Ⓕ Ⓖ Ⓗ Ⓘ 3. Ⓐ Ⓑ Ⓒ Ⓓ

4. Ⓕ Ⓖ Ⓗ Ⓘ 5. Ⓐ Ⓑ Ⓒ Ⓓ 6. Ⓕ Ⓖ Ⓗ Ⓘ

7. Ⓐ Ⓑ Ⓒ Ⓓ 8. Ⓕ Ⓖ Ⓗ Ⓘ 9. Ⓐ Ⓑ Ⓒ Ⓓ

10. Ⓕ Ⓖ Ⓗ Ⓘ 11. Ⓐ Ⓑ Ⓒ Ⓓ 12. Ⓕ Ⓖ Ⓗ Ⓘ

13. Ⓐ Ⓑ Ⓒ Ⓓ 14. Ⓕ Ⓖ Ⓗ Ⓘ 15. Ⓐ Ⓑ Ⓒ Ⓓ

16. Ⓕ Ⓖ Ⓗ Ⓘ 17. Ⓐ Ⓑ Ⓒ Ⓓ 18. Ⓕ Ⓖ Ⓗ Ⓘ

19. Ⓐ Ⓑ Ⓒ Ⓓ 20. Ⓕ Ⓖ Ⓗ Ⓘ 21. Ⓐ Ⓑ Ⓒ Ⓓ

22. Ⓕ Ⓖ Ⓗ Ⓘ 23. Ⓐ Ⓑ Ⓒ Ⓓ 24. Ⓕ Ⓖ Ⓗ Ⓘ

25 (A) (B) (C) (D)   26 (F) (G) (H) (I)   27 (A) (B) (C) (D)

28 (F) (G) (H) (I)   29 (A) (B) (C) (D)   30 (F) (G) (H) (I)

31 (A) (B) (C) (D)   32 (F) (G) (H) (I)   33 (A) (B) (C) (D)

34 (F) (G) (H) (I)   35 (A) (B) (C) (D)   36 (F) (G) (H) (I)

37 (A) (B) (C) (D)   38 (F) (G) (H) (I)   39 (A) (B) (C) (D)

40 (F) (G) (H) (I)   41 (A) (B) (C) (D)   42 (F) (G) (H) (I)

43 (A) (B) (C) (D)   44 (F) (G) (H) (I)   45 (A) (B) (C) (D)

46 (F) (G) (H) (I)   47 (A) (B) (C) (D)   48 (F) (G) (H) (I)

49 Ⓐ Ⓑ Ⓒ Ⓓ   **50** Ⓕ Ⓖ Ⓗ Ⓘ   **51** Ⓐ Ⓑ Ⓒ Ⓓ

52 Ⓕ Ⓖ Ⓗ Ⓘ   **53** Ⓐ Ⓑ Ⓒ Ⓓ   **54** Ⓕ Ⓖ Ⓗ Ⓘ

55 Ⓐ Ⓑ Ⓒ Ⓓ   **56** Ⓕ Ⓖ Ⓗ Ⓘ

Writing Prompt

FCAT 2.0
Reading and Writing Answer Sheets for Practice Test

2

Answer all the questions that appear in Practice Test 2 on these Answer Sheets. Answer multiple-choice questions by filling in the bubble for the answer you select. Write your response to the writing prompt on the lines provided.

1. (A) (B) (C) (D)   2. (F) (G) (H) (I)   3. (A) (B) (C) (D)

4. (F) (G) (H) (I)   5. (A) (B) (C) (D)   6. (F) (G) (H) (I)

7. (A) (B) (C) (D)   8. (F) (G) (H) (I)   9. (A) (B) (C) (D)

10. (F) (G) (H) (I)   11. (A) (B) (C) (D)   12. (F) (G) (H) (I)

13. (A) (B) (C) (D)   14. (F) (G) (H) (I)   15. (A) (B) (C) (D)

16. (F) (G) (H) (I)   17. (A) (B) (C) (D)   18. (F) (G) (H) (I)

19. (A) (B) (C) (D)   20. (F) (G) (H) (I)   21. (A) (B) (C) (D)

22. (F) (G) (H) (I)   23. (A) (B) (C) (D)   24. (F) (G) (H) (I)

25 Ⓐ Ⓑ Ⓒ Ⓓ   **26** Ⓕ Ⓖ Ⓗ Ⓘ   **27** Ⓐ Ⓑ Ⓒ Ⓓ

28 Ⓕ Ⓖ Ⓗ Ⓘ   **29** Ⓐ Ⓑ Ⓒ Ⓓ   **30** Ⓕ Ⓖ Ⓗ Ⓘ

31 Ⓐ Ⓑ Ⓒ Ⓓ   **32** Ⓕ Ⓖ Ⓗ Ⓘ   **33** Ⓐ Ⓑ Ⓒ Ⓓ

34 Ⓕ Ⓖ Ⓗ Ⓘ   **35** Ⓐ Ⓑ Ⓒ Ⓓ   **36** Ⓕ Ⓖ Ⓗ Ⓘ

37 Ⓐ Ⓑ Ⓒ Ⓓ   **38** Ⓕ Ⓖ Ⓗ Ⓘ   **39** Ⓐ Ⓑ Ⓒ Ⓓ

40 Ⓕ Ⓖ Ⓗ Ⓘ   **41** Ⓐ Ⓑ Ⓒ Ⓓ   **42** Ⓕ Ⓖ Ⓗ Ⓘ

43 Ⓐ Ⓑ Ⓒ Ⓓ   **44** Ⓕ Ⓖ Ⓗ Ⓘ   **45** Ⓐ Ⓑ Ⓒ Ⓓ

46 Ⓕ Ⓖ Ⓗ Ⓘ   **47** Ⓐ Ⓑ Ⓒ Ⓓ   **48** Ⓕ Ⓖ Ⓗ Ⓘ

49 Ⓐ Ⓑ Ⓒ Ⓓ   **50** Ⓕ Ⓖ Ⓗ Ⓘ   **51** Ⓐ Ⓑ Ⓒ Ⓓ

52 Ⓕ Ⓖ Ⓗ Ⓘ   **53** Ⓐ Ⓑ Ⓒ Ⓓ   **54** Ⓕ Ⓖ Ⓗ Ⓘ

55 Ⓐ Ⓑ Ⓒ Ⓓ   **56** Ⓕ Ⓖ Ⓗ Ⓘ

Writing Prompt

FCAT 2.0 Benchmarks in Practice Tests

FCAT 2.0 Reading Benchmarks	Practice Test Questions
LA.910.1.5.1 The student will adjust reading rate based on purpose, text difficulty, form, and style.	
LA.910.1.6.1 The student will use new vocabulary that is introduced and taught directly.	
LA.910.1.6.2 The student will listen to, read, and discuss familiar and conceptually challenging text.	
LA.910.1.6.3 The student will use context clues to determine meanings of unfamiliar words.	Test 1: 4, 25 Test 2: 4, 10, 30, 45
LA.910.1.6.4 The student will categorize key vocabulary and identify salient features.	
LA.910.1.6.5 The student will relate new vocabulary to familiar words.	Test 1: 12, 29, 52 Test 2: 19
LA.910.1.6.6 The student will distinguish denotative and connotative meanings of words.	Test 1: 32
LA.910.1.6.7 The student will identify and understand the meaning of conceptually advanced prefixes, suffixes, and root words.	Test 2: 25
LA.910.1.6.8 The student will identify advanced word/ phrase relationships and their meanings.	Test 1: 2, 35, 46 Test 2: 6, 23, 35
LA.910.1.6.9 The student will determine the correct meaning of words with multiple meanings in context.	Test 1: 23 Test 2: 39, 49
LA.910.1.6.10 The student will determine meanings of words, pronunciations, parts of speech, etymologies, and alternate word choices by using a dictionary, thesaurus, and digital tools.	
LA.910.1.6.11 The student will identify the meaning of words and phrases from other languages commonly used by writers of English (e.g., *ad hoc, ex post facto, RSVP).*	Test 2: 52
LA.910.1.7.1 The student will use background knowledge of subject and related content areas, prereading strategies (e.g., previewing, discussing, generating questions), text features, and text structure to make and confirm complex predictions of content, purpose, and organization of a reading selection.	

(continued)

(continued)

FCAT 2.0 Reading Benchmarks	Practice Test Questions
LA.910.1.7.2 The student will analyze the author's purpose and/or perspective in a variety of texts and understand how they affect meaning.	Test 1: 7, 16, 33, 53, 56 Test 2: 1, 18, 24, 33, 44, 48, 56
LA.910.1.7.3 The student will determine the main idea or essential message in grade-level or higher texts through inferring, paraphrasing, summarizing, and identifying relevant details.	Test 1: 3, 6, 10, 26, 37, 55 Test 2: 5, 22, 28, 32, 45, 54
LA.910.1.7.4 The student will identify cause-and-effect relationships in text.	Test 1: 5, 11, 20 Test 2: 2, 21, 36, 51
LA.910.1.7.5 The student will analyze a variety of text structures (e.g., comparison/contrast, cause/effect, chronological order, argument/support, lists) and text features (main headings with subheadings) and explain their impact on meaning in text.	Test 1: 14, 18, 27, 31, 54 Test 2: 17
LA.910.1.7.6 The student will analyze and evaluate similar themes or topics by different authors across a variety of fiction and nonfiction selections.	Test 1: 55 Test 2: 15, 43
LA.910.1.7.7 The student will compare and contrast elements in multiple texts.	Test 1: 24, 30, 50
LA.910.1.7.8 The student will use strategies to repair comprehension of grade-appropriate text when self-monitoring indicates confusion, including but not limited to rereading, checking context clues, predicting, note-making, summarizing, using graphic and semantic organizers, questioning, and clarifying by checking other sources.	
LA.910.2.1.1 The student will analyze and compare historically and culturally significant works of literature, identifying the relationships among the major genres (e.g., poetry, fiction, nonfiction, short story, dramatic literature, essay) and the literary devices unique to each, and analyze how they support and enhance the theme and main ideas of the text.	Test 1: 45 Test 2: 14

(continued)

(continued)

FCAT 2.0 Reading Benchmarks	Practice Test Questions
LA.910.2.1.2 The student will analyze and compare a variety of traditional, classical, and contemporary literary works, and identify the literary elements of each (e.g., setting, plot, characterization, conflict).	Test 1: 8 Test 2: 8, 11, 13, 38
LA.910.2.1.3 The student will explain how meaning is enhanced through various features of poetry, including sound (e.g., rhythm, repetition, alliteration, consonance, assonance), structure (e.g., meter, rhyme scheme), and graphic elements (e.g., line length, punctuation, word position).	Test 1: 13, 36 Test 2: 7
LA.910.2.1.4 The student will identify and analyze universal themes and symbols across genres and historical periods, and explain their significance.	Test 1: 41 Test 2: 15, 43
LA.910.2.1.5 The student will analyze and develop an interpretation of a literary work by describing an author's use of literary elements (e.g., theme, point of view, characterization, setting, plot), and explain and analyze different elements of figurative language (e.g., simile, metaphor, personification, hyperbole, symbolism, allusion, imagery).	Test 1: 9, 15, 39, 40, 42 Test 2: 9, 41, 42
LA.910.2.1.6 The student will create a complex, multi-genre response to the reading of two or more literary works, describing and analyzing an author's use of literary elements (e.g., theme, point of view, characterization, setting, plot), figurative language (e.g., simile, metaphor, personification, hyperbole, symbolism, allusion, imagery), and analyzing an author's development of time and sequence through the use of complex literary devices such as foreshadowing and flashback.	Test 2: 12
LA.910.2.1.7 The student will analyze, interpret, and evaluate an author's use of descriptive language (e.g., tone, irony, mood, imagery, pun, alliteration, onomatopoeia, allusion), figurative language (e.g., symbolism, metaphor, personification, hyperbole), common idioms, and mythological and literary allusions, and explain how they impact meaning in a variety of texts.	Test 1: 43, 49
LA.910.2.1.8 The student will explain how ideas, values, and themes of a literary work often reflect the historical period in which it was written.	Test 1: 44

(continued)

(continued)

FCAT 2.0 Reading Benchmarks	Practice Test Questions
LA.910.2.1.9 The student will identify, analyze, and compare the differences in English language patterns and vocabulary choices of contemporary and historical texts.	Test 1: 38 Test 2: 40
LA.910.2.1.10 The student will select a variety of age and ability appropriate fiction materials to read based on knowledge of author's styles, themes, and genres to expand the core foundation of knowledge necessary to connect topics and function as a fully literate member of a shared culture.	
LA.910.2.2.1 The student will analyze and evaluate information from text features (e.g., transitional devices, table of contents, glossary, index, bold or italicized text, headings, charts and graphs, illustrations, subheadings).	Test 1: 1, 19 Test 2: 37
LA.910.2.2.2 The student will use information from the text to answer questions or to state the main idea or provide relevant details.	Test 1: 17, 22, 34, 48 Test 2: 3, 16, 26, 29, 46, 50, 55
LA.910.2.2.3 The student will organize information to show understanding of relationships among facts, ideas, and events (e.g., representing key points within text through charting, mapping, paraphrasing, summarizing, comparing, contrasting, or outlining).	Test 1: 28, 51 Test 2: 20, 47, 53
LA.910.2.2.4 The student will identify and analyze the characteristics of a variety of types of text (e.g., references, reports, technical manuals, articles, editorials, primary source historical documents, periodicals, job-related materials, practical/functional text).	
LA.910.2.2.5 The student will select a variety of age and ability appropriate nonfiction materials (e.g., biographies and topical areas, such as science, music, art, history, sports, current events) to expand the core knowledge necessary to connect topics and function as a fully literate member of a shared culture.	
LA.910.6.1.1 The student will explain how text features (e.g., charts, maps, diagrams, subheadings, captions, illustrations, graphs) aid the reader's understanding.	Test 2: 31, 34

(continued)

(continued)

FCAT 2.0 Reading Benchmarks	Practice Test Questions
LA.910.6.2.2 The student will organize, synthesize, analyze, and evaluate the validity and reliability of information from multiple sources (including primary and secondary sources) to draw conclusions using a variety of techniques, and correctly use standardized citations.	Test 1: 21, 47 Test 2: 27
FCAT Writing Benchmarks	**Student essays are scored on all FCAT Writing Benchmarks.**
LA.910.3.1.1 The student will prewrite by generating ideas from multiple sources (e.g., brainstorming, notes, journals, discussion, research materials or other reliable sources) based upon teacher-directed topics and personal interests.	x
LA.910.3.1.2 The student will prewrite by making a plan for writing that addresses purpose, audience, a controlling idea, logical sequence, and time frame for completion.	x
LA.910.3.1.3 The student will prewrite by using organizational strategies and tools (e.g., technology, spreadsheet, outline, chart, table, graph, Venn diagram, web, story map, plot pyramid) to develop a personal organizational style.	x
LA.910.3.2.1 The student will draft writing by developing ideas from the prewriting plan using primary and secondary sources appropriate to the purpose and audience.	x
LA.910.3.2.2 The student will draft writing by establishing a logical organizational pattern with supporting details that are substantial, specific, and relevant.	x
LA.910.3.2.3 The student will draft writing by analyzing language techniques of professional authors (e.g., figurative language, denotation, connotation) to establish a personal style, demonstrating a command of language with confidence of expression.	x
LA.910.3.3.1 The student will revise by evaluating the draft for development of ideas and content, logical organization, voice, point of view, word choice, and sentence variation.	x

(continued)

(continued)

FCAT Writing Benchmarks	Student essays are scored on all FCAT Writing Benchmarks.
LA.910.3.3.2 The student will revise by creating clarity and logic by maintaining central theme, idea, or unifying point and developing meaningful relationships among ideas.	X
LA.910.3.3.3 The student will revise by creating precision and interest by elaborating ideas through supporting details (e.g., facts, statistics, expert opinions, anecdotes), a variety of sentence structures, creative language devices, and modifying word choices using resources and reference materials (e.g., dictionary, thesaurus) to select more effective and precise language.	X
LA.910.3.3.4 The student will revise by applying appropriate tools or strategies to evaluate and refine the draft (e.g., peer review, checklists, rubrics).	X
LA.910.3.4.1 The student will edit for correct use of spelling, using spelling rules, orthographic patterns, generalizations, knowledge of root words, prefixes, suffixes, knowledge of Greek, Latin, and Anglo-Saxon root words, and knowledge of foreign words commonly used in English *(laissez faire, croissant)*.	X
LA.910.3.4.2 The student will edit for correct use of capitalization, including names of academic courses and proper adjectives.	X
LA.910.3.4.3 The student will edit for correct use of punctuation, including commas, colons, semicolons, apostrophes, dashes, quotation marks, and underlining or italics.	X
LA.910.3.4.4 The student will edit for correct use of possessives, subject/verb agreement, comparative and superlative adjectives and adverbs, and noun/pronoun agreement.	X
LA.910.3.4.5 The student will edit for correct use of sentence formation, including absolutes and absolute phrases, infinitives and infinitive phrases, and use of fragments for effect.	X
LA.910.4.1.1 The student will write in a variety of expressive and reflective forms that use a range of appropriate strategies and specific narrative techniques, employ literary devices, and sensory descriptions.	X

(continued)

(continued)

FCAT Writing Benchmarks	**Student essays are scored on all FCAT Writing Benchmarks.**
LA.910.4.1.2 The student will incorporate figurative language, emotions, gestures, rhythm, dialogue, characterization, plot, and appropriate format.	X
LA.910.4.2.1 The student will write in a variety of informational/expository forms, including a variety of technical documents (e.g., how-to manuals, procedures, assembly directions).	X
LA.910.4.2.2 The student will record information and ideas from primary and/or secondary sources accurately and coherently, noting the validity and reliability of these sources and attributing sources of information.	X
LA.910.4.2.3 The student will write informational/expository essays that speculate on the causes and effects of a situation, establish the connection between the postulated causes or effects, offer evidence supporting the validity of the proposed causes or effects, and include introductory, body, and concluding paragraphs.	X
LA.910.4.2.4 The student will write a business letter and/or memo that presents information purposefully and succinctly to meet the needs of the intended audience following a conventional format (e.g., block, modified block, memo, email).	X
LA.910.4.2.5 The student will write detailed travel directions and design an accompanying graphic using the cardinal and ordinal directions, landmarks, streets and highways, and distances.	X
LA.910.4.2.6 The student will write a work-related document (e.g., application, resume, meeting minutes, memo, cover letter, letter of application, speaker introduction, letter of recommendation).	X
LA.910.4.3.1 The student will write essays that state a position or claim, present detailed evidence, examples, and reasoning to support effective arguments and emotional appeals, and acknowledge and refute opposing arguments.	X
LA.910.4.3.2 The student will include persuasive techniques.	X

Index

Photo Credits

"The Hemingway House and Museum" (p. 13) by Associated Press.

"The Six Nations of the Iroquois" (p. 16) by the New York Public Library.

"Carbohydrate Craze" (p. 93) by ©iStockphoto.com/Helen Rubtsov.

"Curious Crop Circles" (p. 104) by ©iStockphoto.com/George Cairns.

"Concerto for the Left Hand," Paul Wittgenstein (p. 167) by Bettman/Corbis.

"Daydreams Save the Day" (p. 175) by ©iStockphoto.com/Amanda Rohde.

"Zora Neale Hurston" (p. 181) by Associated Press.

"The All-American Girls' Baseball League," the 1948 Racine Belles (p. 253) by the National Baseball Hall of Fame Library, Cooperstown, N.Y.

NOTES

NOTES

NOTES

NOTES

NOTES

NOTES

NOTES

NOTES

NOTES